THE FRENCH RIVIERA

Landscapes of the Imagination

Landscapes

THE FRENCH RIVIERA
A *Cultural History*

JULIAN HALE

Signal Books
Oxford

First published in 2009 by
Signal Books Limited
36 Minster Road
Oxford OX4 1LY
www.signalbooks.co.uk

A catalogue record for this book is available from the British Library

ISBN 978-1-904955-58-0 Paper

Cover Design: Devdan Sen
Production: Devdan Sen
Cover Images: Fanelli Photography/istockphoto
Illustrations: © Dorothy Bohm pp.i, xv, 10, 47, 105, 133, 148; (c) Steve Williams pp.110, 136, 146, 174, 186, 218; Julian Hale pp.viii, 93; dreamtime.com pp.xii, 14, 65, 81, 84, 164, 206; istockphoto.com pp.2, 34, 58, 98, 112, 162

Printed in Britain by Bell & Bain Ltd., Glasgow

Contents

From cape to shining cape – the Riviera encapsulated

Preface and Acknowledgements

On a bright morning—and there are many on the French Riviera—try standing on the Pont St.-Louis at the far eastern end of Menton, with the sun rising over the Italian cliffs behind you. Then drive, or walk, westwards along the smart new Boulevard de Garavan, turn right and up onto the Route de Super Garavan, cut through the Domaine des Colombières, touch again the Italian frontier and double back to a viewpoint just below the *autoroute* where it disappears into one of its frequent tunnels. Now look due west. That is the French Riviera you can see.

From here or hereabouts you can see practically all of it. Those hills on the far horizon are the Massif de l'Esterel, above St.-Tropez. The bigger towns are hidden behind their bays: Monte Carlo, Nice, Cannes, St.-Raphael. A succession of capes, brown and green and speckled with white walls and red roofs, push out into the blue sea: Caps Martin, d'Ail, Ferrat, d'Antibes and Camarat. All along the jagged shoreline and up into the steep wooded hills behind, villas, villas, villas stretch out to the final hazy horizon.

The French Riviera is dense, tiny, spectacular. Despite the developers, it is still Scott Fitzgerald's "hot, sweet South of France". It is also the "Côte d'Azur", a term invented by Stephen Liégeard in his overblown 1887 guidebook, now joined to the "Riviera" like a Siamese twin.

I confess to a soft spot, a prejudice even, for Menton. I now live part of each year here, very close to the Italian border, where I can enjoy the Franco-Italian mix and relish the almost daily dilemma, whether to turn left for a *fritto misto* or right for a *friture mixte*. For a Briton with an urge to find a "continental" base and a working life that has involved frequent visits to both France and Italy, the opportunity not to have to choose between the two but to sample the pleasures (and frustrations) of both in one place was compelling.

But, as the locals love to point out to visitors to this elegant and relaxing coast, just because the sun is shining does not mean that there is no hard work to be done. The Côte d'Azur, they say, is a "miroir aux alouettes", a mirror to catch the eye of larks, a reflective surface glittering brightly to entice the unwary.

So while I can only agree that taking the historico-cultural temperature of the French Riviera might, superficially, seem all too attractive—

such is its sybaritic image—all the same I hope you, the reader, will enjoy following me in the strenuous business of experiencing first-hand the past and present of the French Riviera.

Which prompts one further thought… For any writer researching a book, the more you progress, the less sure you are of what you knew before you started. How much, if anything, did I actually know about the influence of Smollett and Brougham? To what exactly was Somerset Maugham referring in his over-quoted phrase, "a sunny place for shady people"? Monaco? Nice? The whole of the Riviera? And where are Nice, Cannes and Antibes in relation to each other (let alone Agay and Peillon)? I have tried to include, alongside what is more or less well known, facts and insights that are potentially new, unexpected and imaginative in the hope that discovering the landscape of the French Riviera will prove to be as exciting to you, the reader, as it is to me.

I am grateful to my wife, Helen Likierman, for guiding me to the Riviera, and to those members of her family and friends who live and work close by. I thank too the many people who have helped me in a task that might seem to some readers a soft option, by no means least the wonderful photographers, Dorothy Bohm, a brilliant pioneer of the art of landscape photography, and Steve Williams, an architect with an immaculate eye. I have been helped and advised by kind friends (and critics), among whom Tony Beadles, Robert Hewison, Michael Likierman, Tim Suter, Roger Taylor and William Waterfield. Many people along the Riviera have, of course, offered help and information; among them Dominique Dufrenne and the staff of the Nice regional archives. Finally, my children have given me valuable encouragement.

Introduction

Paradise Imagined

Geologists can form a mental picture of a given area on a map on the basis of the data they have to hand. Most of us need to see with our eyes those topographical features to fix a vivid image in our minds. But in the case of the French Riviera these conjured-up pictures, either imagined or real, are likely to be overridden by photographs, illustrations and artists' transpositions that are the stuff of school and guide books, posters, postcards and lushly painted landscapes. We are all too familiar—even without maps or visual experience—with the brilliant blue sea lapping the sand and rocks of the coastline; with those ribbons of densely populated areas just behind; with the browner, bumpier slopes further inland, speckled with clumps of green, rising quickly to white-topped peaks in the distance.

But, however familiar, the landscape from Hyères in the west to Menton in the east sends an immediately attractive message to all of us— casual observers, scientists and artists alike. The ancient mountains of the Maures and the Esterel are perhaps the most naturally beautiful areas: the former lower, full of valleys and ravines and covered in forests of pine, cork oak and chestnuts; the latter higher, more rugged and bare and above all made of bright, jagged terracotta-coloured rock. The newer, higher pre-Alp formations have a softer beauty, though in places cut through with spectacular and dizzying gorges. The flatter land between the hills and the sea is rarer but no less enticing, with its citrus and olive groves, fields of lavender, palms, agaves and succulents: what Tobias Smollett in the eighteenth century called the "plain… blowing in full glory, with such beauty, vigour, and perfume, as no flower in England ever exhibited." And then there are the islands, from Porquerolles off Hyères to Ste.-Marguerite off Cannes, all with their own characters and history, glittering stone slivers chipped off the massive mainland.

It is hard to imagine the French Riviera, this earthly paradise, as inhospitable, harsh, even hostile. Yet that is how it was both imagined and experienced from time immemorial until pleasure-seekers swooped down from the north armed with bank balances and a vision of lotus-eating languor, spotting more potential here than the sardines and olives with which the old inhabitants had to be satisfied. Before modern roads and

trains, the mountains were too steep, too close to the mostly rocky shore for people to prosper or travellers to pass by in comfort. The few safe approaches were by sea, but even then, having arrived, there was nowhere else to go. In the words of Mary Blume, an American journalist and shrewd observer of the Riviera, it was "a fringe, a liminal space, waiting to be invented."

This is the story, then, of long harsh centuries blasted out of our collective memory over the last couple of hundred years by a gale of high spending and turbulent glamour.

There is a certain apt delight in discovering that the very first human contact with this coast, a million or so years ago, was, one supposes, a consequence of its warm welcome. The original European man and woman settled in a network of caves close to modern Menton. Millennia later, finally and due largely to curious and passionate Englishmen, the sweet microclimate of this sheltered area just to the west of today's Italian frontier finally spread its reputation as the mildest, most benign place to live in the whole of Europe. Menton became a very British haven.

But how much of the French Riviera is "real"? How much "imagined"? By which I mean, to what extent does it have a distinct and definable identity—or is it just an incoherent and indefinable sum of all our personal imaginations, like a screen onto which we project our mental images?

What the Riviera is definitely *not* is Provence, the Roman administrative centre with its grand monuments and its rich cultural and political back history. No use consulting Pagnol or Giorno, Daudet, Bosco or Mistral to define the Riviera—and certainly not Peter Mayle. The Riviera is Matisse and Picasso, not Cézanne and Van Gogh. It is yachts and speedboats, not barges and skiffs. It is sardines and Rosé de Bellet, not *boeuf en daube* and Châteauneuf du Pape. It is movie and rock music celebrities, not bullfighters and dead popes.

Perhaps the most significant identity problem is that the Riviera is seen—or imagined—differently by different *nationalities*, rather than by individuals. Perhaps that should read *was* seen or imagined, since the glitz so beloved by the media (yachts in Monaco harbour, the Cannes Film Festival and the swimming-pooled homes of the stars) have become the common currency of contemporary imagination.

Yet there are significant differences of perception. For the French, the essence of the imagined Riviera is probably still the St.-Tropez duo of Françoise Sagan, through the prism of her novella *Bonjour Tristesse,* and Colette, entertaining guests on the terrace of La Treille Muscate. For Americans—for those of an older generation at least—a similar but harder-edged image is conjured up by Scott Fitzgerald in his novel *Tender is the Night.* For the Russians, it is tempting to say that the Monte Carlo Casino is still their talisman. Even Anton Chekhov was hooked. But again the new generation would relate better to all the bling that newly-won roubles can attract with the help of fancy shopkeepers and estate agents.

For the British, the Riviera has left a more fragmented impression on the collective memory. One lasting image derives from Somerset Maugham. The British mind, steeped in nostalgia, envisages a craggy old man entertaining Noel Coward and the Windsors, all talking scandal in penetrating upper-class voices on the patio of his Villa Mauresque. But nothing in Maugham's fiction encapsulates the Riviera like his life. Graham Greene and Maugham are alike in that respect, although some of Greene's lighter fiction, such as *May We Borrow Your Husband* or *Loser Takes All,* have Riviera settings. Greene's use of the term *Côte d'Ordure* (rubbish coast) did not help to establish him as a popular "Riviera figure". Neither he nor Anthony Burgess, his fellow novelist who lived in Monaco, did much to endear Britons to the Riviera (and vice versa) or to encourage the tourist trade.

Many other writers from earlier generations who are still admired by many British readers, such as H. G. Wells or Katherine Mansfield or even Daphne du Maurier, alluded to the Riviera, or parts of it, but their work cannot constitute any kind of mental template or paradigm of our imagined Riviera today. Tobias Smollett is too esoteric, the eighteenth century too much of a bygone time and his travel account too little read today to survive as a modern guide, however influential he was in his time and however entertaining his descriptions and insights still are to his few twenty-first-century readers. Cyril Connolly came nearest perhaps, but the seedy figure of his anti-hero Naylor, out of his depth and drifting in *The Rock Pool* of his fictional seaside town, in reality Cagnes, scarcely provides a totemic portrayal of the modern Englishman's ideal lotus land. So in the end British people today are probably left with much the same image of exaggerated "glamour" as everyone else.

Dismissing the Riviera as spoiled and overbuilt has been a constant

Dreaming of paradise – "the hot, sweet South of France"

refrain, not just of recent times but from the moment the British started to implant their villas in the prettiest spots along the coast. This is true of people of all nationalities. In the middle of the nineteenth century Prosper Mérimée was just one of many who deplored the taste of much of the "foreign" development of Cannes. Things were always better "before". Following in the tradition of the nineteenth-century writer Guy de Maupassant, the popular inter-war novelist Henry Bordeaux was railing in the 1920s against the threat of building speculators:

> Cimiez hill, above Nice, used to be covered with olives and pines, oaks and cedars, a wood dedicated to Diana and then to Francis Assisi. With its ruins, its gardens, its cloister and its church adorned with the pictures of Louis Brea, the Provençal Angelico, it surpassed Fiesole in beauty, by virtue of the nearby sea. Were our industrial era to have any care for art or respect for the past, it would have been preserved intact, for the embellishment of the Côte d'Azur, which would benefit from a place of meditation, prayer and noble reverie, far from the banality of the Riviera. Whereas it has been unworthily massacred and handed over to the executioners, that is to say the architects and builders. Today it is no more than a flowering of hotels and villas.

If that were true of the 1920s, how much more is it a fair description of the modern Riviera. Yet the opposite is also true. The buildings *make* the Riviera. The Riviera is dazzling, densely built-over, showy. That is how we all imagine it. That is what we expect of it now. That is what we experience. There is no return, and can never be, to a "pristine" state of nature, which is itself a myth, so great has been the human impact on the exotic and colourful flora that also define any image of the Côte d'Azur since the earliest days of pre-historic man in his Roquebrune caves. The Riviera is no more and no less than all the things we see today, demanding our awed attention, flattering our senses—mimosa, palm-trees, swimming pools, terraces, stuccoed hotels, balconied villas and awning-lined apartment blocks, beach umbrellas beside the age-old shining blue sea.

Yet this is still only the surface picture. It is a picture of the Riviera from outside, from above. The Riviera is also an integral part of France. In the historical context, that is something quite recent, since Nice and the territory to the east only became French in 1860. But the question remains, is the Riviera just another part of France, with its geographical peculiarities of course, in the same way as other departments and regions have their own history and topography?

The land along this coastal strip has been used to operating independently of "central" control. The Roman occupation was an important exception, but even then the numbers of occupiers was small and they had a specific task, to defend Roman access and trade routes, with little concern for the local inhabitants. After the Roman retreat and before the eighteenth century the pockets of inhabited land were tiny compared with the wide swathes of rocky, scrubby hillsides and boggy river estuaries. Communities were isolated. Mosquitoes drove everyone mad, and getting around was dangerous and slow (little has changed). Above all, it was a dull place, poor and uncultured, dilapidated and neglected by the outside world. It was waiting to be "rescued". Divided between French and "Italian" spheres of influence, it was not a coherent society even within its contentious borders.

But the French Riviera is not an island, not even metaphorically. It is not politically or socially isolated, even while it strives to be different. Most of the people who live here are after all French, however international the image may be. One group of French people who have given the Riviera its particular quality is made up from the *Pieds Noirs*, the white (and often xenophobic) former inhabitants of French North Africa. They tend to share a right-wing political stance with another group of now-native incomers, namely Corsicans. And, of course, they find allies among many of those with Italian backgrounds, a high proportion of whom have lived on the Riviera, particularly but not exclusively in Nice, for many generations.

On the social level, the modern French Riviera cannot escape being part of the great divide that in many ways has always defined French attitudes and politics. France has for more than two centuries been split socially between left and right; between those who support the Revolution and those who favour the old, monarchical, Catholic ways; between *Dreyfusards* and *anti-Dreyfusards*; between urban and rural. Those traditional divisions have been just as apparent in the south as elsewhere. But there are local twists.

The xenophobic tendencies apparent on the French Riviera have their origins in long-standing fears of neighbours, either Italians on the other side of the modern border or, often expressed in more extreme form, suspicion of the people from the other side of the Mediterranean, the "Saracens" and their successors. The patronizing attitudes of northern visitors, arriving without so much as a by-your-leave, with their money and acute sense of social distinctions, have sometimes exacerbated the long-established tensions. One consequence has been an almost unashamed reliance by local politicans on populist nationalism. They appeal to the shared sense that no-one else, even (perhaps especially) the authorities in Paris, understands the Riviera. They make political capital out of the suspicion that all outsiders are bent on exploiting the Riviera and should be furiously resisted whenever and however they try to impose their alien standards on local customs.

Graham Greene, when he openly denounced the corruption these attitudes led to in his 1982 Zola-esque pamphlet, *J'Accuse*, railed against what he called the "dark side" of Nice, a city which he described as the "preserve of some of the most criminal organisations in the south of France". Greene's main concern was the way a vicious member of the *milieu*, or criminal underground, had used corrupt officials, policemen, lawyers and magistrates to act in his favour and turn a blind eye to his crimes that included kidnap and physical violence. The context was a divorce, but Greene had his sights on the corrupt criminality of a whole gamut of legal and political authorities, who used the Riviera citizens' fear of the outsider for their own nefarious ends.

The mayor, Jacques Médecin, who was mentioned in Greene's pamphlet, was the son of the previous mayor. He was involved in the politics of the far right despite being nominally a member of the Gaullist party. Médecin ran Nice like a warlord. In 1990 he fled France after being in office for twenty-four years but was extradited from Uruguay four years later. Having spent a short time in prison, he went back to Uruguay, only to die there of a heart attack. Jacques Médecin was more than just a symbol of the kind of murky politics endemic in Nice—and to a lesser extent in other cities of the Riviera. He embodied that long tradition of Riviera separatism.

In the same year that he died a French member of parliament, Mme Yann Piat, who had ambitions to be mayor of Hyères and expressed her ambition to clean up the city, was murdered in a *milieu* killing. She had just visited the Interior Minister to complain about local extortion and planning rackets. A number of writers and journalists were later condemned for libel for saying openly what others were whispering, that the killing was blatantly political. The case has never been solved, despite an official enquiry that claimed that Mme Piat was killed merely as a result of a dispute over the ownership of a bar.

Undoubtedly those were the "bad old days". But criticisms remain directed at the kind of politics Greene fought against, even if the corrupt elements no longer flaunt their immunity or openly threaten their opponents, sure, as they once were, of their own security behind a "wall" of mutual protection. The outside world, with its standards of democracy and accountability, its drive towards economic and social interdependence, has certainly reduced—but not eliminated—the "special" nature of this traditionally isolated corner of south-east France.

If the change has gone, according to some, too far the other way, counteracting the Riviera's unique identity, the concept of no change at all is an unattractive one. The essence of the Riviera conjured up in the photographs in this book is seductive, elegant and very much man-made. The sea is all the more spectacular etched with the wakes of speedboats or rocking an elegant yacht, or even showing off a glitzy (but enviable) gin palace. The hillsides are never more beautiful than when they are fashioned into exotic gardens where statues and fountains disport among brilliantly coloured flowers and shrubs, the most exotic imported from hot places all around the world.

Beauty = truth = goodness… but is it even relevant to introduce the moral equation in the context of the French Riviera? Why should a lotus land, even a paradise for playboys (if that were all the Riviera is), be subject to such interrogation? On the other hand, why should it be immune? The trouble is there is no simple moral yardstick. With regard to the Monte Carlo Casino, the issue used to be black and white—neither Victorian tub-thumping preachers like Charles Henry Spurgeon nor Queen Victoria herself had any truck with gambling dens; while for the citizens of Monaco, by contrast, the international gamblers have always been a lifeline, benign suckers who keep their tiny principality economically afloat. Now the consensus is mostly neutral. Let competition flourish. Let the Casino be both a thing of beauty or ugliness, so long as it is also a source of revenue.

Another question: does the Riviera encourage creativity, stimulate the artistic impulses—or does it suck them dry, induce a *farniente* ease that deadens the urge to imagine and create things that will set the world ablaze? The obvious answer is that it can do both. Henri Matisse created his Riviera chapel; Katherine Mansfield used Menton to tease out the subtlest interpretations of her distant childhood; Ferdinand Bac coalesced all his worldly experiences into a Riviera garden. But where is the really great Riviera novel or poem? Where are the really great Côte d'Azur buildings? Why do so many artists associated with the Riviera come to it only in their maturity, often for the last years of their life, when their original talent was nurtured far away in harsher climates?

There are no simple answers of course. The small, dense, beautiful Riviera does not even have to be answerable to interrogations of this kind. It is what it is, and it is what we all make of it.

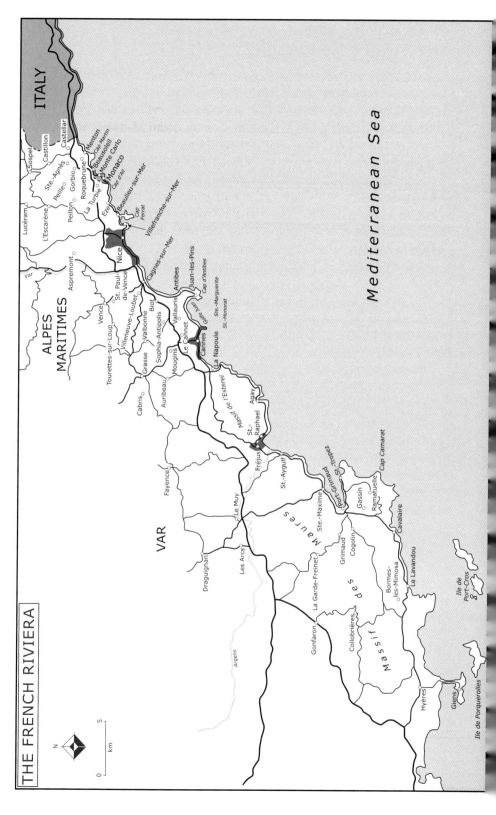

THE FRENCH RIVIERA

N

0 — 5
km

ITALY

ALPES MARITIMES

Sospel
Castillon
Lucéram
L'Escarène
Castellar
Menton
Ste-Agnès
Gorbio
Peille
Cap Martin
Peillon
Roquebrune
Beausoleil
Monte Carlo
Aspremont
La Turbie
Monaco
Èze
Cap d'Ail
Vence
St. Paul-de-Vence
Beaulieu-sur-Mer
Var
Tourrettes-sur-Loup
Villefranche-sur-Mer
Cap Ferrat
Villeneuve-Loubet
Cagnes-sur-Mer
Nice
Grasse
Valbonne
Biot
Cabris
Sophia-Antipolis
Vallauris
Antibes
Auribeau
Mougins
Juan-les-Pins
Cap d'Antibes
Le Cannet
Ste.-Marguerite
Cannes
Golfe Juan
St.-Honorat
La Napoule

VAR

Fayence
Massif de l'Estérel
Agay
Le Muy
St.-Raphaël
Draguignan
Fréjus
Les Arcs
St.-Aygulf
Ste.-Maxime
Port-Grimaud
St.-Tropez
Gonfaron
La Garde-Freinet
Grimaud
Cap Camarat
Collobrières
Cogolin
Gassin
Ramatuelle
M a s s i f   d e s   M a u r e s
Bormes-les-Mimosa
Cavalaire
Hyères
Le Lavandou
Giens
Île de Port-Cros
Île de Porquerolles
Argens

Mediterranean Sea

Chapter One
VIA AURELIA
THE ROMAN RIVIERA

People now called rather haphazardly "Ligurians" were the first known inhabitants of the French Riviera in historical times. Traces of occupation go back three thousand years or so. Not much is known of these aboriginals, only that they built fortified villages, notably on the site of modern Nice.

Some centuries later, Greeks from overcrowded Phocaea moved, first into Massilia (Marseille), then outwards to Hyères and Nice, as they tended to do wherever there was a chance of a little industry or commerce. The Greeks brought the vine (thoughtfully informing the earlier inhabitants what could be extracted from the wild stock indigenous to the area) as well as olives and other products of their advanced civilization. The Celts, who were at the same time putting down roots as far south as the Riviera, preferred the wilder hill country up from the coast—and to raid rather than trade.

Across in "Italy" things in this pre-Christian period were a great deal less predictable. The Punic Wars spilled over into Liguria and along the Mediterranean coast. Roman control, however, was consolidating all the time. The temptation the Romans felt to intrude into someone else's territory became irresistible as their power base ceased to be threatened. When, in 25 BC, the Celts suddenly descended on Massilia like wolves on the fold, the Greeks made the logical but dangerous decision to ask the Romans for help. That help once granted, the Romans decided they liked what they saw and turned the whole area into their very first "Provincia".

In H. G. Wells' novel, *Meanwhile: the Picture of a Lady* (1933), set in a fictional Hanbury Gardens on the Italian side of the modern border, a discursive intellectual visitor reflects on the Roman road that connected not just Italy and France but the remote past and the present.

> Over everything hung a promise of further transformations, for the Italians had a grandiose scheme for reviving the half obliterated tracks of the

The Trophy of the Alps – ruined but still haughty symbol of Augustan power

Via Aurelia as a modern motoring road to continue the Grande Corniche. Everything passed here and everything went by; fashions of life and house and people and ideas; it seemed that they passed very swiftly indeed, when one measured time by a scale that would take in those half disinterred skeletons of Cro-magnon men and Grimaldi men who lay, under careful glass casings now, in the great cave of the Rochers Rouges just visible from the dining-room windows. That great cave was still black with the ashes of prehistoric fires, as plain almost as the traces of yesterday's picnic. Even the grisly sub-man with his rude flint-chipped stakes, was here a thing of overnight. His implements were scattered and left in the deeper layers of the silted cave, like the toys of a child that has recently been sent to bed. With a wave of his ample hand Mr. Sempack could allude to the whole span of the human story.

The Roman conquest did indeed change the human story of the Riviera. But it did not "pass very swiftly"; rather it was the catalyst for the many waves of change to come. And it left an indelible mark on the landscape. Charles Lenthéric, *Inspecteur Général des Ponts et Chaussées* and a prolific writer on the ancient monuments of France, visited the Fréjus area in the latter half of the nineteenth century. He almost believed he was in Italy, as his *The Riviera Ancient and Modern* (1895) testifies:

> The whole effect of this southern landscape is much more Italian in the classical sense of the word than are many celebrated sites in Italy itself. The character of the land is the same, the sky is the same, the general air of sadness is the same as on the banks of the Tiber, and the Roman ruins scattered all around render the resemblance still more striking. Thus does the port of Caesar and Augustus remind us on the coasts of Provence of all the vicissitudes, of the prosperity and the decay of imperial Ostia, and of the other ports of Claudius and Trajan.

There are other reminders of the great days of Rome along the Riviera, but not many, and none as spectacular as the architectural relics in Nîmes, Arles or Aix. One monument, however, exerts enormous power over the imagination still, for all that it has been systematically ruined and only partially restored.

Le Trophée des Alpes

By 14 BC Roman power had finally asserted itself. All the annoying indigenous tribes were rendered inoperative. To prove their point, the conquerors put up one of the most assertively powerful monuments anywhere. This is the Trophée des Alpes, Trophy of the Alps, a massive structure dedicated by the Roman Senate to the cult of personality of the Emperor Augustus, formerly known as Gaius Octavius Thurinus. In boldly cut letters an inscription on the base listed (as Pliny the Elder recorded in his *Natural History*, Volume III) all the forty-four defeated tribes, some as far away as on the Adriatic shores, as if daring them ever to make another attempt to rebel. Its impact was not instantly effective. Resistance from those tribes was a by-product of bullying Roman rule for over a hundred years more. Even so, the Roman tide flowed inexorably in. Rome was an ultimately irresistible force, and the Trophy was its symbol.

The triumphal monument had a square base, each side over 130 feet wide. Above it a ring of columns supported an upside-down cone, so that on the very top, no less than 160 feet above the ground, a statue of the Emperor Augustus, flanked by two captives, could survey his territories and deflate any ambition to topple him or the power of Rome. Towering almost 5,000 feet over the port of Hercule Monoikos (Monaco)—the association with Hercules being a clever piece of political branding—Augustus glowered at the hilly countryside all around.

Even today it is not hard to imagine the fear this inspired. The Trophy itself, though sadly truncated and tamed, is still formidable. A small museum by its side in the village of La Turbie explains its fate, for as the Roman Empire declined and fell, so did this magnificent monument. Visigoths, Vandals and other "barbarians" passed through, knocking bits off it. Christians then took against its dedication to the pagan Apollo and, around the year 700, the Monks of Lérins came by to destroy the statues. Louis XIV gave orders for it to be blown up and succeeded at least in part. From then on it was open season. The stones were simply removed to build churches, houses, bridges, roads…

The rot was stopped soon after the Nice region became attached to France in 1860. In 1900 a local archaeologist began serious excavations, later bringing in the more famous and experienced Jules Formigé. Finally, in a kind of paradigm of the Riviera, rich Americans came to the rescue, and in the 1920s, thanks to the generosity of Dr. Edward Tuck, a financier from New Hampshire who had come to live in Paris and Monte Carlo, restoration to its present form was completed in 1934.

The Trophy of the Alps is still impressive enough at a mere 115 feet high and missing most of the colonnade and all of the cone and statue at the top, to make one conscious of Roman power. It is the most startling evidence of the period of Roman occupation. But there are still many other, less spectacular, traces.

VIA JULIA AUGUSTA

Soon after the Romans saved Massilia and decided to keep it for themselves, they started their familiar road-building programme. The first Roman road headed west, towards Spain. This was the Via Domitia, started in 121BC by Gnaeus Domitius Ahenobarbus. But what was needed most was a proper through road, a freeway all the way from Rome to Gaul, taking in the new Provincia. If the Roman legions had to march all those many miles to the outposts of their Empire, they should be given every modern facility.

The Via Julia Augusta was duly built on the orders of Augustus between 13 and 12 BC. It began in Emilia by the River Trebbia and thrust its way through to the River Var, on the western side of Nice.

There has recently been an intensive programme (at a cost of almost half a million euros) to "revitalize" this key road—particularly the section of it between Ventimiglia, just inside Italy, and the Trophée des Alpes at La Turbie, above Monaco. (The plan had in fact been conceived long before, as H. G. Wells knew when he was writing in the 1930s.) In 2006 the local authorities finally turned debate into action, designating nine sites of special interest. To mark its public launch, historians and elected dignitaries from both sides of the national border walked in procession, in slow and ragged imitation of the legionaries, along the whole route.

Their starting point was the Roman town of Albintimilium (Ventimiglia), which flourished from the second century BC and sported a theatre, public baths and noble houses with fine mosaics. The Romans shifted its original "Ligurian" centre from the heights of Collasgarba down to the estuary of the Nervia river, a more favourable site, especially for trade. The site of the forum is yet to be discovered. The east-west high street, or *decumano massimo*, ten feet wide and paved with slabs of white limestone from the quarries of La Turbie, was one part of the Via Julia

Augusta that presented no challenge to the engineers constructing the military road. It had sidewalks (*crepidines*) and an open sewer or drain (*cloaca*) down the middle. Beyond the Provincia Gate, unearthed remains suggest a smaller version of the Appian Way's avenue of tombs.

Immediately to the west of Albintimilium, the Roman road-builders faced far more severe challenges. This was the first attempt to overcome the isolating terrain of the Riviera, the succession of steep, rocky, inaccessible valleys and gullies that made any east-west journey virtually impossible. Milestones marked off their road's laborious progress.

As early as the middle of the eighteenth century, the archaeologist Giovanni Paolo Ricolvi was digging up milestones from the times of Augustus, Hadrian and (much later) Caracalla. He found them in fields and woods. He pulled them out of walls. Then he studied their scarred inscriptions. In the church of San Michele in Ventimiglia three of these cylindrical milestones are preserved. Two are used to contain holy water, the third is part of a pillar. Each originally displayed the distance in miles (each mile being 1,480 metres) from the centre of Rome.

The Girolami Rossi Archaeological Museum (named after the nineteenth-century excavator) is housed in the Annunziata Fort in Old Ventimiglia. It not only has an impressive view from its terrace out over the Mediterranean, but also contains an exciting number of Roman artefacts. Many of the sculptures, inscriptions, sarcophagi and reliefs were donated by Thomas Hanbury, the British trader, adventurer, collector and gardener (see Chapter Ten). The museum also contains some fine Roman glassware, notably an extraordinary dish engraved with the figure of a centaur with a fish's tail. Seen against a background of the blue sea beyond the museum window, it seems to come alive. In the British Museum in London you can see a white glass jug with blue filaments that came from an Albintimilium tomb, while a whole marble tomb belonging to one M Sabrius found its way to Liverpool's Public Museum.

After the flatter ground of the Latte plain, the next traces of the Via Julia Augusta can be seen in and around the Hanbury Botanical Gardens in Mortola Inferiore. A tiny fragment of paving survives in the lower section of the garden, and there are other traces of Roman roads and buildings in the area, but you have to be a dedicated searcher to track them down, and even then the results are not spectacular.

Further traces of the old Roman road are preserved on the site of the

Palaeolithic caves at the Balzi Rossi (Wells' "Rochers Rouges"), right on the modern frontier. Again, the site promises a little more than it can deliver. Whatever the traces visible a hundred years ago, today life in the Palaeolithic era has to be inferred rather than witnessed from the scooped-out caves in the cliff faces. The retreating sea, the construction of the railway and modern building have made even the precise location of the Roman road difficult to discern. It was certainly hacked into the cliff face. The only fragment that remains on this site is just visible below the railway line. The two parts of the Balzi Rossi Museum are, however, worth a quick visit and help to fill in the visual gaps.

It is here that the road crosses into modern France and the town of Menton. Most of the locally excavated Roman remains have been transferred into museums such as the Musée de la Préhistoire.

On the west side of the town, in Roquebrune-Cap Martin, there is a prestigious first-century funerary enclosure dating from between 100 and 40BC and known as the Villa Lumone after a local nobleman. Decorated with black and white stones and red brick, it was built right beside the road, next to milestone number 599, and reminiscent, as in Albintimilium, of the tombs along the Via Appia. The belief was that the dead person would regain a small fraction of life when looked upon by living passers-by; inscriptions on the tombs would attempt to attract people's attention. Sadly only a remnant of the Villa Lumone tomb has survived, while the Via Julia Augusta is well and truly buried, beneath the Route Nationale 7.

What appears to be a small Roman triumphal arch, just as the road begins to curve out of Menton onto Cap Martin is in fact quite false, an amusing folly from 1882. Continuing further westwards, the Roman road climbs up behind modern Beausoleil to the hills above Monaco. This is where it meets the beginning of an even older road that stretched, in pre-Roman times, towards and into Spain. It was known as the Herculean Way, more of a succession of paths and tracks than a proper road. Above Beausoleil stands a very ancient fortification known as the Mont des Mules, but it is hard to make out from the stones how much predates the Roman road and how much bears traces of Roman engineering.

And then the Via Julia meets the great monument at La Turbie, skirting by it close enough for travellers to be sure to reflect on its symbolic as well as literal power, before soldiering on towards Nice and further west.

CEMENELUM AND ANTIPOLIS

Five hundred years before the Romans, the Greeks from Marseille had settled beside a large bay, known now as the Baie des Anges. Here they founded a settlement they called Nike (Nice), after their goddess of victory. At least that is one story. Antoine de Beatis, in his account of his travels with his master, Cardinal Luigi of Aragon, in 1517 subscribed to the "popular" view that "Nizza" derives from "neither (ne) here nor there (za)", reinforcing his opinion by pointing out that the emblem of the city is an eagle with one leg on the ground and the other is "standing nowhere". (De Beatis was a better amanuensis than etymologist.)

The Romans preferred to build higher up on the hills behind the sixteenth-century city. Cemenelum (now Cimiez) became their regional capital. The ruins of some of its amphitheatres, aqueducts, baths and villas were not impressive enough to inspire much enthusiasm among early travellers, who tended to comment more on the fact that a public highway was driven through them than on their aesthetic qualities.

Antibes—the city across the bay or "Antipolis"—is also a Greek foundation later developed under Roman rule. The most important surviving remnant is the square Roman tower which forms part of the Château Grimaldi (now housing the Musée Picasso).

Traces of Roman life have also been found on the larger of the Iles de Lérins, formerly known as Lero. Pliny mentioned a port and town here. Recent excavations near the Fort Royal have uncovered houses, paintings, mosaics and ceramics from around the third century BC to the first century AD.

FORUM JULII (FRÉJUS)

Fréjus was a thriving Roman settlement, a garrison town founded by Julius Caesar, and the harbour to which Augustus despatched the 300 splendid ships of Anthony and Cleopatra's defeated fleet after the battle of Actium in 31BC. It is by far the most important Roman site on the French Riviera, with extensive architectural remains. It marks the end of the coastal stretch of the Via Julia Augusta. Charles Lenthéric, in his magnificent account of the buildings and landscapes of the ancient and modern Riviera written 130 years ago, pointed up the significance of this Roman port, noting that "Fréjus was then the last maritime station served by this strategical route [the Via Aurelia], the chief advantage of which was that it followed faithfully the coast of the Mediterranean, and so remained constantly under the protection of the Roman fleet, while at the same time it kept the access to Gaul always open."

The port itself is now half a mile inland. Over a century ago the land between silted up, leaving the old town high and dry. Lenthéric said it was "not even a decaying, it is a dead city, stifled, like so many others on this coast, by the mud and the alluvium of the very river to which it had before owed its existence." The Butte Sainte-Antoine, built over massive embankments retained by walls, is, however, a fine reminder of the past glory. It was probably the residence of the maritime prefect or local magistrates and survives in truncated form—although a Roman bollard (a stubby stone post carved out of bluish Esterellite) remains, showing on its base the marks of centuries of mooring ropes. "Augustus's lantern"—a thirty-foot high tower topped by a six-sided pyramid, is said to be a landmark to show the entrance to the harbour. Lenthéric stressed that it was never a lighthouse but was "a sort of sea-mark to direct the course of vessels in the outer port where navigation was sometimes difficult… perhaps the faces of the prism were utilised, like those of the famous tower of the winds at Athens, for the purpose of sundials, and the top of the pyramid may have been surmounted by a vane or a flagstaff."

The arena, a rather poor-man's provincial Coliseum, also survives. Despite placards announcing its restoration, it has today a neglected air, still reminiscent of the time when Victor Hugo stumbled across these same Roman remains behind a hovel in a walk outside the town (*Voyages*, 1839):

> I walked on under this vault and stepped into a vast circular enclosure completely surrounded by a magnificent pile of shattered tiers of seats, broken arcades and filled-in vomitoriums. This is the Fréjus arena. Among the reticulate blocks is a tangle of wild fig trees and terebinths, wrapped around by garlands of brambles. The wild animal pens, shut up behind reed fences, house some old casks. I saw a peasant come down the almost new steps of the emperors' staircase. I was at the very spot where writhed, two thousand years ago, lions, gladiators and tigers. Now tall grass is growing there, munched peacefully all around me by a herd of thin horses, meandering about the amphitheatre with bells around their necks.

The Fréjus arena – little changed since Hugo's time

Even more impressive was, and still is, the aqueduct that brought water over hilly country for a distance of 26 miles. Hugo was bowled over:

> The original aqueduct could not have been more beautiful than this giant ruin stretched over the whole plain, running, falling, getting up again, here showing in profile a series of three or four arches half buried in the ground, there throwing up to the sky a single, broken arch or a huge buttress like a druidical peulven, then majestically rising up in a semi-circle on top of two massive squares of stone, transfiguring the ruin into a triumphal arch.

It is a pity that these and the many other fragments of Roman civilization in Forum Julii seem such an embarrassment to the people of modern Fréjus, more interested apparently in selling dried lavender and Provençal tablecloths to tourists than cleaning the ivy and litter from the stones or placing signs to guide visitors through the invading apartment blocks and car parks. The one complete triumph—an object of exceptional beauty—is the two-headed (Hermes) Carrara marble bust, discovered only in 1970 and now in the Archaeological Museum. The left-facing head is that of an elegant, composed figure, perhaps a Bacchus, though he seems too sober; the right-facing head is a highly realistic Pan/faun with pointed ears, a curly beard and an enigmatically smiling, almost smirking, expression on his sensuous lips. There are other noteworthy examples of Roman art here, including a panther mosaic and a head of Jupiter, but the Hermes is the finest. It has been adopted as its symbol by the town of Fréjus.

A little inland, up the Argens river, on the "wide, green, ague-stricken plain" (in Lenthéric's phrase), is the spot where Anthony managed to persuade the Roman governor, Lepidus—who happened to be an old friend—not to oppose him in the struggle for power and wealth among the successors to the murdered Julius Caesar. The deal struck at Forum Voconii (modern Le Cannet-des-Maures) was of great historic importance, since it led to the break-up of the Roman Republic, then to a period of military rule and finally "the Roman world became the slave of an autocrat," again in the words of Charles Lenthéric.

FRAGMENTS

A little further along the coast from Fréjus, at Les Issambres, on an inlet close to a Gallo-Roman villa, where mosaics were found showing a dolphin swimming between two tridents, is a unique example of a fish farm. Fish were lured into one tank, then trapped in a series of ponds, where the depth of the water was regulated by walls and gates.

In Vence two much-recycled Roman columns have ended up, one behind the cathedral and the other in the Place du Grand-Jardin. They were most likely either part of a triumphal arch or supports for a temple dedicated to Mars. Inscriptions on the plinths show that they were offered by the people of Marseille to Vence at the beginning of the third century AD. In *Secret French Riviera* (2007) Jean-Pierre Cassely recounts their subsequent history:

> As was the custom, the columns were reused to support the vaulting of the cathedral choir. In 1756, after the building was enlarged, they were abandoned. One of them was then used to help hold up the roof of the former fish merchant's shop… as for the second column, it was snapped up to decorate what is now the Place Godeau.
>
> Strangely enough, the reference to the god Mars evoked by these columns sometimes leads to misunderstanding. Antony Mars was a dandy from Vence, during the *belle époque*, and has no connection with the god of war nor with the short form of Marseille in popular use today.

Another curious object from Roman times pointed out by Cassely is the Mausoleum of the Golden Goat, near Biot. Thirty feet high, it is one of several tile-roofed tombs in this out-of-the-way spot.

> It is said that in the evenings, in front of a crevice in the rock known by the herdsmen, a goat with golden horns attracted passers-by with its capricious leaps. Drawn into the cave with its tunnels and galleries, such a man would lose his bearings and fine himself alone, abandoned by the animal. He would indeed find a treasure of golden ingots, pearls and gold coins, but would die of hunger and thirst, lost in the innermost depths of the labyrinth. The source of this legend is a true story. In 714, a Saracen known as the "King of Majorca" buried in this same cave his treasure pillaged in Provence. Obliged to flee the region, he abandoned

his precious booty but left a plan of where to find it engraved on a silver (some say golden) bell.

Maybe! But did anyone ever find the "treasure"?

Fragments like these remind us of the ebb and flow of Roman power, its transience. Monuments such as the Trophy of the Alps or the arena and aqueduct in Fréjus recall a time when the Romans seemed unbeatable, although their modern ruined state tells us otherwise. But the tombs, the milestones, the temple pillars propping up a covered market, the mosaic floors and town drains all attest to a society that enjoyed four hundred years of stability and relative prosperity, before plunging back into hazardous obscurity.

Villefranche-sur-Mer – hillside villas

Chapter Two

A Paradise at War

The Riviera as Battleground

It may seem strange to a visitor to the French Riviera today how many of its towns and villages owe their origins to violence or the threat of violence. Sir Frederick Treves, in his highly coloured account, *The Riviera of the Corniche Road* (1921), wrote:

> …the spoiled and petted Riviera has been the scene of almost continuous disturbance and bloodshed for the substantial period of some seventeen hundred years… it has now become a Garden of Peace, calmed by a kind of agreeable dream-haunted stupor such as may befall a convulsed man who has been put asleep by cocaine.

Those long convulsions began with the Roman conquest of the Ligurian indigenous peoples but increased in intensity after the fall of the Roman Empire. When the imposed peace vanished, the country was, in Treves' words again, "overrun from Marseilles to Genoa by gangs of hearty ruffians whose sole preoccupation was pillage, arson and murder." Not surprisingly, there are few written records from the centuries following the Roman retreat.

Most active among the first wave of "ruffians" were the Lombards, who came out of the mountains to the north to do their pillaging. At some period towards the end of the eighth century an even greater danger started to emerge in the shape of seafarers. In folklore—and still indeed today—they are generally and generically referred to as "Moors" or "Saracens"—Malory's "horryble peple" in the *Morte d'Arthur*. They came from coastal territories all along the eastern and southern Mediterranean. One legacy is a string of fortified and inaccessible hill towns and villages (the *villages perchés* that are such a tourist attraction today—see Chapter Eleven).

The Saracen incursions and their occupation of some quite large areas in the south-east coastal region of France are just one small part of the

The Emperor has landed – from Golfe-Juan to this memorial in Laffrey

massive struggle between newly Islamic raiders from North Africa and the many, often feuding, Christian powers throughout mainland Europe and the Mediterranean islands. The Saracens' most enduring foothold in the Riviera was their so-called *fraxine*, or stronghold, which evolved into the modern town of La Garde-Freinet. Charles Martel's victory at Poitiers in 732 pushed most of the Saracens south into Spain, but this particular prominence behind Grimaud in the Maures hills provided a solid, fortifiable base from which to exert a wider influence for another couple of hundred years. Their fortress has all but disappeared, although their legacy of flat tiles and the cork industry lasted much longer. Being a tiny outpost, however, there are few remaining signs of their more important intellectual and scientific achievements, nor (in literature at least) of their traditional codes of chivalry and courtly love, only oral memories of heroic resistance… and disasters.

Among the small reminders of the Saracens' presence in the region are some place-names and words and expressions in the French and Provençal languages (such as *chiffre* and *épinards*). But Arabic terms are far less conspicuous than in Spanish or even Sicilian.

THE MIDDLE AGES

The two-hundred-year heyday of the Saracens was ended by an early Count of Provence, Guillaume le Libérateur (956-93). His intervention did little, however, to restore the calm that had briefly characterized the Roman occupation. His son, also Guillaume, failed to put a stop to feudal jealousies and strife, such that the Comté de Provence became a byword for dynastic instability. There were no clearly dominant rulers, no single regional power that attracted wide allegiance. The Dukes of Savoy or Milan, the Doges of Genoa, the Counts of Ventimiglia, the Grimaldis (see Chapter Three) and many other rulers of territories with insecure boundaries and conflicting interests fought and bargained and betrayed each other. Pettier rulers such as the Lords of Eze and other fortress village *seigneurs* would use the confusion for their own ends, conducting feuds and raids on each other and only making alliances to further some temporary interest of their own. The details of these complex and confused times are too exhausting to contemplate and best left to historical researchers—or the imagination.

Some coherence was introduced at the end of the fifteenth century.

While Nice and the territories to its east remained under the control of the Dukes of Savoy, the "Estates" of Provence attached themselves to the Kingdom of France as more or less equal partners. It was not long before Provence was cut down to size and found itself imposed upon not just by French troops but also by the French language. In 1543 Nice found itself under siege from both French and Turkish troops. It was then that one of the most enduring legends of resistance began.

The story of Catherine Ségurane has many variations. It is generally agreed, however, that she was a washerwoman who played some role in the town's fierce resistance. She may or may not have seized an enemy standard by knocking out its bearer with the stick she used to thrash clothes. But her real fame is for standing on the rampart and baring her (capacious) bottom to the enemy forces below. The Turks, it is claimed, were so outraged by this feminine indecency that they turned tail and fled. Sadly the story has not been shown to be definitely true (one contemporary witness Jean Badat, who described the action, did not mention the mooning), but what is sure is that the besieged forces triumphed.

In 1691 the French did, however, annexe Nice, only to return it to Savoy five years later. Less than twenty years on, overall suzerainty was granted to the Kingdom of Sardinia.

In 1793, at the height of the French Revolution, there was yet another temporary shift of ownership. The French occupation was then itself threatened in 1800 when sailors from a British frigate briefly captured Monaco. Indeed, in the final years of the Napoleonic war British troops even occupied Nice. But in 1814, with Napoleon on the run and banished to Elba, back went Nice and its territories to the King of Sardinia. Once again, after a turbulent couple of decades, the River Var, just to the west of the city, marked the border.

NAPOLEON AND AFTER

Echoes of the Corsican emperor haunt the Riviera. We have Napoleon to thank, for instance, for the Grande Corniche, the high road between Nice and Menton. For several months in 1794 he stayed in a house between Nice and Villefranche, enjoying a flirtation with the landlord's daughter. A plaque at 6 rue Bonaparte marks the spot. There is a modest ten-foot high obelisk in St.-Raphael, where Napoleon landed in 1799 after his expedition to Egypt. He passed through in the other direction, in April 1814, on his way to exile on Elba.

The most potent reminder of Napoleon Bonaparte's power—and vulnerability—is in Golfe-Juan. Golfe-Juan is now a rather downbeat resort town in the centre of a large natural harbour stretching from Cap d'Antibes on its eastern side to the Cap de la Croisette on the western outskirts of Cannes. In 1815 the beach here had just a few fishermen's huts and potters' sheds; it was a meeting place for local traders and muleteers. They would have been surprised to see at three in the afternoon on 1 March, seven ships appear suddenly—a square-rigged brigantine, the *Inconstant*, with forty guns, four three-masters and a couple of feluccas, the small, narrow boats with triangular sails that used to ply the Mediterranean. This motley fleet, carrying eleven hundred men, was bringing back the Emperor Napoleon after a five-day sail from Portoferraio, on Elba. Here he gave the order to march first towards Cannes and Grasse, then further north. The route taken by Napoleon as far as Laffrey, a small village to the north of Grenoble, is now known as the Route Napoléon.

A concrete blob marks the spot where he landed; the tiny blue mosaic embedded in it is hard to detect among the competing colours of bus stops and posters and café tables. A short distance inland a statue of Napoleon— like a mini-Nelson's column (same hat, same stare, different man)—found its current resting place after years of displacement and mutilation. Every year the town re-enacts the 1815 landing. Stands are put up along the sea front, then, hand on breast and frown on face, a small actor, accompanied by uniformed volunteers, steps onto the sand. Bands play, people cheer. If only the welcome had been as warm a couple of hundred years ago. At least the Emperor did not have to find his way across the busy street along the front, under the railway line and through the one-way system, stuck behind delivery vans and stationary people-movers (though he would not have been able to enjoy a *bouillabaisse* either at the Michelin-starred Chez Tétou).

The ambiguous reception Napoleon received is down-played in the modern re-enactments. But it is fair to say that not many facts about this crucial moment in European history can be verified for sure. One story has it that Napoleon's small contingent of followers were victims of a hold-up by highwaymen. Another story tells that they themselves waylaid the coach of the Prince of Monaco, newly restored to his principality, and demanded money with menaces. This version has it that Napoleon, realizing that the Prince of Monaco was in much the same predicament as himself, let him carry on unmolested. Perhaps that is why the Museum of the Prince's Palace in Monaco houses such a rich collection of Napoleonic mementos.

What is certain is that Napoleon was not received warmly by the garrison in Antibes, nor did his arrival in Cannes kindle much enthusiasm. This coolness appears to have influenced his decision to travel north very circumspectly. Nevertheless, in only just over a couple of weeks he was back in Paris to a tumultuous welcome... eventually to meet his Waterloo.

A great deal of detail about Napoleon, important and trivial, can be found in the Musée Naval et Napoléonien in Antibes: toy soldiers, a miniature pendant by Barrault showing the emperor's pudgy cheeks and receding hairline, his hats and uniforms, and a tableau of him disembarking at Golfe-Juan.

Where the emperor landed was, of course, only just inside France. It was four and a half decades later, in 1860, during the reign of Napoleon III, that the territory of France—after an overwhelming vote by the *Niçois*—was extended eastwards to the line of the current Italian-French border in what appears, at last, to be as permanent an arrangement as any in the region's turbulent history.

The last part of the nineteenth and early years of the twentieth century were a time of unparalleled peace and prosperity. It was the time of the tourist boom, not just the fashionable élite of the *belle époque* but of expanding middle-class tourism too. Hotels were constructed wherever there was land, some on an epic scale like the Excelsior Regina, where Queen Victoria stayed in Cimiez, up above Nice. All the more crushing therefore was the impact of the First World War. The fighting may have been far away in the north, but the effect on the holiday boomtowns on the Côte d'Azur, particularly Nice, was almost as devastating.

The wounded started arriving on the Mediterranean coast within weeks of the outbreak of war. The Casino de la Jetée-Promenade—huge, garish, even Moorish, a dancing and gaming palace that became as much the visual symbol of Nice as the Eiffel Tower in Paris—was invaded by thousands of filthy and putrid soldiers. At least that was how many of the locals saw it. Owners of the smartest hotels complained they were being picked on—surely the cheaper establishments would be more suitable. At the same time their supply of rich Russians and Germans completely dried up, and only very slowly did some kind of winter season get under way again. Some hotels like the Negresco, the Ruhl and the Winter Palace reverted even during the most deadly years of the war to welcoming tourists instead of housing wounded soldiers. By 1917, the complaints were mostly that the Riviera had become too much of a pleasure ground again, ignoring the suffering of the wider world.

What served the Riviera well was the Americans' decision, after their entry into the war, to declare the bigger towns as leave centres. This was the preamble to the interwar years boom, the time when American visitors invented the summer season and ushered in a new era of prosperity. Not until the Second World War did the Riviera become, once again, a battleground.

The Maginot Line

The decision to build a line of fortifications from the English Channel to the Mediterranean was finally taken in 1930, after years of debate following the trauma of the First World War. Most of the building effort went into the northern section, especially in Lorraine, but the line from Switzerland to Menton also involved a massive programme of forts, blockhouses, trenches and tunnels. The Maginot line was made up of *casemates* (gun emplacements), *petits ouvrages* (smaller fortifications close to the frontier) and *gros ouvrages* (forts with massive protection, tunnels and artillery). Many of all three types survive, a formidably impressive witness to a military project imbued with the spirit and force of the mountainous land in which it took shape. In the words of the historian, Christian Corvoisier, quoted in the tourist literature:

> From the picturesquely dilapidated military forts and barracks to the dark trenches and hollow concrete domes, today's visitor couldn't, in a single day, take in all the treasures of this vast labyrinth of fortifications dedicated to the vertiginous and the useless.

"Useless" is a little unfair, because in 1940 the Alpine forts succeeded in holding at bay the initial thrust of the Italian invasion. Indeed, it was the French troops on the line from Lac Léman to the Mediterranean who were most shocked by the sudden armistice, believing themselves impregnable. The main significance of the forts, however, is their survival as monuments of military architecture.

Within the Alpes Maritimes alone there were more than eighty defence works, eight of them major forts, the *gros ouvrages*, in the Maginot line. Furthest north, guarding the upper Tinée valley, is the Rimplas fort, a prototype built in 1927. It was the key to resisting any incursion on Nice from the mountains—but it was never finished. The nearby Frassinea fort, built in the second half of the 1930s, was an altogether more effective obstacle to enemy incursions. It housed thirty soldiers and contained a two-month supply of rations and ammunition. Water came from a natural spring inside the fort. Today it is being meticulously reconstructed and is well worth the long and winding drive to reach it.

Further east loom the fortifications of the Col de Tende and the Massif de l'Authion. The latter inherited a huge nineteenth-century fortification dominating what is now (since its creation in 1979) the National Park of Mercantour. Its strategic importance was already apparent when French and Piedmontese troops clashed here during the French Revolution. It is one of the wildest, scariest and most atmospheric sites in France. If you drive up from the south, past Sospel and the Col de Turini, then on up, you enter a magical landscape of bare peaks and forested valleys with views to the high Alps on one side and the glinting Mediterranean on the other. On clear sunny days it seems the most benign of places. But it takes only a little imagination to picture the frozen, isolated soldiers huddled in their magnificent but grim and snowbound stone fortifications in the depths of winter.

Astonishingly, this apparent remoteness proved a fragile form of defence. In the summer of 1944, when German troops retreated from the coast up to the safety of the Massif de l'Authion (see p.32), they found themselves being shelled—by the US Navy.

In 1947 France annexed from Italy a strip of mountainous land to the east, taking in the high crests overlooking the Tinée valley. As a result the great Maginot forts finally lost their strategic importance. At the same time, the hundreds of forts and smaller military emplacements built by the Italians from the nineteenth century onwards also lost their purpose—though many remnants of the *vallo alpino*, the Alpine Wall, including the central Colle Alto fort and its satellites close to the Col de Tende, provide useful targets for long-distance walkers along the 3,000 plus miles of marked trails in this wild border-land.

To the south, the Maginot forts were again products of traditional

A Maginot fort – "vertiginous and useless"

military defence systems. Several in the Bevera valley towards Sospel—
Barbonnet, Agaisen and St.-Roch in particular—played roles in the Second
World War. Barbonnet from the air looks like an Iron Age fort. Built
between 1883 and 1886, it is pentagonal in shape and surrounded by a
broad ditch. When it became part of the Maginot line, a huge artillery
bloc was added. Agaisen and St.-Roch are no less impressive. Again, it is
easy to imagine in the time-suspended atmosphere of these gargantuan
concrete hulks how up to two hundred soldiers huddled like submariners
inside a construction that would even have impressed Jules Verne.

But for the sheer panorama, it is hard to beat the most southerly of the
gros ouvrages, the Fort de Ste.-Agnès. Its lumpish concrete towers stare
down from their mountain peak above the Mediterranean like giant tubby
Easter Island statues. Ste.-Agnès was the most heavily armed of all the
Maginot forts and dominated the Riviera coastline. At the June 1940
armistice it was forced to cease hostilities. But this great fort never lost a
battle.

THE PONT ST.-LOUIS

If you take the high road from Italian Latte into French Menton, you will cross the Pont St.-Louis and probably not notice it. You are even less likely to notice the holes in the cliff wall facing you on the right just after you have crossed the barely perceptible, but precipitous, gully over which the bridge passes, ushering you across the international border. Had you been a member of the Italian armed forces in June 1940, one of the mighty army dispatched by an eager Mussolini to regain the "lost Italian" territory from Menton to Nice, you would surely have seen those two holes, because behind them were two guns pointing straight at you, one machine gun and one anti-tank gun.

Inside the hollowed-out cliff, without a rear exit because money and time had run out before one could be built, were nine French soldiers, commanded by a young lieutenant. They were trapped inside with very little food or drink, and they had to make their own fresh air by pedalling furiously on an adapted bicycle to re-circulate stale air filtered through a drum of carbon.

Nowadays on many a Sunday afternoon a young part-time soldier with a passion for military history waits beside the bridge to entice any interested passer-by into this deadly cave-cum-machine-gun post. He will explain how, even before the French "declared an armistice" on 22 June 1940, Mussolini rushed to try and cross the long border between triumphant Italy and humiliated France. A blizzard was helping put a stop to his troops' advance over the Little St. Bernard Pass. The only alternative was the cliff-bound road to Menton—since the new coast road had not yet been built and the railway line had been put out of action. But the view across the Pont St.-Louis up the road past the customs house and into Italy was an excellent one for the tiny contingent of defenders, their fingers crooked on the triggers of their two guns, ready for the first glimpse of an Italian soldier or tank. The result was a stand-off.

As soon as the armistice took effect, on 25 June at 08:45, an Italian colonel, prompted by Mussolini's impatience, walked down the road towards the inconvenient defenders waving an enormous white flag, trailing a retinue of officers and men. He blustered to the French lieutenant that the war was over; Menton belonged to the Duce; his impatient mass of men and tanks and guns should have free access, so please be sensible, pack up, get the hell out and let us by. Lieutenant Gros was having none of it. So for several more days the stand-off continued—the Italian army huddling around the corner in the protection of a quarry hacked out of the tall cliffs, the handful of French soldiers continuing to stand by their guns, ready to shoot at the first sign of the enemy.

Only after Italian troops had painstakingly infiltrated into France over the cliffs and down the other side, and once the French authorities themselves had succumbed to the inevitable, did the resisters of the Pont St.-Louis surrender. As the young guide is proud to tell you, "this was one of the most heroic actions of the French army in its entire history."

Occupation

The Italian occupation of the south-eastern corner of France is one of the odder aspects of the Riviera's involvement with warfare. The Italian connection had always been strong, although personal relations between local French and Italian people were traditionally prickly. For the Italians the occupation was seen—and declared, often aggressively—as no more than the recovery of what had "always" been theirs. Menton became Mentone again. They even built an elegant stone stairway from the promenade up to the Church of St.-Michel, San Michele, razing a number of old houses to do so. The town, this gesture said, is ours to do with as we like.

The French *mentonnais* were summarily evacuated to make room for "colonizing" Italians. On 3 June 1940, 15,700 reached Antibes and Cannes, only to be sent, four days later, on to the eastern Pyrenees (although by October many had trickled back). The Italian occupation had meanwhile begun on 24 June. Teaching was now in Italian. Signposts marked the distances to Rome. Everyone was issued with Italian identity cards. The Lira was the only legal currency. Obviously all this was a cause of great resentment and, later, recriminations.

The upheaval of the summer of 1940 affected everyone, on all sides of the conflict. Field Marshal Philippe Pétain, aged 84, for one, gave up his retirement job as a farmer and wine grower in Villeneuve-Loubet, near Cagnes-sur-Mer, to go and govern France from its new capital, Vichy. (One shudders to think what the old man would have made of the enormous pyramid-shaped flat blocks of the Marina Baie des Anges that now dominate what was once his skyline.) In the far south, Pétain was able to rely on a solid constituency of sympathizers. In her *Côte d'Azur: Inventing the Riviera* (1992), Mary Blume tells a story of the modish painter Kiki

Kisling, who had a drink in a Bandol café with the French actor Raimu—who was probably little more than "fashionably" antisemitic. The date was 3 September 1939.

> "Here we are about to die for Polish Jews. I don't know that you think
> of Polish Jews, my dear Kisling, but I couldn't give a damn."
> "I am a Polish Jew."
> "Not really, dear boy. Well, well, good old Kisling! We'll go to Poland
> and beat the pants off the huns."
> Even Kisling had to smile. But he let Raimu pay for the drink.

The Jews in general paid heavily for French indifference—and outright hostility. "Mort aux Juifs" was often seen scrawled on walls and trees both in the inter-war years and during the occupation. As early as 1925 a newspaper specializing in race-purity rants called *L'Action Gallo-Romaine Contre le Péril Judéo-Maçonnique* hit the streets of Nice (but failed after three editions). Marshal Pétain presided over a society which became increasingly dangerous for Jews and other refugees, although at first the southern Free Zone was a haven. One Paris newspaper referred to the Côte d'Azur as the "ghetto parfumé". The (Jewish) wit and playwright Tristan Bernard arrived in Cannes in August 1940 as part of the Great Exodus and was to stay for the next three years, remarking: "Nous ne sommes pas à Cannes mais à Kahn." Another of his *bons mots* did the rounds: "Tous les comptes sont bloqués. Tous les Bloch sont comptés"—which translates as, "All accounts are blocked. All the Blochs are counted." Wit was no defence against Nazis and their French collaborators; nevertheless, when Bernard was finally arrested, he turned to his wife and said, "Relax, *mon amie*, we have been living in fear, now we are going to live in hope!"

Immediately after the fall of France, John Taylor, British Consul in Nice, managed to arrange two coal ships to take off fellow countrymen in a hurry. The writer Somerset Maugham reluctantly boarded the *Saltersgate*, remembering to bring his dinner jacket, though ditching his tails. Later he told the BBC:

> We were of all classes. There were invalids, some so ill that they had to
> be carried on stretchers, but they had to be taken back and none knows
> to what fate because it was impossible to get them on ship… As we were

so short of water, none was available for washing… Then the food began to grow scanty and toward the end we were reduced to a piece of bully beef and four biscuits for our midday and evening meals… Altogether four people went out of their minds.

The journalist Mary Blume spoke to another passenger on the *Salters-gate*, Guy Hamilton, who had driven his Rolls Royce into the sea to stop it falling into Italian hands. "Maugham," Hamilton said, "made the fatal error of being evacuated on a coal boat wearing a detachable collar which because of the dirt immediately had to be detached. So he was not at his best in a shirt and gold stud." It took twenty days for the ship to get to England.

The early months of the *zone sud* were comparatively relaxed. Remaining British residents were able to form a committee, chaired by the Duke of Westminster, to help British soldiers and others escaping from the occupied north on their way to Spain. The local authorities were sometimes ready to issue medical certificates to the wounded to permit them to leave. Neutral Monaco provided a more or less safe haven for supporters of the Allies as well as for Nazi sympathizers; some were spies; most remained indifferent.

It was especially hard for the Jews who had fled south—but not, in the first three years, as hard as things became after September 1943, when German occupation followed the Italian after the Allied invasion of North Africa. The Italians had tended to ignore the zealous efforts of the Vichy prefect to round up and remove the Jews. An Italian-born Jewish banker, Angelo Donati, even played a prominent role protecting Jews and planning their escape into Italy.

Many intellectuals, including Jews and communists, gathered in Nice after the events of 1940. On a famous occasion the left-wing writer André Gide planned a lecture at the end of May 1941, but ran into opposition from the Légion Française des Combattants, Pétain's cheerleaders. In the end Gide delivered an angry denunciation of censorship but did not give the lecture. Later, Sartre came down to the southern zone to try and persuade first Gide then André Malraux to become more active in the Resistance, but without success. Malraux simply said he relied on "Russian tanks and American planes to win the war."

Despite some tolerance of refugee intellectuals, the long-standing antisemitism in Nice was hard to contend with. On 3 June 1942, in an atmosphere of public apathy and police connivance, the synagogue was ransacked. There were no protests and no attempt to bring the perpetrators to justice.

The arrival of the Germans themselves a year later condemned thousands to the extermination camps. In Nice the arrested Jews were taken to the Hotel Excelsior, from there to Drancy and, in most cases, on to Auschwitz. In all, about 5,000 Jews were transported from Nice, few ever to return. Only in Monaco did life continue more or less undisturbed. In fact, 1943 and 1944 were years of unprecedented prosperity.

But these years were also the high point of an increasingly active French resistance on the Riviera. The resistance movement was slow to start, even in the southern zone. Many French people there were not so unhappy that the left-wing Front Populaire was no more, even if they may have underestimated the controls the Germans were inflicting on the new right-wing authorities. In the far south, the refugees from the north, who included many Jews and other persecuted minorities, were not always made welcome by the humiliated but still intensely nationalistic French population. At the same time the need to smuggle people out of France or to give them shelter was the impetus for the creation of networks among those who, for humanitarian, political or personal motives, were determined to resist in any way they could the imposition of fascism.

The veteran writer Peter Leslie (*The Liberation of the Riviera*, 1980) has told the story of one remarkably brave resister, a schoolmaster from the mountain village of Peille, Ange-Marie Miniconi, who turned a sense of angry humiliation into "a guerrilla army of more than 600 men under the eyes of the Germans—and then used it to liberate Cannes." Fortunately for France, there were enough who shared those ideals and the courage to fight back to make the Allied landings, when they came, a success.

THE CHAMPAGNE CAMPAIGN

When it finally came on 15 August 1944, for most of the local population the Allied invasion was the first real time of upheaval. Winston Churchill opposed the American plan, preferring to attack German forces in Italy. His view did not prevail, and in the end the Anglo-American landing on the Riviera coast was a well-planned and deadly assault and soon over. It can hardly be compared in its scale or emotional impact today to Omaha or the other Normandy beaches. The reason why so few physical traces survive on the beaches of St.-Raphael of Operation Dragoon (dubbed the "Champagne Campaign") or of the German resistance, is not its insignificance, rather that, after the inevitable confusion of the first assault, the Allied advance was so unusually swift.

The operation was first codenamed "Anvil" and then, when that became so familiar as to be useless, "Dragoon"; but "no evidence exists," say Adleman and Walton, the American historians of the campaign, "that DRAGOON ever misled anyone, either." The landings certainly came as no surprise to the French. Attitudes to German occupation were already changing in anticipation. Almost everybody now wanted to be seen as part of the Resistance. Many continued to dig the antitank obstacles and dugouts and accept the hot meals in return, but they were also a good source of intelligence material for the Allies. This was confusing to the German occupying forces. According to Patrick Howarth:

> The Germans mistook French cooperation for agreement and misread perfidy for the surprising degree of resistance on August 15. But the inhabitants were neither passive nor perfidious. They were simply being Frenchmen. Insensitivity to this point was almost as serious a handicap to German plans for the defense of Southern France as the missing or inaccessible stores of men and materiel.

When the operation began, first the paratroopers and then thousands of infantrymen in gliders dropped out of the night onto the rugged territory around the town of Le Muy, behind Fréjus. Success was almost immediate despite the inevitable casualties and confusion. Even the fact that many landed up to thirty miles from their drop zones played into the invading forces' hands, because the Germans concluded that many *more* troops were attacking them than was in fact the case. They never did get organized enough to make a coherent defence. One American group surprised themselves by landing near St.-Tropez, but they surprised the German defenders more, so that, by the time the town was bombarded and then attacked by troops landing from the sea, the job of taking the town had effectively been done.

Le Muy itself was of great strategic importance to both sides, as it controlled a network of roads. The American commander, the quietly charismatic General Robert T. Frederick, moved in hard and fast, inducing an equally fast German surrender. The even more important town of Les Arcs was less of a pushover but was still captured quickly. St.-Tropez was damaged by American bombs, but the Carlton Hotel in Cannes, it seems, was spared after an appeal from a *New York Times* journalist.

Patrick Howarth (a colourful character who was a Special Operations Executive (SOE) Controller, a diplomat, banana grower, historian, poet and much else) quoted an American Red Cross official as estimating that "the period between the initial welcome and the asking of the question 'Why don't you go home?' usually lasted about three days. The Americans expected the French to admire them and be grateful to them for the fact of liberation. The French found this attitude difficult to endure."

The fact is that on the Riviera, as elsewhere in France, there were local scores to be settled, polical agendas to pursue and secrets to hide. The liberation itself created a new and volatile situation, fresh opportunities for revenge, denunciation and cover-ups. General Frederick was lucky to have a free hand, since the real action was moving up northwards, and the people of the Riviera were lucky to have him. In the words of Adleman and Walton:

> He was in a position to make serious mistakes. The complicated people and politics of these Mediterranean communities were literally begging for a scapegoat upon whom to blame the violent public disorder, the low foodstocks and the almost complete lack of new clothing, fuel and transportation. The Germans were gone so the Americans could have easily filled this role. They could have kept the residents of the Riviera from an uncomfortable self-scrutiny.

By keeping his distance and remaining a strictly military commander, Frederick avoided the worst mistakes. Some of the loudest complainers were expatriates who suddenly felt they were owed favours. They were out of luck. He also had under his command a rough tough unit called the First Special Service Force whose members—the Forcemen—had their own ideas of fair play and loyalty, tolerating no interference at all with their urge to fight hard and party hard afterwards. But for all the American troops this period of the war was a curious mix of danger and reward.

Monaco was technically "off limits", but not to soldiers determined enough in their pursuit of pleasure. Nice developed into a kind of instant resort even while the fighting was still going on. An American colonel remembered:

> We had taken over the Hotel Negresco but they [the management] kept the entire staff on duty. They were willing to work if we would supply the food; you see, there was plenty of money around but no food. It was amazing; you could be up in the hills in a foxhole being shelled, living the doughboy's life with C-Rations, grenades and all the rest of it, then get into a truck and drive thirty miles to a completely different world. You'd walk into the main dining room of the Hotel Negresco in dirty fatigues and your old jump boots and the waiters would flock around to serve you.

This is the same officer who became so adept at improvising the bringing of supplies into the Riviera that he and his men became known as "Colonel Graves and his Five Thousand Thieves". The problem was that everything brought in through the southern ports went straight up the Rhône to support the main northwards thrust. A fellow colonel in the increasingly isolated First Airborne Task Force recalled: "We were very light on transportation in those days… so we began to 'requisition' everything we could find. We took some bicycles to push our fifty caliber machine guns and we took a few civilian cars too. As a matter of fact, I ended up with a Cord front-wheel drive that had belonged to Charlie Chaplin and I put jeep wheels on it and this became quite a sight up and down the Riviera."

For Menton, the last town in occupied France, the ordeal went on to the bitter end of the campaign. The SS occupied the town on 29 August. Six hostages were shot. Bread had long since run out. Shells rained down onto Menton and the villages just inland. Once again there was a large-scale evacuation.

In the end a kind of stalemate was reached. The American Task Force became stretched to its limit once it had reached the Italian frontier, while the Germans, some of them holed up in the Maginot forts such as Agaisen and Barbonnet, did not have the resources to counter-attack. There was a short period of intense activity in mid-October, but this was cover for a

German retreat. Sospel up in the hills above Menton was evacuated at the end of the month. Apart from some long-range shelling (to the consternation of the German soldiers on the Massif de l'Authion, for example), the Alpes Maritimes sector finally became quiet. The First Special Service Force was pulled back to Villeneuve-Loubet and formally disbanded in December. The surviving men of the Task Force itself were replaced to become involved in the Battle of the Bulge, the last big German counter-attack. Casualties had been high; a third of its men were killed and wounded in the campaign. It was not Champagne all the way.

WAR AND PEACE
Today the only fighting on the Riviera is between criminals and the police or between rival gangs. That is a sign of peace. The Riviera has survived its moments of war very well. Monaco, especially, came through un-scathed, richer than ever. The occupation pointed up ancient divisions and prejudices, but it did not create them. Today the intensity of those conflicts is much reduced. The Riviera is no longer a battleground.

The power of the foreigner remains the most important influence on social life on the Riviera, but it is the power of money not of weaponry. The Roman harbour in Fréjus, the Vauban forts, the Maginot fortifications, the hilltop villages, the museums of Napoleonic mementos, even the occasional warship cruising by on its way to Toulon or showing the flag off Villefranche, these are all part of the pleasure circuit, tourist attractions featured in glossy brochures. Only by making an intellectual effort is one reminded of the bloodier times in which they were created.

Chapter Three

A DYNASTIC RECORD

MONACO AND THE GRIMALDIS

As a family, the Grimaldis have been big players in the south of France and the part of what is now Italy from Genoa to Naples, for the past nine centuries. They are the longest-serving reigning dynasty in Europe (and probably the world). The official family website describes their origins:

> The Grimaldis emerged from the Crusades as one of the four major ruling families of the Genoese urban nobility, essentially warriors, shipowners, and bankers. Genoa experimented with several political systems to organize its City-State and, around the 11th century, chose the *Commune*. As such, the City was led by a committee of consuls who were generally chosen among the feudal families that had settled down in the City. Grimaldo, who gave his patronymic name to his descendants, was the youngest son of Otto Canella, a Consul of Genoa in 1133. In turn, Grimaldo rose up to become consul three times, in 1162, 1170 and again in 1184. Oberto Grimaldi, son of Grimaldo, is the first of the family known to use the patronymic *Grimaldi*.

During the power struggles between the papacy and the Holy Roman Empire the Grimaldis backed the pro-papacy Guelph party against the emperor—an unfortunate choice because in 1270 the Guelphs were forced into exile. The Grimaldis and their allies took refuge in Guelphic towns of the western Riviera, around Nice. This began the expansion of the House of Grimaldi in Monaco, Boglio (Beuil) and Antibes during the thirteenth and fourteenth centuries.

The alliances, dramas, skulduggery, assassinations and betrayals during the several centuries of the Grimaldi family's seizure and occupation of Monaco were every bit as complex and bloody as the carryings-on in neighbouring Provence. It started with a classic demonstration of the art of dirty tricks. François Grimaldi (called *Malizia*, "the Cunning") was the

33

Monaco – a ghost town with real people

first of his family to capture the rock of Monaco. On the night of 8 January 1297, dressed as a Franciscan monk, he was invited into the castle, threw off his habit, drew his sword and let in his cousin Rainier with a group of men behind him. The event is commemorated on Monaco's coat of arms, where the supporters are two monks armed with swords. A statue of the "Cunning One" stands at the top of the ramp up to the Prince's Palace. But François only held on for four years.

Thirty years later, with the help of the Guelphs, who had staged a comeback, Charles Grimaldi re-occupied the rock. A decade after that he took over the neighbouring territory of another family, the Spinolas, then bought the lordships of Menton and Rocquebrune.

Until 1860 this was roughly how things stayed, except for a hiatus between 1793 and 1814, when all revolutionary hell broke loose, and for a period immediately afterwards, when the principality was placed, briefly, under the "protection" of the Kingdom of Sardinia.

THE STORY OF MONACO

The story of Monaco goes back way before the Grimaldis. The rock that dominates its western side, the site of the thirteenth-century fortress and then the Royal Palace, was also the site of caves—in St. Martin's Gardens— where man lived well over a million years ago.

The derivation of the name itself is uncertain. Perhaps the most plausible candidate is that "Monaco" comes from the Greek, Heracles Monoikos ("Hercules alone" or alternatively "Hercules with one temple"), since the Greek settlers here did consecrate a temple to him. But Monaco could also have its origins in some Ligurian language, although it does not seem to be associated with the name of any known tribe.

The port was in continuous use for several centuries by Phocaean and Carthaginian sailors and traders. Julius Caesar embarked from its harbour on his way to lead his campaign in Greece, but this was a rare moment of international renown. After the fall of the Roman Empire, Monaco was part of the wider social, political and economic decline. For a long time after the back-stabbing in 1297 Monaco enjoyed very little stability or real independence. In 1489 the French King and the Duke of Savoy recognized its independence, only for it to be lost again in 1524, when the principality was put under the protection of Spain.

The next century, the seventeenth, was not a happy one. It began badly for Honoré I, who in 1604 was thrown into the sea by his subjects for ignoring their poverty. Monaco's reputation for wealth only began in the reign of Honoré II (who became prince in 1612). This Honoré's tactic was to get close to France, and in 1641 a treaty with King Louis XIII gave Monaco "friendly protection" while keeping the principality's rights and privileges. But there were still the occupying Spaniards to dispose of. When this was achieved by an armed revolt, a period of relative prosperity began.

The Great Apartments of the Prince's Palace date from this period. By the time Honoré II died in 1662, they were brimming with paintings, tapestries, silverware and fine furniture, though the principality consisted still of little more than a spruced-up castle and a few mean streets on an almost inaccessible rock. The glamour deserted the court on Honoré's death. Most of the artists and intellectuals packed up and left, and a great many of the treasures were sold by his grandson to pay for a mission (unneeded, as it turned out) to the pope to intervene in the complex issue of the Spanish succession. The principality returned to its more usual condition of being both remote and poor. Only in 1730 was a road suitable for carriages built between Monaco and Menton—a rather late boost even for internal trade and communication.

In 1731, with the death of Antoine I, the male line of the Grimaldis of Monaco died out. He had three children but they were mere daughters. An arrangement was made whereby the eldest of these girls, Louise-Hippolyte, known as Coco, married a Norman noble, who gave up his own name and coat of arms for those of the Grimaldis. This was the only way the Grimaldi name and dynasty could survive, according to the terms of an agreement first drawn up in the fifteenth century. When the wife of this new recruit to the family died, he became Jacques I of Monaco. His last years were spent in his Paris house, the Hôtel Matignon, today the official residence of the French prime minister.

In the mid-eighteenth-century War of the Austrian Succession Monaco was again a victim, put under siege by Austrian and Sardinian forces, though not for long. The next crisis was less threatening. In the summer of 1767 the young Duke of York, brother to George III, fell ill suddenly on his way to Genoa, put into the harbour at Monaco, but died a few days later in the Prince's Palace—in one of its most sumptuous rooms.

These minor setbacks did not disturb the peace and prosperity that reigned until the French Revolution, when a very sudden upheaval introduced "people power" to a still feudal principality. French troops ensured that the traditional rulers were driven out, the riches of the palace were dispersed and paintings and other works of art were sold at auction. The Palace itself was used first as an officers' billet, then a hospital, then a home for the poor. Indeed, "Monaco" ceased to exist. For a brief period it was officially called "L'Hercule".

Various Grimaldis were imprisoned, then freed. Two young princes were drafted into the French army. The only member of the princely family to be guillotined was the unfortunate wife of Prince Joseph, the second son of Honoré III, Marie-Thérèse de Choiseul-Stainville. She postponed her execution by claiming she was pregnant. But then in a moment of honesty she confessed that she had lied, in order to give herself time to cut her hair off and send it as a memento to her children. Her whole head followed. Marie-Thérèse's execution took place just one single day before the reign of terror ended. Eventually, as the French Revolution was itself overturned, the Grimaldi family's privileges and sovereignty were restored. Honoré IV returned to Monaco in March 1815. This was the moment of Napoleon's arrival from Elba and the Prince's enforced meeting with the Emperor in the middle of the night.

In November of the same year, an impoverished Monaco was suddenly placed under the so-called protection of the King of Sardinia. Successive Grimaldi princes tried over the next decades to reverse this humiliating state of affairs. But their attempts to cope with an increasingly dire economic situation were met by popular demonstrations; the people of Menton (still within the administrative orbit of Monaco) were particularly incensed.

The success of their popular revolution in 1848—among many such popular revolutions in Europe that year—encouraged the *Mentonnais* and the people of neighbouring Roquebrune to appeal for their independence. As it turned out, neither the authorities in Turin nor their old rulers in Monaco succeeded in controlling, let alone annexing, this little rump of newly independent territory. It was only when the county of Nice and Savoie decided to join France twelve years later, in 1860, that the new Prince of Monaco, Charles III, formally gave up his claim. By renouncing his rights over Menton and Roquebrune he secured an indemnity of four million francs and a guarantee of total independence for Monaco under his sole authority. Not since Honoré II had the principality, albeit now in much smaller form, been so free.

MONTE CARLO AND THE CASINO

Monaco was free but wretchedly poor. Not even the lemons of Menton were going to help boost the revenues of the principality any more. Charles III and his mother, Princess Caroline, saw even worse economic times ahead if they let things drift. But they did have a cunning plan in mind. Already in 1856 they had the bright idea that was to shape Monaco's future—and, indeed, present. What was badly needed was a source of regular income, but the taxes they could hope to impose on the much reduced population were at their absolute maximum. So, they reasoned, why not try… gambling? Two things were in their favour. The first was that casinos were illegal in France and Italy. The second was that the railway was coming. The story of the establishment of Monaco as the gaming capital of Europe has often been told. Briefly, what happened was this.

The initial venture was premature and misguided. The Nice-Menton railway link was still over a decade away, and the pair of businessmen given the first concession, the Parisian journalists Léon Langlois and Albert Audet, were a couple of chancers. They set up their tables in a villa called Bellevue in the middle of the orange groves of the Condamine district. Legend has it that in their first week, 15 to 20 November 1857, just one sole gambler came along—and won two francs. Since it needed a four-hour ride in a bumpy *diligence* to get from Nice to Monaco, with the extra hazard of a trek down the precipitous path from La Turbie, this might not seem so surprising.

When the pair abandoned their lost cause, a series of equally unsuccessful attempts was made to make the venture pay, until Charles III approached a man called François Blanc, the son of a poor Avignon tax collector who was reputed to have set up a highly successful gambling operation in the German principality of Hesse-Homburg. In Patrick Howarth's account:

> On 31st March 1863 François Blanc went to Monaco, stated his terms
> for buying the casino concession, said he would return for his answer at

3:30 p.m., as he intended catching the 4 o'clock steamer to Nice, kept to his schedule, and bought the concession for 1,700,000 francs.

Shrewdly, Blanc calculated that when his German casino closed for the winter Monaco would provide continuity of profit—certainly once the new *corniche* road to Nice was completed. Luckily for Charles III and the Grimaldi family, they had a sharp lawyer, M. Eynaud, who insisted that the profits be shared with the principality. In his *Riviera: the Rise and Rise of the Cote d'Azur* (2005) Jim Ring tells the story of the deal like this:

> Despite his reputation as the genius behind Bad Homburg, Blanc cut a curious figure: a small, bespectacled man with a straggling moustache, nervous manner and heavy provincial French accent, he was obliged to stand throughout the negotiations because of a boil on his behind… In exchange for the concession the Prince acquired shares in a new company to be established to run it, an annual fee, and a share of the profits. In retrospect, this looks like the deal of the century. "Monaco," wrote Eynaud presciently to Prince Charles, "is about to experience an entire and brilliant transformation."

This transformation did indeed happen, and fast. In 1866 the area where the new casino was established was dubbed Monte Carlo, in honour of the prince. Within three years all taxes were abolished, to general rejoicing, in anticipation of the boom that would be provided the following year when the promised railway would arrive. By the end of the decade over three hundred thousand visitors a year were pouring into Monaco. "Rouge perd, noir perd, Blanc gagne toujours" (Red loses, black loses, Blanc [i.e. white] always wins) was the catchphrase of the time.

A veil of respectability was drawn over the venture by calling it the Société Anonyme des Bains de Mer et du Cercle des Etrangers à Monaco— sea bathing being generally considered a healthier pursuit than gambling. This never fooled the critics. Nice, Cannes and Monte Carlo were referred to popularly as "the world, the flesh and the devil". Both the Bishop of Gibraltar and the Dean of Canterbury expressed their outrage. Rude name calling has gone on ever since; recently the "serpent in paradise" has been dubbed "the world's money laundry" and even, snobbishly, "Billionaire's Benidorm".

Queen Victoria definitely disapproved. She particularly did not approve of the first (but not last) visit to the casino by her son and heir, the Prince of Wales, in 1875. In 1882 she wrote in her diary after a rare visit by herself, not to the casino of course, but to the principality:

> One saw very nasty disreputable looking people walking about at Monte Carlo, though many respectable people go there also for their health. The harm this attractive gambling establishment does cannot be overestimated. The old Prince of Monaco derives his income from it and therefore does not wish to stop it, though efforts are being made to do so.

Such efforts were, of course, futile. François Blanc laughed all the way to the bank, married one daughter off to a Radziwill and another to a Bonaparte and indulged himself with mansions and racehorses until his death in 1877.

Soon a newer, bigger and glitzier casino designed by Charles Garnier, the architect of the Paris Opera, was constructed to reflect the enormous prosperity and fame of Blanc's enterprise. It also acted as a magnet for opera and ballet (in time attracting Diaghilev) as well as super-rich investors such as Sir Basil Zaharoff and, later, Aristotle Onassis, anxious to annex some of the profits. It was the smart place to honeymoon (as my own father and mother did in 1937, cautiously amassing enough winnings each evening to pay for a reasonable meal) or just to see and be seen.

British attitudes were a strange mixture of the horrified and the attracted. John Addington Symonds, author of the *History of the Italian Renaissance*, was an early visitor to Monaco:

> There is a large house of sin blazing with gas lamps by night, flaming and shining by the shore, like pandemonium or the habitation of some romantic witch… Splendid women with bold eyes and golden hair and marble columns of Imperial throats are there to laugh, to sing songs, to tempt… The croupiers are either fat sensual cormorants or sallow, lean cheeked vultures, or suspicious foxes. Compare them with Coutts men.

On Christmas Eve 1880 a leading article in *The Times* fired a broadside of scatter-shot in order to denigrate the casino and decry its pernicious influence.

The respectable tradesmen, merchants, bankers, and professional gentlemen in the Riviera have long been of opinion that the Casino is a dangerous rival, and intercepts much of the expenditure that should naturally flow to them. The English are accused of excessive economy, and of doing as little as they can to encourage the arts and manufactures of the region, or even to help in its charities. No doubt many of them go there to economize. So the particular complaint of the Riviera shopkeepers may not come to much. This is an affair of the whole world. Monaco invites all nations, and they respond to the call. The result is the annual wreck, it is said, of a million pounds sterling, of the people represented by that sum, and of many a manly character that might have figured in the world's history but for this early extinction. The scandal is immensely aggravated by the cloud of witnesses. All nations are there, and, in the sight of all of them, France allows and even encourages a gigantic, indeed unequalled, system of depredation upon the simplicity of the young and. inexperienced, the wealthy and the high-born.

The effect of such attacks was negligible, indeed probably counterproductive. It was an Englishman, Charles Wells, who in 1891 "broke the bank": after three days of wins he pocketed a million francs. Hailed as a national hero on his return to London, he went back like a moth to the flame to win another three million francs before, some months later, losing the lot. The publicity he gave the casino was enormous.

It is said that, in the same year, the casino launched the career of a young adventuress who became one of the most famous and richest courtesans, Caroline Otéro. She was thirteen and knew nothing about roulette when she walked into the gaming room, put ten *louis* on red, got bored while the wheel went round and round and only noticed she had won when the other gamblers called out to her. Still bored, she left her winnings on red. It came up twenty-one times in a row and she walked out with the (modern) equivalent of £25 million. Almost inevitably, the green baize was also her undoing. Though she lived until she was 97, dying in Nice in 1965, she ended up penniless.

Of course, the casino's reputation for sleaze was also well founded. Prostitutes were part of the scene from the start, as were the moneylenders, fraudsters, pickpockets and every kind of petty criminal. The most pernicious were the so-called *entraîneurs*, enticing guests to spend, and risk, more than they could ever afford.

The legends—and reality—of the suicides have haunted Monte Carlo since gambling began there. The English Baptist preacher Charles Haddon Spurgeon, who preached his fire and brimstone messages to crowds of 10,000 or more all over Britain, thundered against the iniquity of Monte Carlo in his own magazine, *The Sword and the Trowel*. In June 1879 he let rip:

> If our readers will only imagine the Crystal Palace transformed into what is called "a hell", with all its fascinating surroundings, they will have some idea of the prominence and perilous power which Monte Carlo possesses… Well did one of the magistrates of Nice exclaim, "This gaming is the plague of the country, and the plague is gangrened. The ravages of vice extend every day."… A commercial traveller coming on business to Mentone went to Monaco. As usual, he just put down a five-franc piece. His own money soon went. That of his employer followed, and there he was! He could not bear the disgrace, and, therefore, putting a pistol to his head he rushed, at the early age of thirty, unbidden, into the presence of his Maker, a self-murderer. Another poor wretch, before taking his own life, wrote these words on a blank leaf—"*Monaco, thou wilt yet slay many others!*"

Spurgeon did not, of course, neglect to add how the corpses of the suicides were "buried by stealth after sundown". Six years later the *London Daily News* reported the story of how

> a clerk of a German counting house passing his honeymoon on that *littus avarum*, the Riviera, came to Monte Carlo. He had £1,000, his employer's money, in his possession. Distrusting his own virtue, he did what is generally safe—he gave the sum to his bride to keep for him. Then he left the room for a time, and on returning found that the unhappy girl had played away all of the £1,000. He also learned that she had drowned herself in the sea at the foot of the rocks. A more dreadful end to a honeymoon cannot be imagined; nor can any defender of Monte Carlo deny that but for the temptations so publicly offered the miserable woman might now be a happy wife.

It was not just foreigners who inveighed against the evils of gambling in general and of the Monte Carlo Casino in particular. In the early 1890s a newspaper was established in Nice, Cannes and Menton with the express purpose of highlighting the dangers posed by Monaco, although copies of *l'Indiscret* were hard to sell and the venture soon closed.

On 30 March 1912 the *New York Times* reported that the casino was having one of its worst seasons on record and that "the popularity of this resort is already on the wane." The writer accused the Monaco authorities of a "perfect conspiracy of silence" to hush up the losses and resulting suicides, reporting one witness who saw a man shoot himself on a bench on the casino terrace, then watched as two policemen hauled the body out of the light and dragged it away to a waiting room in the nearby station. But this was all wishful thinking on the part of the moral critics. Nothing—neither bad seasons nor suicides—could halt the steady progress of the gambling bandwagon.

The attraction of the gambling tables of Monte Carlo was by no means limited to gullible clerks, weak-minded addicts and the excessively rich. On 13 April 1891 the Russian dramatist and writer Anton Chekhov wrote happily to his sister:

> I can't tell you how thrilling the game is. First of all I won eighty francs, then I lost, then I won again, and in the end was left with a loss of forty francs… I have been here since the morning, and it is twelve at night. If I had money to spare I believe I should spend the whole year gambling and walking about the magnificent halls of the casino. It is interesting to watch the ladies who lose thousands… This charming Monte Carlo is extremely like a fine… den of thieves. The suicide of losers is quite a regular thing.

Almost at the same time he was writing a little more censoriously to his brother: "I love wealth and luxury, but the luxury here, the luxury of the gambling saloon, reminds one of a luxurious water closet. There is something in the atmosphere that offends one's sense of decency and vulgarizes the scenery, the sound of the sea, the moon."

Even so, when Chekhov was staying in Nice in the late 1890s, he and a group of friends would spend hours at the Monte Carlo Casino desperately trying to beat the system with a perfect "martingale" (doubling the stakes after each loss) before finally giving up.

Between the two world wars the image of the casino remained ambivalent. Some, like the consumptive, moody and hypersensitive writer, Katherine Mansfield, used language reminiscent of the Victorian scourges when she recounted, in February 1920, a trip in a "kerridge and pair" to Monte Carlo:

> *Monte is real Hell.* To begin with it's the cleanest, most polished place I've ever seen. The villas are huge and they have strange malignant towers… All the shops are magasins de luxe, lingerie, perfumes, fat unguents and pawnbrokers and pâtisserie. The Rooms are the devil's headquarters. The blinds are down, there's a whitish glare from the electric light inside—carpet on the outside steps—up and down which pass a continual procession of whores, pimps, governesses in thread gloves—Jews—old, old hags, ancient men stiff and greyish, panting as they climb, rich great fat capitalists, little girls tricked out to look like babies—and below the Room a huge outside café—the famous Café de Paris with real devils with tails under their aprons cursing each other as they hand the drinks. There at those tables, sit the damned.

Nine years later Evelyn Waugh arrived in Monaco in an unseasonable snowstorm to embark on a Mediterranean cruise. He was fascinated by the way, at the end of each flurry of snow, "there appeared an army of busy little men in blue overalls armed with brooms and hoses and barrows; they sluiced and scraped the pavements and brushed up the lawns; they climbed the trees with ladders and shook down the snow from the branches… The snow was put into barrels and packed into hampers and taken right away, across the frontier perhaps, or into the sea, but certainly well beyond the imperium of the Casino."

Waugh was equally intrigued when he came across a 'Tir aux Pigeons' competition down by the sea.

> The competitors were for the most part South Americans with papal titles. They made very interesting gestures with their elbows as they waited for the little cages to collapse and release the game; they also had interesting gestures of vexation and apology when they missed. But this was rare. The standard of marksmanship was high, and while I was there

only three birds, fluttering erratically with plucked tail and wings, escaped the guns, to fall to the little boys below, who wait for them on the beach or in rowing-boats and pull them to pieces with their fingers… On the balcony above the terrace sat one of the Casino pigeons, privileged and robust, watching the destruction without apparent emotion. The only convincing recommendation which I heard of this sport came from one of the visitors at the Bristol who remarked that it was not cricket.

Virginia Woolf paid the customary visit to the Monte Carlo Casino in 1935, recording her experience in a diary entry dated Tuesday 28 May:

A bright blue and white day: carved parapets gleaming; little embayed town on the sea. I saw domes & pillars & told L[eonard, her husband] this was the Casino; so we went in, & then paid nothing but went into a florid but dingy hall, set with seven or eight tables, something like great billiard tables, at which sat a dingy sweaty rather sordid crew, with their faces all set & expressionless watching the gold bars sweeping this way & that in the middle. They had something peculiar. One couldn't place them. Some were dingy old governesses in spectacles, others professors with beards; there was one flashy adventuress; but most were small business men—only rather, not very vicious. It was a blazing hot Sunday morning about 12, & this, we thought is the way our culture spends its holidays. Vicious, dull, & outside lurid. So on.

And *so* VW! The story goes that even the brilliant economist John Maynard Keynes, a fellow member of the Bloomsbury set, became so obsessed by gambling at the casino that he ended up without enough money to get back to England. This was *before* he published his groundbreaking *General Theory of Employment, Interest and Money*.

The American writer and Algonquin wit, Dorothy Parker, managed one apposite quip: "the Monte Carlo casino refused to admit me," she declared, "until I was properly dressed, so I went and found my stockings, and then came back and lost my shirt."

In British and American imaginations Monte Carlo became a symbol of raciness, where High Society and the *nouveaux riches* could mix with less discomfort than elsewhere. One of the most devastating portraits of a Monte Carlo snob-cum-social climber is the ghastly Mrs. Van Hopper in the early chapters of Daphne du Maurier's *Rebecca*. Our innocent heroine is forced to connive with the social ambitions of this woman to whom she is paid companion until she is "rescued" by the sinister and cynical Maxim de Winter, who only happens to be in Monte Carlo to relive his honeymoon, but is really on his way to the more culturally acceptable Italy and Greece. It is presented as the young heroine's redeeming feature, the ability to see through Monte Carlo's flimsy glamour, where women in "black satin" dresses are no match for a genuine if slightly dowdy young woman whose sensible clothes are packed in a "Revelation suit-case and… stout hold-all", ready to leave as fast as she can for a better life at home.

This echoes the comparison Sir Frederick Treves made in the very early 1920s of the difference between Monte Carlo and Menton.

> Mentone is a quiet place that appears to take its pleasure demurely, if not sadly… Perhaps its nearness to Monte Carlo makes this characteristic more prominent. If Monte Carlo be a town of scarlet silks, short skirts and high-heeled shoes Mentone is a town of alpaca and cotton gloves and of skirts so long that they almost hide the elastic-sided boots.

This has a much later echo in Graham Greene's 1955 novel, *Loser Takes All*, the story of a young man who is enticed to Monte Carlo, starts winning big money, and is finally persuaded that he is better off poor but reconciled with his girlfriend. Once again, glamour and wealth lose out to true love—this British image of the fatal lure of the casino has become a cliché.

A SUCCESSION OF PRINCES

When Prince Albert I succeeded his father, Charles III, in 1889, he inherited a thriving economy based on income from the casino. But he also brought to Monaco skills that were very different from those of all his predecessors. Albert was a scientist, an oceanographer and palaeontologist. The impressive Oceanographic Institute, founded by him in 1910, was only one of several museums and institutes of which he can claim to be the founder. He even set up an International Institute of Peace in an

Monte Carlo
Casino – "Blanc
gagne toujours"

early effort at conflict resolution. In 1911 he gave Monaco a constitution—altogether a very different image for the principality than the incarnation of the devil so roundly condemned by such as Charles Haddon Spurgeon and Queen Victoria.

An opera house had already been created in 1869. In the same year Albert had married the vapid Lady Mary Victoria, Marie-Victoire de Douglas-Hamilton. The succession issue was complicated. Albert's marriage to Marie-Victoire was not made any more likely to succeed by his taking an American mistress, the widowed Duchesse de Richelieu (born Alice Heine, daughter of an American-German-Jewish banker from New Orleans who lived in Paris). Marie-Victoire, in her turn, fell for a dashing Hungarian count. After a bitter and almost bankrupting divorce, the marriage was annulled. Charles III was blind and depressed but still alive—and kicking against his son's liaison. Alice did, however, get to meet Queen Victoria, a rare American to do so, during a brief encounter in 1882. But in the end Charles died, taking his antisemitic hostility with him, and Alice married her Albert. It was she who became the driving force behind many of the changes in Monaco introduced as counterweights to the gambling. Unfortunately a visiting British opera composer caused a scandal (and caused Albert, when he found out, to slap Alice's face in public—in fact at a performance of Massenet's *Le Jongleur de Notre-Dame*). Her crime was to start an affair when the prince was off on an oceanographic expedition. The customary Grimaldi marital hostilities were resumed. Alice's memory was erased in Monaco by her vindictive husband, even to the point of a rose she helped to create being renamed. Yet she was still formally the *Princesse de Monaco* when she died in London in 1925.

The son of Albert I and Marie-Victoire, Louis II, became a distinguished soldier, reaching the rank of general in the First World War. Louis' daughter, Princess Charlotte, married Prince Pierre de Polignac, and it was their son, Rainier, born in 1923, who was the male heir (Rainier would come to the throne when his grandfather, Louis II, died in 1949).

Meanwhile, the late 1920s and 1930s were politically traumatic years. Prince Louis had never cared about his job or the *Monégasque* people. He may or may not actually have said, as reported, "let them have live bullets instead of a constitution," but that was certainly what he felt like saying. A popular revolution was barely avoided. In a report from Monaco headlined "The Land of Chance", a special correspondent of *The Times* filed a scathing piece for the edition of 9 April 1929. The National Council had brought out the gendarmes—again—and, while admitting the unrest was "not without a seasoning of Tarasconesque humour", the reporter noted that it was beginning to have an effect on the rest of the Riviera. Violence was very bad indeed for tourism—especially for the Monte Carlo Casino with its "processions of excited gamblers and its cascades of gold".

The lack of democracy and the price of water, gas and electricity were becoming a combustible mix in Monaco. Nevertheless, set against the profits from the casino and the high spending of the rich (who included the prince), the paradox of poor and frustrated citizens should not have been beyond any reasonably caring and competent government to solve. Instead, things reached the point when vocal citizens were actually accusing Prince Louis of "besmirching the fair fame of Monaco".

Even Prince Louis' hand-picked delegates to the token Assembly rejected his 1933 budget, in which funds to preserve his luxurious lifestyle took precedence over public services. At the same time he was feuding with his daughter Charlotte over everything, she was herself in bitter conflict with her ex-husband, including over the upbringing of her son Rainier. It was a dysfunctional family *par excellence*, echoing the marital, legal and political quarrels from decades, even centuries, past and destined to carry on for decades into the future.

During the Second World War Monaco was formally neutral, though occupied on 4 July 1940 by Italian forces, who were welcomed by the large numbers of Italian expatriates who worked in the principality. Russian residents tended to sympathize with anyone who was fighting the Red Army, both Italians and Germans. The Ukrainian-born Diaghilev dancer, Serge Lifar, became notorious in Paris not just for his scene-stealing but also for accepting German patronage and protection, which resulted in his taking refuge in the more congenial surroundings of Monaco, where he directed his Nouveau Ballet de Monte Carlo. Prince Louis' loyalties were ambiguous. Basically pro-French, he saw Vichy France—and German investments—as his best means of protecting Monaco's fragile independence. At almost seventy, Louis, in the time-honoured way of the Grimaldi family, sought solace and distraction from the dilemmas posed by the war in the arms of a woman, in his case an actress half his age.

The young Prince Rainier remained in France during the occupation years at Montpellier University. He was formally made heir to the throne in June 1944, once he had become twenty-one. He promptly enlisted in the Free French forces. He fought bravely and ended a colonel. Meanwhile, on 3 September 1944, exactly five years after the outbreak of war, American soldiers entered Monaco, which the Germans had already evacuated. (The novelist Irwin Shaw, incidentally, claimed he was the first to liberate the Tip Top Bar.)

The Americans decided to respect Monaco's neutrality rather than turn it into a rest camp for their soldiers. Reversing their policy in the First World War, they declared it off limits to all personnel. Even the Supreme Commander General Eisenhower, when he arrived on the Riviera in the summer of 1945 for a few days of rest, stayed at the Eden Roc rather than in Monte Carlo. None of this stopped Monaco becoming a thriving centre for the black market. It took the Americans some time to realize that the people responsible were the same as those, such as the Minister of State, Emile Roblôt, who had been the most enthusiastic collaborators with the Germans. When General Frederick, commanding the American forces on the Riviera, set out with a couple of jeeploads of soldiers and policemen to arrest him in his villa, Roblôt escaped by the back door.

Later, an American captain claimed that Prince Louis and his ministers were so keen to keep their distance from France and so impressed by the Americans that they made a bid to have the USA take over Monaco. General Frederick was apparently shocked and referred the matter to the State Department. Captain Joseph Welsh, who had accompanied the general to a meeting with the Monaco bigwigs, later recalled:

> I don't know how we kept straight faces until we got out of there, but we did. When we got back to headquarters we just exploded. Somebody on the staff, it might even have been Frederick, suggested that we cable Washington to tell them that if they wanted a forty-ninth state, we were ready to supply it!

Not surprisingly, the annexation "project" died the death. What the State Department could not have anticipated was that, almost exactly a decade after the end of the war, there would be a very different kind of American takeover in the form of a beautiful blonde superstar.

But first the new prince, whose hour had finally come in 1949, had to face up to a series of dangers that constantly threatened his tenure as ruler of Monaco. One problem was the same one as had affected the family since the beginning if its long reign—women. Rainier had a long-standing relationship liaison with another (much less famous) film star. For six years he lived with the glamorous Gisèle Pascal, the daughter of Nice flower sellers and star of films with titles such as *Après l'amour, Mademoiselle s'amuse* and *La femme nue*. Though they shared a villa at Beaulieu, she kept up her career and he, with no opportunity to do a proper job, kept himself busy skiing, diving and cutting ribbons. His first job as prince was to contest the will by which Louis had left half his—or Monaco's—fortune to the actress whom *he* had just had time to turn from mistress into wife. Gisèle Pascal, after an awkward time when she and Rainier shared a weekend villa in St.-Jean-Cap-Ferrat, went off in the opposite direction, returning to the stage and marrying her leading man.

"Woman trouble" for Prince Rainier was not confined to having a possibly unsuitable mistress. In the early 1950s threats were multiplying on every front. His scheming and hostile elder sister Antoinette took the opportunity to hatch a scheme to put her own son Christian on the throne. On another front, Aristotle Onassis, the Greek billionaire shipowner, was plotting to take over the ailing casino—although the property owned by the Société des Bains de Mer was what he really had his eye on. To make matters even worse, another company on which the principality's income depended, the Société Monégasque de Banques et de Métaux Précieux, went into spectacular bankruptcy, and one of those most suspected of fraud turned out to be the prince's sister's lover. This was to be the pretext for Antoinette's coup against her brother. It was Onassis who persuaded Rainier that the whole business should be hushed up as bad for business.

Politically there was danger too. The ultimate threat to impose, as it were, the divine right of the prince to rule absolutely and without fetter was in fact exercised—though only once—by Rainier. He had been boxed into a corner by the machinations of Jean-Charles Rey, his sister's lover and the most powerful member of the National Council. The issue was the apparently trivial one of building a "Marinarium" for Jacques Cousteau to carry out underwater research. But Rainier's "coup d'état" had the unfortunate side effect of alienating General de Gaulle, who objected strongly to Rainier's unilateral appeal to French citizens to use Monaco as a tax haven. When Rainier capitulated, two-thirds of the French capital invested in Monaco was transferred to Swiss banks and property values plummeted. Rey remained on the Council.

Rainier counter-attacked by confronting Onassis, who was fortunately distracted by his affair with the temperamental opera diva Maria Callas. The prince turned for help to a surprising figure, his former enemy Rey, who had just become his brother-in-law. They plotted to turn the principality into the majority shareholder of the Société des Bains de Mer, while at the same time briefing French newspaper editors that Onassis was a mere speculator who had no interest in the long-term future of Monaco. The plan worked. Onassis boarded his yacht *Christina* and sailed away without, literally, a backward glance. As his American private chaplain and friendly adviser said to the embattled prince, "Perhaps it is time for you to get married."

Indeed, after these difficult times, the Philadelphia-born on-the-up film star Grace Patricia Kelly did not turn up a moment too soon. She may have had a chequered past herself for such an apparently demure actress, but she did have what was really needed, and that was glamour. What is more, she had a shrewd grasp of what was required of her.

As soon as she became Princess of Monaco, on 18 April 1955, Grace Kelly became an instant icon, a kind of *Monégasque* Jacqueline Kennedy/Onassis, a great beauty who put a shine on the Grimaldi family image and softened the rigid, authoritarian atmosphere of princely power in Monaco. "Something which is not so well known is that she wrote a personal note to every newborn child in the Principality," gushed the organizer of an exhibition of the princess' memorabilia and personal items twenty-five years after her horrific death in a car accident.

Of course, it was not a marriage arranged without a degree of financial cunning. There is plenty of evidence that all sides saw advantages beyond True Love. The point is that it worked. Monaco's tourist industry boomed; its brand image changed from sleazy to sexy; its tax haven status had never been so eagerly enjoyed. And by giving birth to a boy, Princess Grace ensured that Monaco did not revert to France, since, extraordinary as it might seem, exactly that would have happened if Rainier had died without a male heir and no other male heir were to come onto the scene. The old fifteenth-century rule had never been rescinded.

Grace Kelly, Princess Grace, lived long enough, it can fairly be said, to save—even create—modern Monaco. It is hard, though, if you drive down the same winding road into Monaco from the family retreat, Roc Agel, near La Turbie, not to want to rerun and edit out that horrible moment, one morning in September 1982, when the Princess's green Rover went out of control and plunged over a hundred feet into a scrubby ravine. It was such a humdrum accident, perhaps due to a family tiff, or her notoriously poor eyesight, or more likely a minor stroke, but it caused a massive trauma among the Monaco people as well as in the royal family. Throughout the principality the atmosphere remained brittle until Rainier's death in 2005.

THE RAINIER AND GRACE EFFECT

His Serene Highness Prince Rainier III was 81 when he died. His longest-lasting legacy is that of "the Builder Prince". He was also known for his autocratic tendencies and his single-minded drive to turn his principality into "Monaco Inc.". No doubt some of his austerity was due to his long period as a widower. There were many things courtiers knew they could never raise with Prince Rainier.

"Autre pays, autres lois, autre ambiance" (a different country, different laws, a different atmosphere) is how *Nice Matin* summed up Monaco in a 2007 article. But what is really so different about it today?

The best view of Monaco is from the coastal path that runs around the

Cap Martin, named after the architect le Corbusier, looking across the bay towards the port, the skyscrapers and the backdrop of sheer cliffs. It is a little like Hong Kong, a little like Manhattan, but tiny, almost as tall, it seems, as wide. From the yachts to the cliff-top hotels and villas, it is, even from a distance, a formidable monument to wealth. Much of this is due to the policies of the man who ruled Monaco for all of 56 years.

One of the "Builder Prince's" most impressive achievements was his ability to increase the actual territory of Monaco, its land mass, by a massive twenty per cent. When a country occupies only a couple of square miles, that is quite a feat. He did it by it by pushing back the sea with an enormous concrete landfill, then building on top of it. The Fontvieille section is still expanding, though under financial pressure.

Naturally it helps to have, if not total control, nevertheless a degree of absolute power. There is in Monaco a *Conseil National* of 24 deputies, representing the 8,000 citizens, but it has little power over the "government", which is to say the prime minister and five *conseillers*, or ministers, who in turn have to account to and indeed take orders from the prince.

Monaco cannot, however, be judged by conventional rules. It never has been. Sometimes its reckless disregard of European standards of democracy has brought it near to disaster. But it has survived as an historical anomaly. Its effectiveness depends on its semi-independent status that guarantees its right to control its own (lack of) taxes and its own constitution. There may be 25,000 or so foreigners who live in Monaco (from 124 nationalities), but they know why they are there and what the rules are. The principality functions through the tacit consent of all concerned.

Boom times have become an established fact, and still the money keeps rolling in. So much so that other casinos in French territory along the Riviera, in Nice, Cannes and Menton, have complained that Monte Carlo is taking away their business. A report in 2008 noted a 16 per cent rise in takings in Monaco, while the French casinos, with their more restrictive rules and higher taxes, posted falls of 4 to 18 per cent. The losers said they were hoping that a smoking ban, scheduled to take effect in Monaco in 2009, will even things up a little. But for the seriously high rollers, notably Arabs and Russians, the peculiar attraction to Monaco was predicted to remain the principality's trump card.

The authors of the Cadogan guide to the South of France described modern Monaco thus:

Big-time tax-dodgers agree: it's hard to beat Monaco for comfort and convenience when the time comes to snuggle down with your piggy chips. Unlike most other tax havens, the Principality is not an island, so you can purr over to France or Italy in the Lamborghini in just a few minutes. The grub is good, you can safely flaunt your jewels and there's enough culture to keep you from feeling a total Philistine; the homeless and other riffraff who might trouble your conscience are kept at bay. Security, understandably, is the prime concern… in emergencies the whole Principality can be closed off in a few minutes.

One of Monaco's more caustic residents, the Manchester-born novelist, critic, composer and literary gadfly, Anthony Burgess, sought shelter there in 1976, fearing that Italy had become too violent and that his son would be kidnapped. In an article in *The Times* of 13 March 2005, John Cornwell claimed that Burgess "was furious that he was writing in Monaco in sight of yachts at anchor, but 'not one of these yachts belongs to a man or woman who writes or has written.' There was, of course, that 'carpet bagger' Harold Robbins down the Riviera, he sneered, 'but he is probably not really a writer at all.'"

Burgess, who used Monaco as one of his many means to avoid paying taxes, was referring to a time a few decades earlier when he told an American academic: "Monaco was like Ruritania, before Grace died. An outpost of Hollywood, too, with these yachts arriving. When Grace married Rainier, Americans thought she was going off to become the madam of a high-class gambling saloon…" He described Monaco residents as a "philistine lot mostly". But Burgess also paid his dues; he was a co-founder in 1984 of the Princess Grace Irish Library. He once wrote: "I shall die somewhere in the Mediterranean lands, with an inaccurate obituary in the *Nice-Matin,* unmourned, soon forgotten." This was only partly true; he died in London in 1993.

The "philistines" have not gone away. Yet meretricious Monaco has not just sucked in gamblers and spat them out penniless into the streets or on the rocks, for it has long been a major sponsor of the arts. The Russian impresario, Serge Diaghilev, presented *Scheherazade* in Monte Carlo in 1911 and after the First World War installed his own Ballets Russes. Stravinsky himself, already a frequent visitor, found the Monte Carlo scene to his liking despite vocal protests from members of the Russian colony there. Today the Opera (in Garnier's beautiful addition to the casino), the Monaco Masters music competition, the Ballets de Monte-Carlo, the Philharmonic Orchestra, the Little Singers, the Spring Arts Festival, the International Circus Festival, not to mention the Formula One Grand Prix, the ATP Masters Tennis tournament, and even the international fireworks competition, all carry on that tradition, providing a yearly round of solid, high-class entertainment.

Monaco remains attractive to many British people. Retail magnate Sir Philip Green, Shirley Bassey and Roger Moore as well as assorted Formula One racing drivers all live there. They make up the third largest expatriate community behind the French and Italians. Currently 2,200 Britons live in Monaco out of a total population of around 32,000.

For all that the foreigners are there primarily for tax reasons, they are not immune to the changing image of the principality. The death of Princess Grace was traumatic not just for her surviving husband but for the whole family and for everyone living in Monaco. All three royal children have had their dysfunctional periods. The youngest, Princess Stephanie, who was in the car at the time of the accident, went furthest off the rails, with her miscellaneous lovers (racing driver, bodyguard, elephant trainer… the list went on and on) featuring in all the world's scandal sheets. Princess Caroline's adventures were scarcely more edifying, though losing her second husband in a speedboat accident was a sad misfortune that upset her efforts to follow a steadier path. The only son, now Albert II, finally acknowledged two love children and, much to the relief of the *Monégasques*, and surely of the foreigners who have adopted the principality as their home, decided to marry. His fiancée looks, and dresses, uncannily like Grace Kelly—an omen perhaps, but for what?

So far the signs are positive. Middle age has definitely calmed the current Grimaldis. Albert is a less stiff character than his father. His activities as a member of the Monaco bobsleigh team and on the International Olympic Committee mark him down as an active and influential figure in the sporting world. He expresses respect for democracy in the American mode and seems determined to carry on what Rainier did to Monaco, except with his own environment-friendly twist. In his inauguration speech, Prince Albert declared: "One should never forget that tomorrow's reality is often made of up of yesterday's pipe dreams which have finally been realized. For Monaco and its inhabitants, I wish for a *model society and a society model.*"

Even so, Monaco—a ghost town with real people—has always acted, and will surely never escape acting, as a magnet to satirists and witty writers. A. A. Gill had a literary bilious attack when covering the Grand Prix (the "Scumball rally") in October 2001, describing Monte Carlo as a "money puddle. A cash delta. It is as if all the wealth from the rich northern European pasture has run down the Continent and found its way here, to form a sort of mangrove swamp of avarice before running into the Mediterranean." He wasn't (of course) finished there.

> Monte Carlo is the sort of slum that rich people build when they lack for nothing except taste and a sense of the collective good. The one thing a poor slum has over a rich one is dignity. What Monte Carlo has instead of dignity is CCTV cameras and policemen.

Victoria Coren, poker player and *Observer* columnist, offered similar thoughts to readers in April 2008, but ended less biliously and, it should be said, a bit more fairly:

> It is a strange, lonely place. The streets are always deserted, the residents lurking inside their fortified castles, the beaches carved up for private use. The shops sell nothing but weird clothes embossed with rhinestone poodles' heads. You never see any poor people at all. I imagine that a giant truck pulls into town at 5 am every day and releases an army of them to sweep, clean, paint, empty the bins and get out again before the billionaires wake up.

That image is probably impossible to eradicate entirely. Yet Albert II's enthusiasm for the arts, even his support for the Monaco football team, improve not just his own image but go some way to mitigate the way the Principality is seen beyond its own little claustrophobic world.

Chapter Four

SNOBS, CONSUMPTIVES AND PENPUSHERS

THE BRITISH

"Don't let's go overboard" has been the motto of British travellers over the centuries. Far better to keep things within bounds, not stray too far beyond the familiar. A certain detachment is required to mask any unexpected high emotions or excessive enthusiasm which the destination—or even the travelling itself—might inspire. No grander, yet more typical, example of an Englishman abroad on the Riviera can possibly be found than Lytton Strachey (1880-1932).

His first reaction to arriving in the south of France in 1906 was to write to his friend Maynard Keynes that he was passing along "in a dream looking at peacock-blue seas." But familiar reality immediately intervened, bringing him down to earth again. He declared that he was spending far too much time "talking to imbecile dowagers". In his many letters home he created a whole bestiary of English expatriates in turn-of-the-century Menton society. There are his two aunts, "la tante Elinor" (Lady Colvile, whom his biographer, Michael Holroyd, describes as "a figure of Elizabethan grandeur," bullying her maid "for serving the curry before the rice, or for not putting the Oriental Pickles on the table"); and there is "Aunt Lell" who suffers from *twinges* and whose hands, her nephew Lytton declared, "are enough in themselves to prostrate one" but, seeing her without her wig, he adds, "You can't conceive the difference. She looked terribly old." Then there is uncle Trevor who "makes the most disgusting swilling and squelching noises when he's eating" and a distant cousin Mr. Bax Ironside, known as "Mr Iron Backside"; and Major Horrocks who would buttonhole his victim with descriptions of his many diseases, eczema being his star turn. There are still others in Lytton's *galère*.

"Mrs Hodgson is a relief, as her nostrils are apparently amputated, so that I can recognize her pretty well. But Miss Scott, and Miss Egerton,

An international crowd along the Promenade des Anglais

and Miss Duparc!—They have all long red noses, they are all 45, and they are all hopelessly respectable and insufferably cheerful…" Lady Dyer, meanwhile, was something between a vicar's wife and an ex-governess, dressed in a long velvet cloak with fur edges and a round yellow straw hat trimmed with mauve chrysanthemums; she was "a complete vulture. Her red pointed nose and her moulting fur added to the effect."

This *aperçu* of Côte d'Azur life was written at the high point of a trend that had been started in the late eighteenth century by one British doctor in Nice, Tobias Smollett, given a boost in Cannes by a former Lord Chancellor, Lord Brougham, in the middle of the nineteenth century, then given a final fillip in Menton by another doctor, James Henry Bennet. These are the trio of stepping stones that thousands of British people used to enable them to pluck up courage and cross over to the Riviera, "reinventing" it as a winter retreat. In doing so, they turned the whole French Riviera into a playground for the well-born and wealthy and a spacious sanatorium for the unhealthy. It became the done thing to stay for a season on the Côte d'Azur. As Arnold Bennett put it, "nobody could believe the Riviera who has not seen it." It certainly would not do to be the one left out.

First Comers

There were British visitors to the French Riviera before Tobias Smollett, but no-one stayed nearly as long, or offered as perceptive insights or as trenchant comments, as the dyspeptic Scottish doctor, novelist and author of *Travels through France and Italy* (1766). The poet John Milton and the diarist John Evelyn had both dropped in during a sea passage to Italy (the *de rigueur* destination of all aesthetes and intellectuals in the mid-seventeenth century), but if their imaginations were fired by the experience, they left little trace of it.

Dr. Smollett, however, stayed in Nice from early December 1763 to early April 1765, taking a few months off in Italy from the autumn of 1764. He had a good opportunity to observe at first hand the foibles of the natives and the way *Niçois* society worked. Smollett is very funny, whether about the ladies of Nice parading around with their *cicisbeos* (gigolos) or about Piedmontese mules with an aversion to horses and an urge to "always march upon the brink of the precipice," or about the plagues of insects in summer:

Notwithstanding all the care and precautions we can take, we are pestered with incredible swarms of flies, fleas, and bugs; but the gnats, our couzins, are more intolerable than all the rest. In the day-time, it is impossible to keep the flies out of your mouth, nostrils, eyes, and ears. They croud into your milk, tea, chocolate, soup, wine, and water: they soil your sugar, contaminate your victuals, and devour your fruit; they cover and defile your furniture, floors, cielings, and indeed your whole body. As soon as candles are lighted, the couzins begin to buzz about your ears in myriads, and torment you with their stings, so that you have no rest nor respite 'till you get into bed, where you are secured by your mosquito-net. This inclosure is very disagreeable in hot weather; and very inconvenient to those, who, like me, are subject to a cough and spitting. It is moreover ineffectual; for some of those cursed insects insinuate themselves within it, almost every night; and half a dozen of them are sufficient to disturb you 'till morning.

Smollett is always astute in his observation of everyday life and ever ready with expressions of joy, outrage or amusement and, of course, full of the prejudices of the time. He tells the story of a 200-pound logger-head turtle ("which in the West-Indies are eaten by none but hungry seamen, negroes, and the lowest class of people") that was floating along in the sea fast asleep until some Nice fishermen caught it and brought it on shore.

The whole town was alarmed at sight of such a monster, the nature of which they could not comprehend. However, the monks, called minims, of St. Francesco di Paolo, guided by a sure instinct, marked it as their prey, and surrounded it accordingly. The friars of other convents, not quite so hungry, crowding down to the beach, declared it should not be eaten; dropped some hints about the possibility of its being something praeternatural and diabolical, and even proposed exorcisms and asper-sions with holy water. The populace was divided according to their at-tachment to this, or that convent: a mighty clamour arose; and the police, in order the remove the cause of their contention, ordered the tortoise to be recommitted to the waves; a sentence which the Francis-cans saw executed, not without sighs and lamentations.

For all that he had a sharp tongue, Tobias Smollett could wax as lyrical as the next man about the beauty of nature along the Riviera coast. He it was who set the scene for travellers to come. Even the Norfolk-born agriculturalist and keen recorder of facts, Arthur Young (though unable to suppress his negative reaction to the "savage, sombre air spread over the whole…" where the "pines, and evergreen shrubs, that cover the greatest part, cover it with more gloom than verdure") could not escape the thrilling sense of anticipation felt by the first-time visitor to the Riviera. In his case, as expressed in *Arthur Young's Travels in France* (1792), it was the fact that he was entering (Sardinian) Italy that particularly inspired him.

> The first approach to that country so long and justly celebrated that has produced those who have conquered, and those who have decorated the world, fills the bosom with too many throbbing feelings to permit a bush, a stone, a clod to be uninteresting. Our percipient faculties are expanded; we wish to enjoy; and then all is attention, and willingness to be pleased.

Thus primed, he was ready to appreciate the best features of Nice.

> The sea-view is fine, and, for enjoying it in a greater perfection, they have an admirable contrivance, which I have seen nowhere else. A row of low houses forming one side of the street, a quarter of a mile long, has flat roofs, which are covered by a stucco floor, forming a noble terrace, opens immediately to the sea, raised above the dirt and annoyance of a street, and equally free from the sand and shingle of a beach. At one end some finely situated lodging-houses open directly on to it. The walk this terrace affords is, in fine weather, delicious.

As a result of the Smollett effect, Young unearthed as many as fifty-seven English families wintering in Nice—but only nine French. They were, however, even as he arrived, "dismally alarmed" by the Revolutionary "disturbances". Young predicted that in the coming winter there would be "nine English and fifty-seven French". He also discovered that Smollett's reputation of having "libelled" the climate (itself almost libellous, since Smollett was on the whole very complimentary in this respect) had affected French sensibilities more than English imaginations; a former

English consul, Lord Shelburne, believed that, "if he (Smollett) were to go again thither the Nissards would certainly knock him on the head." Fortunately, perhaps, the good doctor was long dead.

In the years following Smollett's visit another pair of men from Norfolk visited the Riviera and returned to write up their impressions. The botanist, James Edward Smith (1759-1828), noted in the environs of Nice "several very pleasant villas, mostly destined to accommodate strangers", and how "the whole neighbourhood has the air of an English watering-place." He found Hyères "mean, dirty, and crowded" but was charmed by Cannes, "a little sea-port, whose houses are bathed by the waves of the Mediterranean." Dr. Edward Rigby (1747-1821) was also interested in agriculture. He deplored the "decay" of Fréjus but enjoyed a wholesome English dinner of "plain roast beef and boiled potatoes, with some special good draughts of porter" in Nice—a meal all the finer for its familiarity.

After the Revolution and the end of the Napoleonic wars the British returned to the Riviera—with added arrogance. The number of visitors multiplied fast. Tradesmen and shopkeepers, tutors and music masters all moved in to supply the demands of foreign, largely British, families who were only there for the climate—and to keep each other company in a simulacrum of native society. Churches and cemeteries were built. Missionaries began to ply their trade.

Following the harsh, frost-bound winter of 1821/2, the financing of the Promenade des Anglais was a triumph for British (English) society, a concrete, lasting legacy of Anglo-Saxon "ownership" of Nice—or, if that is too strong, it was at least a statement that the English visitor was a key stakeholder in the town's future development. The Rev. Lewis Way, a hyperactive organizer and proselytizer, persuaded his fellow British residents of the wisdom of providing relief work for the many local families hit by the effects of the frost on sales of oranges. Eventually the wide, gently curving road reached a length of six miles along the shore of the Baie des Anges. English visitors walk—or drive—along it still.

In 1828 one Englishman, after a long stay in Novia Scotia, visited a relative in Nice and found the old town "narrow, dirty, and stinking", while the English quarter on the other side of the Paillon river was "open and clean". This was the Croix de Marbre area, also known as Newborough or Little London.

When the 26-year-old John Ruskin travelled through Nice in the spring of 1845, he too was not impressed, neither by the town nor specially by the people who lived there.

> They seem not unamiable, not blackguardly… but kept down by the povery of a sterile country with no commerce. You cannot conceive anthing so comfortless as the aspect of things. Not dirty—inside at least the houses seem exceedingly clean—but left without a vestige of repair or paint for these last hundred years—no glass in the windows—the supply of air being limited by their smallness—torn plaster for walls—loose tiles for roof—no signs of agriculture—no indian corn—no farming—no vines—no gardens—they live by shopkeeping & innkeeping… Their only mode of living is by making clothes, utensils, &c. for the country people around, and by selling them wine & so on at fair time and keeping skittle grounds on fair days… It is well to have seen the country. I will take good care not to come again.

The young Ruskin managed to be every bit as disparaging about the *Niçois* as the middle-aged Smollett, but he did start to work up some enthusiasm as he set out eastwards.

> The Corniche above Nice and Monaco is far finer than I thought, but then I saw it today in lovely weather, from a carriage perfectly open—cliffs & sea & sky seen at once. It is very superb, and the entrance here among the indian figs and heavy laden lemon trees, with crowds of peasantry coming home with their orange baskets full of yellow fuit & glittering leaves upon their heads, & the intense, purple sea are more to me than I could have conceived… I was sauntering about at Nice as carelessly in the sun as in the shade. I could sit in the open carriage at the top of the pass with no greatcoat and run out here for a walk before dinner without a moment's rest.

This was the greatest attraction for the fog- and snow-bound English. The sun was what they came for. Nice was being taken over by Anglo-Saxon sun-seekers. There is the famous story told by Alexandre Dumas *père* in the mid-nineteenth century, when an innkeeper answered the question, "Who are the new guests?" with "Sono certi Inglesi, ma non saprai dire si son Francesi o Tedeschi…" (They are certainly English, but I can't say if they are French or German). When in 1860 the eastern Riviera, from Nice to Menton, became French, the British colony was on the whole indifferent, perhaps rather positive about the change. The climate remained the same and that was the main thing.

Meanwhile the formidable ex-Lord Chancellor Lord Brougham had almost instantly established Cannes as the new fashionable place to go for winter. In the dying days of 1834 he was—unusually for him—stopped in his tracks by junior officials. They refused him entry to Sardinian territory on the grounds that there was cholera in France (perhaps his cause was not helped by his railing at the "beast-ridden and priest-ridden Government of Sardinia").

As night approached, Brougham and his family tried to stay in Antibes, in a noisy and dirty *auberge*, then in the Château Salé (the acute accent is important here), whose owner explained that, having welcomed during the Revolution the family of General Bonaparte, he could not with any decency receive an Englishman. It was too far to go on to Grasse. Then Brougham remembered the fishing village he had seen and rather liked earlier in the day. The party galloped back to Cannes and found shelter with Père Penchinat, the proprietor of the Auberge de La Poste-aux-Chevaux. The moonlight gave it a certain charm, disguising its dirty corners, and the smell from the *marmite* was extremely enticing to the hungry English. Soon they were enjoying fish soup, toasts rubbed with garlic and wine as bitter as it was tasty.

Within a week Lord Brougham had shaken off his aristocratic anger and fallen for the charm of the Riviera. He bought himself a plot of land on which to build an enormous villa, and spread the word to English society. They flocked down to keep him, and themselves, company.

Brougham even funded the building of a harbour, and not just to import more easily the turf for his lawns, though that was important to him. By the time he died, thirty years later, the population of Cannes had more than tripled to ten thousand. The British called it the "Cowes of the Mediterranean". A statue to the "inventor" of modern Cannes still stands in a busy square, high on a plinth, dressed in legal robes and clutching a rose. He also merited, if that is the correct word, a verse in his honour by Stephen Liégeard:

Honneur à Brougham l'orateur
D'Albion la plus belle gloire,
Du port il fut l'instigateur,
N'en perdons jamais la mémoire.

I do not believe this can be improved by translation.

Once again, the first instinct of the English coming to Cannes and other resorts along the Riviera was to recreate as much of familiar England as possible; not just the croquet lawns, cricket pitches and tennis courts, but horse racing, gooseberries, Protestant churches, Tudor half-timbering, grocers and hygienic drains. The Scots made sure they had their Free Church and imported haggis. The price of meat doubled in Nice from 1860 to 1870. In 1861 Hyères sported six language teachers, three music teachers, three drawing teachers, two piano renters, nine carriage renters and three photographers, all relying on the high-spending visitors. Letting apartments and houses became, in the words of one researcher, "a passion—from the richest to the poorest, all want to let."

The eccentric guide-book writer and student of manners, Augustus Hare (1834-1903), spent some time on the Riviera, particularly in Menton(e) in the winter of 1860-1. He was concerned that his dinner

Lord Brougham
– pillar of the Cannes community

should be "stripped of its oil and garlic, and has had some extra cooking bestowed on it." One saving grace was a developed aesthetic sense, deploring the "hideous villas" in Cannes and the "effacement of all the natural beauties of the place". He deplored just as vehemently the "hideous and stuccoed villas in the worst taste" which had turned Mentone from a "picturesque fishing town" into somewhere "vulgarised and ruined" with "pretentious paved promenades". Hare was nothing if not a snob.

Edward Lear's take on Nice, where he came for the winter of 1864-5, was even more eccentric:

> There was an old person of Nice,
> Whose associates were usually Geese.
> They walked out together,
> In all sorts of weather.
> That affable person of Nice.

Lear wrote to the teenage daughter of a friend, Anna Duncan, in January 1865, enclosing a photograph of himself in Nice, dressed in loud check tweeds and a bowler hat and earnestly writing in his notebook, with the message:

> I got home very safely last night, and partly this was owing to the care taken of me by two remarkably large & amiable Frogs, whose arms I took, & who saw me down the lane... Nothing could exceed the genteel & intelligent expression of their countenances, except the urbanity of their deportment and the melancholy and oblivious sweetness of their voices. They informed me that they were the parents of nine and forty tadpoles of various ages and talents some of whom were expecting shortly to emigrate to Malvern and Mesopotamia.

In 1868-9 he stayed a little further down the coast, observing:

> There was an old person of Cannes,
> Who purchased three fowls and a fan;
> Those she placed on a stool,
> And to make them feel cool
> She constantly fanned them at Cannes.

The English were big spenders, on fowls and much else. The disposable income of the "guests" was generally welcome to their "hosts", despite distorting local prices (so it is good to know that an elderly *cannoise* could afford three fowls as well as a fan). Tradesmen and shopkeepers were adept at raising their prices to foreigners, while keeping them down for their local customers. Prosper Mérimée wrote to a friend in 1862: "Le métier d'écorcher les Anglais est meilleur que la culture du jasmin et des tubéroses" (fleecing the English is better than growing jasmine and tuberoses).

Some of the British on the Riviera were spectacularly rich, though distinguished by little else than money and a title. This did not make them any the less desired. Marie Bashkirtseff, herself from a family whom the Russian nobility would not receive, had an adolescent passion for the Duke of Hamilton, who was himself quite content with his huge yacht, the *Thistle*, his Italian mistress and his cigars.

THE GREAT INFLUX

Among the many British visitors to the Riviera looking not just for a cheap life in the sun but for something more enriching was a handful in search of the kind of spiritual peace that would stimulate their imaginations and inspire creativity. Robert Louis Stevenson (1850-94) visited Menton on three occasions, in search of a cure for his sick lungs and inspiration for his books. Later he was to move to the western end of Riviera, where he bought a tiny chalet in Hyères, calling it La Solitude. He remembered the time he spent there in 1883-4 as the happiest of his life—though, given his melancholy nature and poor health, this happiness could only be relative. At least *Treasure Island* had just given him a welcome financial boost. And he was productive there, writing many of the poems to be collected in *A Child's Garden of Verses*. He and Fanny, his wife, would play a game together, whereby she played the role of Scheherazade, inventing stories during an afternoon walk, then recounting them to her husband, the Sultan, who had been taking a nap. Some of these ended up in his *New Thousand and One Nights*.

Promoting the Riviera as the best place to cure diseases of the lungs was the brainchild of James Henry Bennet (1816-91). His appeal to the British to come to Menton was calculated and self-interested—he was a doctor determined to build up a successful practice—but it was not false.

Dr. Bennet genuinely adored Menton, remembering in *Mentone, the Riviera, Corsica and Biarritz* (1862) that his first vision of the town, from a boat near the shore, was of how

> all the details are blended into one harmonious whole, the two bays becoming one, and the little town scarcely dividing them. The grandeur of the semicircular range of mountains, generally steeped in glorious sunshine, also comes out in broad outline. These mountains positively appear to all but encircle the Mentonian amphitheatre in their arms, thus to separate it and its inhabitants from the world at large, and to present it to the blue Mediterranean waves and to the warm southern sun.

Once landed, he noted the troops of girls and women coming down "daily from the mountains with large baskets of oranges or lemons poised on their heads", generally barefoot but with "apparent ease"; he described them as looking "very picturesque" despite carrying loads he estimated at a hundredweight. "Only the strongest and healthiest girls can undertake the work," he observed, "and that only for a few years. They will go to and from the mountains, a distance of from three to six or eight miles, several times a day, and gain about fifteen pence daily. The olive, he wrote, "imparts an Eastern charm to the place," reminding him of Jerusalem and the "sacred scenes of the Holy Writ".

Dr. Bennet was convinced of the curative powers of the Menton sun for patients suffering from tuberculosis. The dry air, he believed, retains the body's electricity and so the "nervous system is stimulated, and buoyancy and cheerfulness of mind follow." Sadly, although his theory was apparently convincing—his own health certainly improved after he had first gone to Menton to "die in a quiet corner... like a denizen of the forest"— the science was flawed. This did not become generally apparent until decades later. The fact was that seriously dry *mountain* air was of much greater value. The appeal of Menton's microclimate was meanwhile immensely popular, so that hotels and sanatoria sprang up all over the town and surrounding hills, following Bennet's endorsement. Many came as much for the benefit of familiar comfort and social company as for any certainty of cure. Even Dr. Bennet saw among "members of the same nation... a feeling of solidarity, of a common origin and object, that exists among the passengers of a ship on a long sea voyage."

He followed up his first successful book with another, later also published in a German translation and then in America, *Winter and Spring on the Shores of the Mediterranean* (1875), which included whole passages from his first book but elaborated on the medical value of spending winter—indeed years on end—under the protection of the Menton sun and his medical care. The kinds of people who answered his appeal were not always the liveliest, contributing to Menton's reputation as dowdy. In 1912 Thomas Cook and Son published a *Travellers' Handbook for the Riviera*, which referred to Menton as a "dull place" with "no keen edge to its breeze, no crisp freshness in the breath of its sea… a kind of gloom pervades it, which is somewhat depressing." The guide quoted a "well-known writer" referring to Menton as "that stuffy morgue". Even now the old joke persists about the town's nickname, *double Menton,* referring to the amount of double chins on view.

Much in the spirit of Lytton Strachey, Sir Frederick Treves poked fun at the "class of English lady—elderly, dour, unattached—known by the not unkindly term of 'aunt'".

They are propriety personified. They are spoken of as "worthy". Although not personally attractive they are eminent by reason of their intimate knowledge of the economics of life abroad. To them those human mysteries, the keeper of the *pension*, the petty trader and the laundress are as an open book. They fill the frivolous bachelor with reverential alarm, but their acquaintance with the rate of exchange, the price of butter and the cheap shop is supreme in its intricacy. These "aunts" are to be found in larger numbers in Mentone than in any other resort of the English in France.

In Menton Dr. Bennet established a practice that flourished even to the extent of being endorsed by Queen Victoria herself, who visited the town in March 1882. She spent happy hours in his steeply terraced garden, just a short distance inside Italian territory (ignoring any passport requirements), sketching and walking. She was sad to leave, noting in her journal, "Alas! already far away from beloved and beautiful Mentone! It is too sad to watch the beautiful mountains and vegetation… disappearing."

The nine visits of the queen to the Riviera between 1882 and 1899 were the climax of British social dominance. According to Michael

Nelson's *Queen Victoria and the Discovery of the Riviera* (2001), half of the entire time she spent abroad was in France, and of that three-quarters was spent on the Riviera. She visited Cannes, Grasse, Hyères and Nice (Cimiez) and made excursions up and down the coast as well as to the foothills inland. She threw flowers at Nice's Carnival, gave money away to any poor people she came across and (despite her age and poor health) went some way to convincing local people that the British did have—and not just believe they had—a touch of class. Even as she was dying, Queen Victoria said, "Oh, if only I were at Nice, I should recover."

Following in the footsteps of the poet and critic Algernon Swinburne, who came to Menton twice in the early 1860s in search of improved health, two British artists/writers with decadent habits and styles and weak lungs went there in the 1890s, expecting to breathe their last in that town of consumptives. One, Aubrey Beardsley, art director of *The Yellow Book* and illustrator of Oscar Wilde's *Salome*, died there of tuberculosis in 1898 at the age of 25 and was buried in the Old Château cemetery. Richard le Gallienne, a minor writer, poet and part-time actor, who also contributed to *The Yellow Book*, survived far longer (he was only asthmatic). He was to die, in poverty, in Menton in 1947, aged 81.

The English needed, of course, their own newspapers. Competition was fierce as titles multiplied: the *Cannes Gazette*, the *Menton and Monte-Carlo News*, the *Riviera Daily*, the *Continental Weekly*, *Barnett's Riviera Weekly* (subtitled "A Fashionable, Newsy, Picturesque, and Independent Chronicle for Anglo-Saxon Sojourners in Europe") and many more. The format was, however, almost completely uniform, with lists of arrivals and departures and society gossip, often in mock-heroic style, as well as an editorial and gleanings from international newspapers on the inside pages, and a front page consisting entirely of advertisements. Most of these would be small ads. The front page of the *Cannes Gazette* on 9 March 1894 ran advertisements for English grocery stores, an American dentist, the local circulating library, the Cannes cricket club, a "Manufactory of Imitation Old Furniture", Monsieur A. Carli (Baritone and Guitarist vocal "At Homes" arranged), English tailors, butchers, hatters and a purveyor of Lawn Tennis requisites. All the journals and gazettes closed at the end of the season around late April and re-opened for business in November.

In the years preceding the outbreak of the First World War the Riviera changed from being an extended sanatorium for invalids (who found themselves sent off to the drier Alps instead) and more of a pleasure ground. As *The Times* correspondent noted in an article on 18 March 1911:

> There is idling in plenty, and good idling—the idling of the aged states-man at 'La Bastide', the idling of the overworked average man, for whom it is enough to lie in a long chair in the sun among the acacias and the orange- trees or to stroll in some pinewood between the mountains and the sea. But the life of the ordinary English holiday-maker is fairly stren-uous, especially in Cannes and westward of Cannes, he and she are almost sure to be playing golf or lawn tennis or croquet, winding up perhaps with a little billiards in the evening, for, though there is exhibi-tion play of the finest in all the towns along the coast, people are not content to watch. And then there are the motorists and motoring—let who so dare call idling. The increase in the floating population of those who come and go in motor-cars is one of the most striking changes in the life of the Riviera. They do not take villas; very likely they do not stay more than a few days in any one place. But they come in very large numbers, and on the whole, perhaps, they get the very best that the country has to offer to those in normal health.

Not all visitors to the Riviera, however, belonged to the idling classes. One exception was a young Polish-born sailor who was to become the British writer Joseph Conrad. He spent time on the Giens peninsula, below Hyères, late in 1874—with tragic consequences. There he enjoyed a passionate affair with the daughter of a Polish hotel keeper before sailing away on his seafaring adventures. A year to the day after he left her, Thérèse Chodzka killed herself. For her it had not been just a fling. The man who was not yet Conrad returned many times to Marseille and the coast along the Riviera, fascinated by that "charmer and deceiver of audacious men", the Mediterranean. Three years after her death, perhaps to the very day, he tried—but failed—to kill himself. He became a British citizen, changed his name and began to write in English.

Conrad's novel, *The Rover*, published in 1923, is a story of revolution and Anglo-French derring-do and mystery set on the Giens peninsula. In it Conrad recalled his "young misery", transferring to his fictional hero, the Master Gunner Citizen Peyrol, a man with a dark past and a waistcoat stuffed with looted coins, a fancy to buy up all this land to the furthermost field, away over there where the track lost itself sinking into the flats bordering the sea where the small rise at the end of the Giens peninsula had assumed the appearance of a black cloud... all that soil from which he had sprung: houses, woods, vines, olives, vegetable gardens, rocks and salt lagoons.

But it is not the "people of landsmen with their houses and animals and activities" who count for him. It is the sea and the "craft that belonged to it" which cheer his heart.

...here he beheld a perfect serenity, nothing sombre on the shore, nothing ominous in the sunshine. The sky rested lightly on the distant and vaporous outline of the hills and the immobility of all things seemed poised in the air like a gay mirage. On this tideless sea several tartanes lay becalmed in the Petite Passe between Porquerolles and Cape Esterel, yet theirs was not the stillness of death but of light slumber, the immobility of a smiling enchantment, of a Mediterranean fair day, breathless sometimes but never without life.

Conrad could capture with accuracy but with no apparent effort the essence of any place he knew around the world. In *The Rover* he evoked the timeless beauty of this corner of the Riviera with all the skill and passion of a man who knew it intimately.

LATE COMERS

After the First World War the *belle époque* was well and truly over, nowhere more conspicuously than on the Riviera; only St. Petersburg felt equally deprived, but with less hope of a fast recovery. Yet it took just a single heartbeat for the Riviera to re-invent itself. The newspapers catering for foreigners had had a lean time, but in a year or two many were back in business or replaced by newcomers. By March 1923 the *Menton and Monte-Carlo News* (looking exactly as it had always done) needed six pages for its "List of Visitors in the Hotels of Menton" and three more for Monte Carlo, plus a page for a "list of residents and visitors in villas and apartments".

Arnold Bennett (1867-1931), famous for his novels set in the Potteries, also enjoyed the good life on the Riviera. He had been in Menton and more usually Cannes even before the war, enjoying seeing and being seen on the Croisette, thinking presumably to himself a thought expressed in his poem, "A Night on the Riviera": "This peace is my peace and this kingdom mine!"

Another avid stroller along the Croisette was Rudyard Kipling, who regularly over-wintered in Cannes with his wife from the early 1920s until he died in 1936. He described the town as "like the third act of a music-hall revue". P. G. Wodehouse (1881-1975), creator of Jeeves and master of the English style of humour, had even ruder things to say about Cannes on his first visit there in 1925: "the most loathly hole" was one description in a letter to his stepdaughter. He went on: "Of all the poisonous, foul, ghastly places, Cannes takes the biscuit with absurd ease." Jim Ring, in his literary guide, puts this down to homesickness. In fact, Wodehouse soon began to mellow: "Cannes doesn't seem so bad after all. I think the secret is not to go into it… We went to the Casino last night and I won 500 francs… Italian musicians have been singing under our window this morning. All very jolly."

It was typhoid that killed Bennett, a perforated ulcer that ended Kipling's life, and extreme old age that finished off Wodehouse. But still, even well after 1918 consumptives came to the Riviera to find their last rest home—those at least who had not yet got the message that mountain air was better for them. Most came to wilt more or less resignedly but gracefully in villas, hotels and sanatoria in Menton, in an atmosphere of lemon blossom and almond cakes. One visitor with a peculiarly fine awareness of her surroundings and her condition was the New Zealand-born writer, Katherine Mansfield (1888-1923), married to the British critic and editor, John Middleton Murry.

Mansfield's tuberculosis brought abrupt changes of mood, from elation to terror and back again, heightening her acute sensory and literary sensitivity. Palms were at one moment "hideous (like Italian profiteers)" and then they were "superb things… sometimes they are bronze, sometimes gold and green, warm deep tiger-gold—and last night, under the moon in a little window, they were bright silver." This was written in February 1920 from the Villa Flora in Menton, a place she once called "heaven from dawn to dawn". Even the birds were "much milder here, much quicker, properly on the qui vive…" She revelled in the "lovely little town, small and unreal like all these places are, but even here there are real spots. The colour and movement everywhere make you continually happy." If only that had been true, for even in Menton Mansfield could suddenly declare herself to be "out of my mind with misery".

Mansfield also stayed at the Villa Isola Bella in Menton, near the eastern end of the platform of the local Garavan railway station. Beneath the house (on whose wall is a plaque remembering her stay there) is a small and not very airy room. She probably never went in there herself, but for over forty years, every year, a New Zealand writer is free to use it. These are the Katherine Mansfield Fellows, and they are funded to stay in Menton, hopefully inspired to write something special, for nine months.

One of the earliest fellows was the poet Fleur Adcock, who was a little put out by the Spartan conditions and the trains that "boom all night,/a dozen metres from the bed", preferring "this fuzz/that blurs and syncopates the singing buzz/of crickets, frogs, and traffic in my ears." ("Villa Isola Bella", from *Poems 1960-2000*)

Among New Zealand's finest writers who have taken advantage of the fellowship there has been (so the novelist and poet Damien Wilkins, the 2008 Fellow, told me) a touch of ambivalence. Mansfield left her native country aged eighteen, never to return; and would not London, her main home abroad, not provide a more stimulating creative environment? Perhaps that explains a strain of melancholy in many of the fellows' works, when they reflect on their time in Menton…

> Fast forward again
> top-heavy *Alpes*
> *Maritimes* grind
> the sky small. One
> more dull day scraped off
> off a slaty sea.
> (Allen Curnow (1983 KM Fellow), "A Nice Place on the Cote d'Azur",
> from *The Bells of Saint Babels*, 2001)

Vence also sheltered its share of consumptives, among them D. H. Lawrence. He did not take to being nursed in the Villa Ad Astra sanatorium (which happened to be opposite a cemetery) and moved to another villa his wife Frieda had rented, the Villa Robermond. Here he died in 1930 and was buried in the Vence cemetery, though his body was later taken out, burned and the ashes (probably the real ones, though there were theories that his wife's lover had replaced them) taken to New Mexico.

One of the most devastating portraits ever written of the dark side of that inter-war Riviera life is Rebecca West's in her novel *The Thinking Reed*, begun when she was staying in Antibes with her young son by H. G. Wells in the mid-1920s, but not published until 1936. This was a case not of bodily sickness but of moral decline. When rich young Isabelle and her even richer husband Marc go to the Cap d'Antibes for their honeymoon, they fall in with people who epitomize the worst excesses of futile hedonism. She attacks first the falsity of their friendships:

> Whether they were French, Russian, English, or American, endearments flowed from them as freely as rheum from an irritated mucous membrane. This was only in part due to mercenary motives, for a considerable proportion of them were so rich that they had no need to curry favour with their friends. It came rather from their intention, never formulated but governing all their actions, to treat each phenomenon till it became indistinguishable from all others of its kind. They hampered friendship by taking its special vocabulary and distributing it as largesse among all human beings, so that it could not perform its function of building up strong preferences… They… had taken vows of wealth, unchastity, and disobedience to all standards.

And apart from anaesthetizing themselves with alcohol, West wrote, the Riviera crowd are crippled by anti-intellectual philistinism.

> The passion which men bring to debates regarding free will and determinism, or capitalism and communism, which never wearies of the controversy and longs to burn its opponents at the stake, was here directed to interminable arguments as to whether Gordon Lloyd had a right to do what he did on Ferdy Monck's yacht at Saint-Tropez last week, and whether Laura had really said what Annette said she had at the bridge-party at Super-Cannes just afterwards.

As a result they become "more driven and irritable than the people in the world outside". When Marc and Isabelle go to spend the day with a couple on Cap Ferrat before going on to a party in Monaco and an evening losing money at roulette at the casino, the endlessly repetitive roundabout of the beautiful life is bound to end in tears of boredom, frustration and guilty conscience.

> They lay on mattresses on a marble bench, a little Capuchin monkey skipping backwards and forwards over their bodies. They patted it in tenderly, feeling pity for its animal folly. But it began to seem a very long time until lunch, and after they had discussed for some time whether Gordon Lloyd had had a right to do what he did on Ferdy Monck's yacht at Saint-Tropez last week, and were unable to follow through by discussing whether Laura had said what Annette said she did at Super-Cannes, because Laura herself was present, the backgammon boards were brought out. Then the menservants came up with cocktails, which recalled a children's party by their light and creamy appearance and sweetish taste, but which acted like a powerful brake on all discontented and aggressive movements of the mind.

The falsity of their temporary happiness is inevitably soon exposed. West's circle makes a neat contrast with Strachey's aunts and uncles in dowdy Menton. But there is a third type of Englishman altogether on the French Riviera, the bohemian rebels who pretend to have talent but make no pretence of having money. Indeed, poverty is almost a badge of honour. Cyril Connolly pinned these characters like butterflies on a board in his novel *The Rock Pool*, first published in Paris in 1936 because it was judged too obscene, and possibly libellous, to risk a brush with British law.

Connolly's creepy anti-hero, Naylor, fetches up in Trou-sur-Mer (Cagnes-sur-Mer on the real map). He is a "writer" looking to experience something to write about, a cadger despite a small personal income that he is aware gives him a certain *cachet*, a small-time snob, thin-skinned and a self-deceiver. In all these respects except money he fits in quite well with the crowd of desperate bohemians, bar owners and hangers-on who are already taking over the small seaside town. At the same time he is looking for love, though sex will do just as well. He trails his Englishness along behind him like a comfort blanket.

> At lunch he propped up the Continental Daily Mail and behind it let his imagination run wild; even that dismal paper, which contrives to

make all the news equally unimportant, from wars and revolution to cricket, British colony garden parties and lists of new arrivals in Riviera hotels, could not affect his elation.

Naylor has literary ambition but is uncertain quite where he belongs in the expatriate literary scene: "All along the coast from Huxley Point and Castle Wharton to Cape Maugham little colonies or angry giants had settled themselves: there were Campbell in Martigues, Aldington in Le Lavandou, anyone who could hold a pen in Saint Tropez, Arlen in Cannes, and beyond, Monte Carlo and the Oppenheim country. He would carry on at Nice and fill the vacant stall of Frank Harris."

His early optimism is evident in his ability to be pleasantly surprised by his wider experiences of the Riviera.

It was customary, in the circles in which Naylor moved, or used to move, to disapprove of Nice—such a horrible trippery place, like Brighton; but he realized that evening how delightful it was; the pink Italian piazzas, the derelict casinos, the Russian churches, the Gothic taverns, the déclassé yacht harbour, the musical-comedy palms, the little seafood restaurants along the front, the Genoese atmosphere of the old town. It was all charmingly dowdy and romantic, like Offenbach.

This nostalgia for the *belle époque* does not survive the disillusion of life in a Trou-sur-Mer, however, full of people left behind by the retreating tide. Cannes, in Naylor's view, is "a fringe of evanescent luxury but not a town". But arriving in Antibes triggers a bilious diatribe.

A belated cicada chirred in a dusty pine; scattered uncomfortable villas gave way to broken rocks; the woods of the cape, spotted with hoardings, came down to the inhospitable beaches, filling the air with the scent of resin, and a shameless chocolate-box sunset disfigured the west. The intolerable melancholy, the dinginess, the corruption of that tainted inland sea overcame him. He felt the breath of centuries of wickedness and disillusion; how many civilizations had staled on that bright promontory! Sterile Phoenicians, commercial-minded Greeks, destructive Arabs, Catalans, Genoese, hysterical Russians, decayed English, drunken Americans, had mingled with the autochthonous gangsters—

everything that was vulgar, acquisitive, piratical, and decadent in capitalism had united there, crooks, gigolos, gold-diggers, and captains of industry through twenty-five centuries had sprayed their cupidity and bad taste over it. As the enormous red sun sank in the purple sea (the great jakes, the tideless cloaca of the ancient world) the pathos of accumulated materialism, the Latin hopelessness seemed almost to rise up and hit him.

Does the Mediterranean quite deserve this? Of course, it is the view of a flawed and envious man, the fictional Naylor. All the same, one suspects that, as with Daphne du Maurier and Rebecca West, this too much protesting must be evidence of some kind of English puritanical reaction to the unavoidable delight which is everyone's first and most powerful feeling faced with the obvious beauty of the Riviera. The desire not to be seduced by its charms, to feel a prick of conscience at the ease by which one is seduced, is a particularly English phenomenon. It is a constant feature of Riviera scenes particularly in the fiction written between the two world wars.

Some of the writers in Naylor's caustic survey have survived the passing of time, while others are all but forgotten now. Aldous Huxley's base was a little outside the Riviera of this book, his Villa Huxley being in Sanary-sur-Mer, not far from Toulon. Edith Wharton's Hyères features in the next chapter. Roy Campbell (1901-57) was a South African-born poet who moved to Martigues, twelve miles west of Marseille in 1928 with his wife and two little daughters, with only £10 to his name, to "start life." Richard Aldington (1882-1962), a poet, critic, novelist and biographer, visited the Riviera many times on holiday, spending a winter on Port-Cros, one of the Iles d'Or, and also visiting Le Lavandou. Aldington is now better known for a controversial biography of T. E. Lawrence than for his other writings, but he did write one novel (*Rejected Guest*, published in 1939) partly set on the Riviera, in which his hero, David Norris, striving for self improvement, is left disillusioned by the warped characters he meets there—a theme reminiscent of Connolly himself.

Of the other writers mentioned in *The Rock Pool*, the snobbish Bulgaria-born socialite Michael Arlen (1895-1956) is painful to read eighty years or so after the zenith of his reputation; his novel *The Green Hat*, sometimes assigned to the "Riviera fiction" category, is really no such thing, but its archly depicted characters are recognizable as Riviera types. As for E. Phillips Oppenheim (1866-1946), he was another immensely successful writer (specializing in gentlemen crooks) who attracts little attention now. Frank Harris' *Life and Loves* is still a popular "dirty book"— but a great deal more fascinating, in all probability, than anything Naylor might have composed. Harris' main Riviera connection is that in 1898 he sheltered Oscar Wilde in La Napoule and encouraged him to work again there. It was a noble but vain effort. Wilde had more fun meeting up with Sarah Bernhardt in Cannes, drinking absinthe and chasing "fisher-lads" who were "strangely perfect". After he had been recognized in Nice, Wilde returned to Paris and died there two years later.

Somerset Maugham has stood the test of time. He was already successful as a playwright, novelist and short story writer when he moved to Cap Ferrat in search of what he disingenuously described as the "simple life"—"despite," as Mary Blume put it, "his thirteen servants, grand guests and dinner parties at which he wore black tie and embroidered velvet slippers from Peal in London and served avocado ice cream made out of fruits grown from cuttings he had smuggled into France in a golf bag." "Willie" Maugham holding court at La Mauresque became a popular symbol of the best the Riviera could offer, though he wrote very little about the Côte d'Azur itself.

His famous off-the-cuff phrase, "a sunny place for shady people", seems to refer to Monaco rather than the Riviera as a whole. Certainly the current prince, Albert II, in a press conference at the London Ritz in October 2007, accepted that Monaco was Maugham's target. "I wish he had never said that," the prince declared. "All we want to say is that we are open for business." The phrase has become such a journalistic cliché that it was guaranteed to be used, for example, when Mark Thatcher was made unwelcome in Monaco; it has appeared as a slogan on T-shirts and as the title of a track on a rock music album; it is even the title of a book on the Gold Coast. But there is another theory of the phrase's origin (which remains obscure—to whom was Maugham speaking when he made the remark? We do not know). A blog from one Francis O'Hara in Nice in May 2007 read: "BUT please will journalists put that tired quote, or rather mis-quote of Maugham's, into the dusty archives… Maugham was in fact referring to parts of Marseille, during the second world war, when France of course was occupied, and contraband trading was rife."

Maugham did not merely entertain the international great and not-so-good. Among his acquaintances were local celebrities, including Matisse, whose paintings he wanted to hang on his walls. Matisse would have none of it. Yet, writes Robert Calder, Maugham "was touched when Matisse gave him a volume of his drawings with a flattering and warm dedication. Maugham, too, was probably one of the few people to own a bathmat designed for him by Matisse."

Another painter on Maugham's guest list was Graham Sutherland, who had a home near Villefranche from 1947. Maugham was Sutherland's first subject as a portrait painter. Later on, Sutherland moved to a house in the hills behind Menton. In a disused building in the town the strips of tapestry were assembled that made up his vast work now hanging in Coventry Cathedral.

Nobs and Snobs

British visitors to the Riviera in the interwar years who were neither creatures nor creators of fiction or works of art were generally neither sunny nor shady but simply their British, usually English, selves transported to a sunnier climate. The class system was no less rigid (except perhaps in the melting pot of the casinos) and attitudes to the natives and to each other unchanged by the temptation to let down their guard in the softer air. The Duke of Westminster lorded it in one or other or his pair of yachts just as he did in his Belgave mansion. The society columns dropped the names of the rich and famous, and many more who were rather less rich and famous, and were read by all and sundry to be sure who was in and who was out. The *Menton and Monte Carlo News* regularly ran satirical sub-Hiawathan verses featuring a character called Profiteera, gently mocking the habits, while appealing to the snobbery, of those on whom nevertheless the paper depended for its income.

> Once again to Montikarlo comes the awful Profiteera
> With the lurid Maridorta from his Palace in Baisworta...
> In the deadly heat of summer, on the sun-scorched courts of Tennis,
> See once more the Profiteera in an Oldarrovian Blaza.

Old attitudes died hard. *The Times* reported on 12 May 1936 that "the campaign against noise has so far proved abortive. The authorities in the coast towns have done their utmost, but the ultimate suppression of noise rests with the police, and the policeman of the south is immune to noises which wreck the nerves of the Anglo-Saxon." Even in the late 1950s the eccentric, domineering TV chef, Fanny Cradock and her submissive husband Johnnie were dishing up the same sneers. In *Holiday on the French Riviera* (1960), an account of a yachting and motoring tour, they professed themselves horrified by Nice officialdom.

> Nice harbour is of particular interest to tourists since it is here that yachts must call (if not at Cannes) for goods supplied for their use afloat *Out of Bond*. The service is naturally invaluable, providing as it does canned foods, wines, spirits, soaps, scents, cigarettes, tobacco, liqueurs and such like free of duty; but it operates so dreadfully inefficiently, is made so obstructive and lackadaisical by men who clearly realise their offices are indispensable and aim therefore to be both pompous and idle that the whole business is well nigh unendurable.

Up the coast in Menton the Cradocks confronted another evil of foreign travel, dirt and smells: "Menton is like a grubby ball dress—once charming, now tatty. The beach resembles all the worst jokes about Southend, with its litter of papers, peels and soiled linen. We still

Gin palaces in Monaco – glitzy but enviable

remember with a shudder the night we were forced to drop anchor in Menton harbour last year. The harbour was filthy and it smelt."

One of the last survivors of the old-fashioned expatriate Britons on the Riviera was the adventurous writer, artist and journalist who made (a now cleansed and prettified) Menton her home in the 1970s, the London-born Lesley Blanch. She was the author of *The Wilder Shores of Love* and lover— later wife—of the Resistance hero, diplomat and novelist Romain Gary (to name but one of her many *amours*). She died in May 2006, aged 102, still in her villa near the Italian frontier, despite it having burnt down to the ground in 1994, only to be lovingly rebuilt. Her villa in Menton-Garavan—"not Provence but Liguria", she would insist—was filled with oriental rugs, icons, and memories of her exotic travels and enthusiasms, and her garden with bamboo and jasmine. This was a Riviera retreat appropriate for a true British eccentric's reclusive final years.

New Comers

It was a British writer who saw the fictional potential of that most modern of Riviera places, the high-tech International Science Park known as Sophia-Antipolis. J. G. Ballard's 2000 novel *Super-Cannes* is set in a kind of copy-and-paste version of Silicon Valley built over five and a half thousand acres of rolling woodland off the A8 autoroute behind Vallauris and Cannes. The real thing (unless it is a virtual deception) was created in 1969. It has four sectors—electronics and computers in one, health and biotechnology in a second, teaching and research in a third, and environmental sciences in a fourth. Ballard's spooky dystopia has no doubt only marginal psychological correspondence, although his "vision of glass and titanium straight from the drawing boards of Richard Neutra and Frank Gehry, but softened by landscaped parks and artificial lakes" is evidence of a writer who takes pleasure in observing accurately. His "Eden-Olympia", a "virtual city conjured into the pine-scented air like a *son-et-lumière* vision of a new Versailles," is a convincing simulacrum of the real thing.

Meanwhile, down on the coast and up in the high villages, the British still come to the traditional Riviera. The majority now come by budget airliner, hatchback and InterRail. But the heady "Sweet South" scent of the *belle époque* is still in the Riviera air. The old and unchangeable attractions still exercise their pull to the south, still whisper intimately into receptive British ears.

Chapter Five

ROUBLES AND ROULETTE
THE RUSSIANS

In the second half of the nineteenth century the Russians began to arrive in force on the Riviera. One immediate effect was that the British, appalled by these noisy, "vulgar" newcomers, huddled ever more tightly together, creating a society even more exclusive of outsiders. The Russians had no such inhibitions.

It all started on a note of high diplomacy. Defeated in the Crimean War, Tsarist Russia yearned for a naval base in the Mediterranean. In October 1856 the Dowager Empress arrived in Villefranche for a "holiday" with a retinue of a hundred. She stayed in a hotel virtually requisitioned for herself and her entourage. The King of Sardinia, Victor Emmanuel, called on her. Dinners, balls, concerts and good-will exchanges followed one upon the other, to the horror of the British.

"Empress-Mother" Alexandra Fyodorovna remained in Nice for six months, her health "much improved". She was not the first Russian to benefit from a stay on the French Riviera, but she set a social trend. From now on the roubles began to talk as loud as the titles.

The coming of the railway to Nice in 1864 increased the volume of traffic between St. Petersburg and the French coast. Three days after its inauguration, Tsar Alexander II arrived in a special train. This gave the impression to some that Russia virtually owned the rail link to the Riviera. The Grand Duke Michael, the tsar's son, convinced that a speed exceeding thirty miles an hour would damage his heart, obliged the railway authorities between the two far-flung places to re-arrange their timetables to accommodate his fears.

THE *BELLE EPOQUE*—RUSSIAN STYLE
Grand Duke Michael is often said to have turned Cannes, his favourite watering-hole, into the most promiscuous society in Europe. In his Villa Kasbek the Prince of Wales met Alice Keppel, his most desired mistress. In

Onion domes in Nice – the Russian Orthodox cathedral

When the Riviera Was Ours (1977) Patrick Howarth tells the story of a Russian aristocrat in Cannes, Count Apraxin, who

> kept a number of distinguished cellists on permanent duty any time of day or night that he chose, and as the music tended to make him feel suicidal a servant had to stand behind his chair to prevent him from shooting himself. Once the crisis had been overcome he would drink seven or eight glasses of a mixture consisting of cognac and a distillation of violets poured over sugar and then fall asleep. He refused to receive any visitors, even the Grand Duke Michael, apart from the Mayor of Cannes, M. Capron, who was permitted to call from time to time.

If the Russians' extravagance was legendary, so too was their imperious disdain for convention. The widow of Grand Duke Constantine commandeered a frigate to sail to Genoa rather than travel with the common people on the steamer (then she remained on board for two weeks while a jetty was built to take off her grand piano in safety). One grand duke killed a police inspector, taking him for a nihilist, but the crime was hushed up. There are stories of predatory widows, drunken escapades and noblemen treating local workers as serfs whom they could flog at will. But this was not, of course, the whole picture.

Individual Russians had already found the Riviera, particularly favouring Nice, even in the years before the Dowager Empress opened the floodgates. One much humbler visitor from the 1840s was the author of *Dead Souls* and *The Government Inspector*, Nikolai Gogol, who made his name exposing the follies of the powerful and rich. As soon as he arrived in Nice at the beginning of December 1843, he was seduced: "Nice is a paradise. The sun spreads over everything, like a layer of oil; there   are countless butterflies and flies, the air is like summer. Utter peace…"

He retreated into the fledgling Russian quarter, setting himself up as a kind of spiritual adviser to Alexandra Osipovna Smirnov, a Russian beauty in her early thirties who seemed more attracted by earthly things; nevertheless he read her what he was writing each morning—his work in progress on *Dead Souls*. He told his friend Yasikov: "I am rowing resolutely into the waves, taking myself on, that is to say taking on the laziness and throbbing anxiety which overtake me…"

But a couple of months later, in March 1844, Madame Smirnov left

Nice. Gogol's health was always poor, but his hopes that the Riviera would give him a boost were unrealized. Despite his urge to dispense more spiritual advice to his ardent admirers, he too left Nice—for ever.

In November 1851 Alexander Herzen and his wife Natalia were in Nice, waiting for his mother and his son Kolia to arrive by boat from Marseille (still the easiest way to make the journey). But in the night the boat struck a rock off the island of Porquerolles. Herzen dashed to Hyères, but in vain. Natalia never recovered from the loss of her son, dying from a broken heart six months later. Herzen's novel *Oceano Nox* was inspired by this tragedy. After his death in 1871 he was buried next to his wife in the Château Cemetery in Nice; "there is no more beautiful cemetery in the world than this mountain," he had written to a childhood friend.

Lev Nikolayevich Tolstoy's acquaintance with the French Riviera was scarcely less sad. He came to Hyères in the summer of 1860 with his brother Nikolai, who was suffering from tuberculosis. They stayed in one villa, while Nikolai's wife and three children put up in another. Nikolai's death shortly afterwards prompted some bitter reflections by his brother Lev in a letter to a friend, Afanasy Afanasyevich Fet:

> On 20th September, our style, he died, literally in my arms. Nothing in life has made such an impression on me. He was telling the truth when he said there is nothing worse than death. And if you think that death is after all the end of everything, then there's nothing worse than life either… A few minutes before he died, he dozed off, then suddenly came to and whispered with horror: "What does it all mean?" He had seen it—this absorption of the self into nothingness… One thing remained for him to the end—nature. The night before he died he went into his bedroom and fell exhausted on the bed by the open window. I came in. With tears in his eyes he said: "How I've enjoyed this whole last hour." From the earth you came and to the earth you will return… I'm spending the winter here for the simple reason that I am here, and it makes no difference where I live.

Nikolai was buried in Hyères cemetery. Lev took his three nephews on expeditions, one to the island of Porquerolles, and finally got down to some writing—but the novel he started here, *The Decembrists*, was soon abandoned (although Turgenev said he had enjoyed the first few chapters).

In fact Ivan Turgenev had already been to Hyères, staying for ten days in the Hôtel d'Europe in October 1848. He too was not happy there, but only because it rained incessantly and a "thick uniform fog, gloomy and grey" prevented him from enjoying the views.

In October 1875 the satirist Mikhail Saltykov-Shchedrin came to stay in the Pension Russe (now the Hôtel Oasis) in Nice. He was not impressed by this "perfumed hole": "There are no gardens, only orchards with miserable orange trees. The famous Promenade des Anglais is a rather bad parody of a boulevard; there is no shade and the miserable palm trees along the side look like leeks."

Almost twenty years on, Anton Chekhov made the first of his four visits to Nice. On the first two he was at the end of long trips and impatient to get back to work in Moscow. In 1897 his wanderlust and a persistent cough encouraged him to return to France, first to Biarritz, which he found too rainy, then to Nice, where "culture oozes out of every shop window, out of every wicker basket and every dog smells of civilisation."

He found himself among a large number of Russians in various stages of ill health, particularly with lung problems, and adopted a quiet routine of staying indoor in bad weather, avoiding spicy food and reading on benches in the sunshine. But he complained of the difficulty of writing in a foreign country, doing more reading than writing, working out ways of beating the odds at the casino, and fighting the cause of Dreyfus, supporting Zola and in doing so quarrelling terminally with his old friend Suvorin, the editor of *New Times*. Two years later, at the end of 1900, Chekhov was back at the same Pension Russe, correcting the last two acts of *The Three Sisters*, while in Moscow rehearsals had already begun on the first two acts.

This was to be Anton Chekhov's last visit. He returned to Russia after just six weeks, only to die, at the age of 44, just after witnessing the success of *The Cherry Orchard*. It was in the first act of this play that he made his only fictional reference to the French Riviera, when Anya complains to Varya (her older, adopted sister) that their mother has been living a miserable life abroad: "She's already sold her villa near Mentone; she has nothing left, nothing. And I don't have any money left either, not a single copeck, hardly enough to get to Paris."

Fictional references to living on the Riviera were almost shorthand for the "good old days". Living on the Riviera implied times of plenty but also a prosperity that had something shifty about it, reputed to attract characters who might not always be what they seemed. In Tolstoy's *Anna Karenina*, Kitty's mother quizzes her daughter's new friend Varenka about her upbringing with the almost coded query, "I've heard you live at Menton with your aunt—I think—Madame Stahl"; and indeed this woman turns out to have an ambiguous past. Even during the *belle époque*, by no means all the Russians living or staying on the Riviera lived the life of grand dukes and duchesses. Places like Menton suggested a degree of comfort and a slightly *louche* lifestyle but by no means great wealth.

One Russian family whose name became prominent at the height of the *belle époque* was the Bashkirtseffs, not because they were conspicuously rich, but through their ebullient, self-promoting and precociously talented daughter. They were not socially acceptable to all, partly because the father remained in Russia (the better to pursue his private pleasures), while the daughter, Marie, was a wild child, dashing about the Promenade des Anglais without a hat and going into the Monte Carlo Casino in short dresses. The family also conducted a feud with a branch of the Tolstoy family, which resulted in Marie's uncle George holing up in Monaco with his mistress.

Marie herself, however, channelled her precocity well. Her teenage diary, full of her enthusiasms, hates, ambitions and caustic observations, was published in 1877. It was described by William Gladstone in his own diary three years later as a book of "true genius". Among all the places the Bashkirtseff family stayed in during their years of wandering around Europe, Nice was Marie's favourite; "nowhere is more splendidly simple and adorably poetic than Nice," she wrote in her diary in 1874.

> One is as if in a nest, surrounded by mountains neither too high nor too dry. On three sides one is protected as if by a stylish and comfortable coat, and, in front of one, one has a huge window, an infinite horizon that is always the same and always new. I love Nice; Nice is my own country; Nice makes me more grown-up, healthy, with good colour. It is so beautiful! ... When the moon shines, it makes a great pathway in the sea like a fish with diamond scales...

Being who she was—vulnerable like Katherine Mansfield and indeed Tobias Smollett to the mood swings of a tuberculosis sufferer—Marie had also confided to her diary (on 23 November 1873): "Horrible town! Boring people! How I hate you! Nice! Nice, how I hate you!"

Marie Bashkirtseff died at the age of 24. But she left her mark, as she was determined to do, fiercely resisting her conventional role as a dependent female facing marriage as the "only career" and fighting against what she dubbed a "commercial operation". Her paintings, perhaps even more than her writing, show both talent and maturity (see p.145), though many of them were destroyed by the Nazis. Today, on the corner of the rue Marie-Bashkirtseff at the end of the Avenue de la Californie, stands a small fountain with an inscription to her memory.

Revolution and Change

The Russian Revolution of 1917, the First World War and then the civil war put an end to the glory days of the Russian community on the Riviera. One poignant reminder of those times is Nice's Russian cemetery, on a gentle slope overlooking the sea, just off the Avenue Ste.-Marguerite. Here is the tomb of the Tsar Alexander's morganatic wife, Katia, the Princess Katerina Yurevsky. He met her when making a visit to a school for the children of impoverished nobility, but the scandal of their relationship began to spread, and she was kept far away from him. However, her status improved to that of official mistress when he found her again in Paris during a visit to Napoleon III. After the empress died, Tsar Alexander married his "démon bleu", as the English-born socialite and novelist, Princess Bibesco, dubbed her in her novel of that name. But it all ended badly when he died in her arms, victim of an assassination, and the princess left Russia to settle in Nice for the last years of her life.

Yet the picture was more complex than a simple one of the overthrow of the tsars and the Russian nobility, of the rapidly ebbing tide of social privilege. Some, but not many, Russians managed to bridge the gap between pre- and post-Revolution.

Serge Diaghilev the Russian impresario was one. In 1911, the year the Ballets Russes were founded, he staged the ballet *Scheherazade* in Monte Carlo. When the First World War put him into financial difficulties, he used his contacts to establish a small permanent troupe of dancers there. From 1922 to 1929, after travelling all over the world, he again made Monaco the base for his dance company. The Riviera also provided a rich source of inspiration. The *Train Bleu*, bringing rich visitors in luxury from the English Channel to the Mediterranean, was the theme for the comic ballet first staged in Paris in June 1924. Contributors included Jean Cocteau (story), Darius Milhaud (music), Bronislava Nijinska (choreography), Coco Chanel (costumes) and Pablo Picasso (curtain). But Diaghilev was already himself part of the Riviera scene.

One much later sign of the post-Revolution decline of the Russian presence on the Riviera was the sale, as late as 1975, of Diaghilev's library (he had died in 1929). His collection contained the first book ever printed in Moscow, the first Russian grammar printed in the western world, and manuscripts of Pushkin's novel in verse, *Evgeni Onegin*, and Stravinsky's *The Firebird*.

Igor Stravinsky was the man most associated with the musical side of Diaghilev's artistic enterprises. Stravinsky himself had visited the Riviera before 1914. Indeed, his ballet *Petrushka* had already caused something of a scandal in conservative circles, especially among the Russian colony at that time. After the Revolution, in 1924, he moved to Nice and lived in the Mont Boron quarter.

The first Russian winner of the Nobel Prize for Literature, Ivan Bunin (1870-1953), was a precociously successful poet, translator (of Longfellow's *Song of Hiawatha* and of Byron's poetry, among much else) and celebrated short story writer. His diary, with its fiercely accurate observations of his personal experiences during the Revolution and the civil war (he had moved from Moscow to Odessa), was published under the title *The Accursed Days*. Bunin left his native country after the turbulent times in his native country and began to divide his time between Paris and Grasse. He found the hills behind Cannes conducive to a literary life (despite a stormy marriage and an affair with a young Russian writer who left him for another woman). He remained in Grasse until the end of the Second World War. Strongly anti-Nazi, he is reputed to have sheltered fugitives in his house there, the Villa Jeanette, throughout the occupation. As his health deteriorated, he had several spells convalescing in the Russian House in Juan-les-Pins.

Another man whose career bridged the revolutionary divide was Vladimir Nabokov. He visited the Riviera, sometimes for years at a time, from as early as 1904 as a four-year-old boy, up until 1960-61, writing *Pale Fire* in Nice. In Cannes, Menton (in the Pension Hespérides), the back country village of Moulinet, the Cap d'Antibes and St.-Aygulf on the Esterel coast, during the years just before the Second World War, he worked on his last Russian-language fiction, *The Gift*, also on *Laughter in the Dark*, novellas, plays and even the first conception of a story that became *Lolita*. His short story *Visit to the Museum* was inspired by a trip to Menton—where he was particularly impressed by the busts of Pushkin and Peter the Great. Of course, the butterflies on this part of the Mediterranean coast were an equal source of satisfaction to such a keen lepidopterist as Nabokov.

In July 1935 the volatile, bisexual symbolist poet Marina Tsvetaeva took a holiday with her son in a Russian pension, the Villa La Favière in Le Lavandou, a village frequented then by more Austrians than Russians. Tsvetaeva was disappointed:

> After two weeks here I am bored… really and truly I don't need this beauty, so much beauty, the sea, the mountains, the mimosa in flower, etc. One tree outside my window is enough… Such beauty forces me into uninterrupted enthusiasm… this eternal beauty wears me down. I have nothing to give in exchange. I have always been attracted by modest things: simple places, deserts, which don't please anyone but give me the confidence to sing their praises and which, I feel, love me. To love the Côte d'Azur is the same as loving a twenty-year-old prince. It wouldn't occur to me.

This reaction is not unique. Not every Russian artist found the Riviera stimulating, even though it might have provided a respite from social turbulence and danger. Sometimes the Côte d'Azur's warm embrace proved just too much of a good thing, a place to which the only response was to relax rather than to create. Others, such as Bunin and Nabokov, had the opposite reaction, finding it easy to create in its indulgent climate.

The Riviera attracted all kinds of Russians, not just artists and writers, but businessmen too. It is unclear if Sir Basil Zaharoff (1849-1936) can strictly be classified as Russian, though he wooed his wife in 1872 by pretending to be a Russian prince; in fact, his DNA was a cocktail of nationalities, and the sources of his wealth equally mysterious and exotic. But he had used Monaco as his base for many years, dealing in arms and oil at a time when the Boer War and then the First World War were excellent for profits. In 1918 his fortune was such that he was able, with Prince Louis' consent, to buy out Camille Blanc and take over his holdings in the Monte Carlo Casino. In *The Grimaldis of Monaco* (1992), Anne Edwards described what happened then.

> Upon acquiring control of the Casino, Zaharoff (who claimed never to set foot inside its doors) immediately had the minimum stake doubled on all bets and appointed his own managing directors. Even though profits rose dramatically, Louis loathed and distrusted Zaharoff. Whether Zaharoff's original takeover of the Casino had been an old man's whim or a desire for greater influence in Monaco, he soon lost his enthusiasm for the project when the married woman he had loved for thirty-seven years was finally widowed and they were wed. Within a year she became terminally ill and her elderly bridegroom refused to leave her side. His interest was sold in 1924 to a group of Paris bankers.

The Russian Orthodox Church tried, in its own way, to consolidate Russian society on the Riviera. An impressive monument to the Russian presence in Nice is the colourful and immense Russian cathedral, built just before the 1917 Revolution (see Chapter Nine). But, as Scott Fitzgerald observed, the post-Revolution decline left a palpable change in the whole atmosphere of the Riviera:

> Most of all, there was the scent of Russians along the coast—their closed book shops and grocery stores. Ten years ago, when the season ended in April, the doors of the Orthodox Church were locked, and the sweet champagnes they favoured were put away until their return. "We'll be back next season," they said, but this was premature, for they were never coming back any more.

Indeed, the congregations at the cathedral dwindled rapidly. Some services began to be conducted in French, while the choir was padded out by French students learning Russian. The French Ministry of Culture recently declared the cathedral's contents part of the "national patrimony", not to be removed without its permission.

In 2008 a delegation from Moscow tried to "reclaim" ownership of the cathedral. In fact, it was originally the property of Tsar Nicholas II, but a 99-year lease ceded it to the Archbishop of St. Petersburg. That lease

A Russian soul at rest in Menton's Old Château cemetery

expired in 2007. The post-Soviet Russian government saw a chance to exercise its influence by "restoring unity" with the central Church authorities in Moscow. Their first tactic was to get legal permission to enter the cathedral and take an inventory. But the Nice religious officials and congregation have so far resisted.

THE ROUBLE'S RETURN

The Russians were down—but not out. As communism retreated and the Soviet Union turned back into Russia, so new money started to accumulate and find its way into the West. The French Riviera was a major beneficiary of this trend. The good old days of the rouble have started to make a comeback.

Between December 1905 and April 1914 there was a four-page weekly broadsheet in Russian—*Le Russe sur la Riviera*—modelled on *The Continental Weekly* and on many other English-language newspapers that published the names of those arriving and leaving for the season, advertisements for language teachers, times of church services and so on. In 2007 so many Russians had returned that the *Riviera Times* began publishing its A-Z guides in Russian, in addition to those in English, German and Italian. *Nice-Matin* now regularly runs stories about fabulous property deals in which Russian billionaires buy spectacular villas like latter-day grand dukes. The biggest ever was the sale reported in the summer of 2008 of the Villa Leopolda, the huge estate bought by the former King of the Belgians, Leopold II, in 1902 for a symbolic franc. The buyer turned out to be the Russian "Nickel King", Mikhail Prokhorov. But his record offer of 500 million euros fell through when the credit crunch hit – not the first but certainly the biggest lost deposit on the unstable Riviera property market in early 2009.

Russian business men still come – to play if not always to buy. There is less evidence, however, of latter-day Russian artistic imaginations being fired by the Riviera sun, even if every summer Cannes hosts a Festival de l'Art Russe, which might feature anything from the circus to jewellery, concerts, plays and exhibitions. Though the Russians are back on the Riviera, it remains to be seen if financial conditions will allow them to recreate in the twenty-first century the glory days of the of the *belle époque*.

Chapter Six

AN AZURE DREAM

THE AMERICANS

When the First World War and then, with dramatic finality, the Bolshevik Revolution, dried up the flow of rich Russians to the French Riviera—the "lost caviar days", as F. Scott Fitzgerald put it—suddenly the grand dukes and princes, the businessmen, landowners, writers and artists were penniless and miserable. It was the moment for the Americans to move in. And they did, slowly at first, but with increasing verve and style, determined to make things happen. Dick Diver, hero of Fitzgerald's *Tender is the Night* (1934), had a theory: "All the northern places, like Deauville were packed out by Russians and English who don't mind the cold, while half of us Americans come from tropical climates—that's why we're beginning to come here."

Mary Blume had much the same opinion:

The gaudy Russians were reduced to quiet domesticity or to the roles of taxi drivers, vendeuses at the new branches of Poiret and Patou, and extras in Rex Ingram's films. In any case, they had become inappropriate. New blood was needed, clean-limbed bodies, youth incarnating the optative mood. The Americans came with their swinging gait, their jazz records, their sweet corn and new canned soups, their way of making the impossible look easy, and above all the briefly contagious national mood of expectation, the belief, in F. Scott Fitzgerald's words, "that there were gay, exciting things hovering in the next hour."

If Lytton Strachey summed up English *hauteur* and wry wit faced with the foibles of his countrymen on the Riviera, one American (apart from Fitzgerald) encapsulated the very opposite reaction, an innocent, heartfelt passion for the sights and sounds of a long-dreamed-of, magical Côte d'Azur. On New Year's Eve 1955 the poet Sylvia Plath was thirty-three years old and about to travel by train down to the southern French coast.

The Carlton in Cannes – old glamour, new money

She was aware, as were most bookish, sensitive Americans, that she was heading for something exotic, thrilling, beautiful. Fitzgerald and many others had prepared the way, but her description has an archetypal, out-of-time quality about it, an expression of the essence of excited anticipation.

> Off into the night, with the blackness of a strange land knifing past. In my mind, a map of France, irregularly squarish, with a minute Eiffel Tower marking Paris toward the north, and a line of railway tracks, like a zipper, speeding open to the south, to Marseille, to Nice and the Côte d'Azur where perhaps in the realm of absolute fact the sun is shining and the sky is turquoise. Away from sodden mud and cutting winds of gray Cambridge, away from the freezing white frosts of a cold gray London, where the sun hung in the white mists like a bloody egg yolk…
>
> …We are leaving the thick clouds and smoky ceiling, we are plunging through into clear moonlight, first edging the thinning clouds like curded cream, then breaking forth pure and clear, in a spinning blueness… The Mediterranean. At last, unbelievable, the moon on that sea, that azure sea I dreamed about on maps in the sixth grade…
>
> Sleep again, and at last the pink vin rosé light of dawn along the back of the hills in a strange country. Red earth, orange tiled villas in yellow and peach and aqua, and the blast, the blue blast of the sea on the right. The Côte d'Azur. A new country, a new year; spiked with green explosions of palms, cacti sprouting vegetable octopuses with spiky tentacles, and the red sun rising like the eye of God out of a screaming blue sea.

Once in Nice, Plath headed along towards that blue sea.

Everywhere little black-clad people walk along the sparkling Sunday morning pavement, sitting in the turquoise-painted deck chairs along the Promenade des Anglais and facing into the rising sun; painted beach blondes pass by in high heels, black slacks, fur coats and sun glasses; old men in navy-blue berets amble stiffly along, smoking pipes, blinding behind dark glasses; someone has brought out a pet monkey, and a little crowd has gathered to watch the monkey jump for the lowest branches of the palm and swing by one long hairy black arm.

There is much more in her diary of this breath-catching, scarcely controllable excitement at seeing the colours and sights and oh-so-European people of the Riviera. Here indeed is the essence of the American image of the Riviera.

First Impressions

The story of Americans on the Riviera in fact goes way back. As Michael Nelson reminds us in his *Americans and the Making of the Riviera* (2008), the first American to visit was also the "most distinguished". Thomas Jefferson (1743-1826), third US president, was on his way to Lombardy to study rice growing when he came to Nice in late winter 1787. He was also self-consciously following in the footsteps of two British writers he admired, Tobias Smollett and Laurence Sterne.

As well as a good letter writer, Jefferson was a meticulous note-taker and note-keeper; he was travelling with his own portable copying machine as well as a "reservoir", or fountain pen. His comments covered the excellent Bellet wines and the hedges of pomegranates, sweetbriar, broom and wild thyme, where the largest olive trees could be found, and which was the last village they grew in, as he headed out towards the Col de Tende and Piedmont. He described Nice as "in fact an English Colony" and Monaco as "a little off the road but worth going to see." In a later memorandum he listed as "Services to My Country" not only the Declaration of Independence and the act prohibiting the importation of slaves, but also the introduction to the United Sates of olive trees and an improved strain of rice, commenting that "the greatest service which can be rendered any country is, to add an useful plant to its culture."

A century later, Americans were not just passing through but were on the Riviera in force. They quickly became famous for their beautiful and lively women. But also among the early visitors from the United States were many less glamorous individuals crossing the Atlantic for a kind of sub-prime Jamesian experience, eager just to see the sights and prove that young Americans could be more independent, and their women much less hidebound by convention, than their European counterparts. A fine fictional example is Amy March, who, in the sequel to Louisa May Alcott's *Little Women*, *Good Wives* (1869), finds herself in Nice, admiring the Promenade des Anglais in a conventional enough way, when she meets up with an old friend, Laurie. As they go together towards the Old Town,

Amy is indignant when Laurie describes it as a "dirty old hole": "The dirt is picturesque, so I don't mind. The river and the hills are delicious, and these glimpses of the narrow cross-streets are my delight. Now we shall have to wait for that procession to pass."

When what is clearly, from Amy's description, a group of Blue Penitents has finally gone by, she conducts her friend up the castle hill, then whisks him off to sketch in Valrosa, up behind the city. Here, May Alcott projects onto her heroine an almost eighteenth-century bucolic scene.

> Here an ancient monastery, whence the solemn chanting of the monks came down to them. There a bare-legged shepherd, in wooden shoes, pointed hat, and rough jacket over one shoulder, sat piping on a stone, while his goats skipped among the rocks or lay at his feet. Meek, mouse-coloured donkeys, laden with panniers of freshly-cut grass, passed by, with a pretty girl in a *capaline* sitting between the green piles, or an old woman spinning with a distaff as she went. Gnarled olive-trees covered the hills with their dusky foliage, fruit hung golden in the orchard, and great scarlet anemones fringed the roadside.

How very different from the Marchs' home life in Boston.

The trigger for Americans at large to come to the Riviera was the 1870 publication in New York of Dr. James Henry Bennet's *Winter and Spring on the Shores of the Mediterranean*, nine years after it had had the same effect on the British. Mark Twain was one of the more distinguished visitors who believed the Riviera climate would improve his health, although when he got there he was his usual sceptical self.

THE LITERARY ELITE

The doyenne of American literati on the Côte d'Azur in the years following the First World War was Edith Wharton (1862-1937). The process of choosing Hyères as her winter base was a long and careful one. She had known the Riviera as a teenager. Even before 1914 she had driven up and down the coast, thrilled at being a pioneer of motoring in her Panhard-Levassor. On one trip she was accompanied by Henry James. After further trips, staying in a succession of hotels (including the Costebelle, southwest of the old town, where Queen Victoria had preceded her), she decided in 1919 to take a lease on (and later buy) the old convent of Ste.-Claire.

It was the garden as much as the view across the pink rooftops and down towards the Giens peninsula and the offshore islands that attracted her. She settled down to a happy routine of planting and writing and looking at the views. As she wrote to Bernard Berenson, "seven hours of blue-and-gold and thyme and rosemary and hyacinth and roses every day that the Lord makes; and in the evenings, dozing over a good book!"

Edith Wharton's fiction had at its core the manners and customs of rich and well-born New Yorkers. The Riviera played a big part in her imagined schemes; sometimes her characters' attitudes to the Riviera were important to establish their personality, particularly their inadequacies. Book Two of the *House of Mirth* (1905) starts with these observations on the dangerous charms of the Riviera's most notorious symbol:

> It came vividly to Selden on the Casino steps that Monte Carlo had, more than any other place he knew, the gift of accommodating itself to each man's humour... As he surveyed the white square set in an exotic coquetry of architecture, the studied tropicality of the gardens, the groups loitering in the foreground against mauve mountains which suggested a sublime stage-setting forgotten in a hurried shifting of scenes— as he took in the whole outspread effect of light and leisure, he felt a movement of revulsion from the last few months of his life.

On Nice's Promenade des Anglais the lawyer Lawrence Selden meets a character called Ned Silverton, who is in "a mood of Titanic pessimism", wondering how "any one could come to such a damned hole as the Riviera—any one with a grain of imagination". There is altogether little hope for relationships in a setting where gossip and scandal reign, and where "conspicuousness passed for distinction."

An echo is heard here of a passage in Wharton's 1900 short story *The Touchstone*, when the indigent hero, Glennard, observes an over-rich friend in their New York club:

> Hollingsworth, lounging away from the window, had joined himself to a languidly convivial group of men, to whom, in phrases as halting as though they were struggling to define an ultimate idea, he was expounding the cursed nuisance of living in a hole with such a damned climate that one had to get out of it by February, with the contingent

difficulty of there being no place to take one's yacht to in winter but that other played-out hole, the Riviera.

A pre-echo, perhaps, of Connolly's fictitious "hole", Trou-sur-Mer, somewhere between Nice and Cannes?

THE VERY RICH

Not to be confused with Dr. James Henry Bennet—or even with fiction, though he was certainly larger than life—is the super-rich American newspaper heir, James Gordon Bennett Jr. (1841-1918). Michael Nelson describes him as "the most eccentric American to live on the Riviera in the nineteenth century." This was the man who fled to France after urinating in the fireplace of his one-time fiancée's parents at a New York reception; who challenged the Duke of Hamilton (whose sister was briefly married to the Prince of Monaco) to a yacht race; who organized a Venetian costume parade and firework displays in Villefranche; who would throw the entire day's mail for his newspaper, *The Paris Herald*, overboard from his yacht whenever he had a hangover; who bought an entire restaurant when he could not get the table he wanted and gave it away to a waiter; who dined with Henry Stanley in Nice, having commissioned him to search for the explorer, David Livingstone; and who took such a fancy to Beaulieu that he virtually founded it as an independent commune and turned it into a resort in its own right.

Richard O'Connor told in his 1962 biography *The Scandalous Mr. Bennett* the story of the reporter and the cow. Gordon Bennett was immensely proud of his new yacht, the 2,000-tonne *Lysistrata* and its many mod cons, including a Turkish bath, owls' eyes that shone from the prow and from the top of the mast, a radio telegraph and a crew of a hundred. "The Commodore", as Bennett liked to style himself, summoned a young man on *The Herald* staff in Paris down to Villefranche, took him far out to the countryside, chose a cow, thrust its lead into the reporter's hands and told him to march it down to his yacht. Here the beast was put into a padded, fan-cooled stall, ready to give milk on the next cruise.

When Gordon Bennett died in 1918 the Riviera lost its greatest benefactor; the presidents of both France and the United States sent their condolences; newly prosperous and independent Beaulieu never looked back.

In the same mould, but a generation later, another heir to an American fortune, Frank Jay Gould (1877-1956), descended on the Riviera. After increasing the value of his share of his father's railway money and surviving a couple of bad marriages and a great deal of whisky, Gould sobered up, met a San Franciscan divorcée, Florence LaCase, proposed to her on the same day, married and moved into the Villa Sémiramis in Cannes. This was in 1923. The couple owned the villa for thirty years, but used it almost exclusively for entertaining. Their real home was to be La Vigie in Juan-les-Pins. What Gordon Bennett did for Beaulieu, so Frank Gould did for Juan-les-Pins, buying up swathes of land, building a casino and the Provençal Hotel. His empire extended to Nice, where he also built a casino and a couple of major hotels, the Palais de la Méditerranée and the Majestic.

There were plenty of stories about Frank Jay Gould, but Florence made the bigger splash. She is credited with introducing water-skiing to the Riviera and launching the fashion of day pyjamas as well as "baccarat pyjamas", which had large pockets for gambling chips. And, as with Gordon Bennett, the Goulds' guest-list was star-studded (though the Scott Fitzgeralds made themselves unwelcome by overdoing the riotous behaviour).

After the Second World War the Goulds built a new house next to La Vigie and let the old one out. Picasso was a tenant for a while and painted frescoes on the walls. When he left, Gould had them painted over. He died in 1956. Florence sold the Villa Sémiramis to the Cannes authorities, who transplanted the palm trees on to the Croisette, where they still grow. She died in 1983, aged 87, the last link to the spectacular marriage of American capitalism and Riviera sun.

One particularly enjoyable Gould legacy is the complete eighteenth-century pharmacy in the Palais Lascaris in the old town of Nice. As you come into the labyrinthine baroque palace off the Rue Droite (and extremely narrow), you see through a door on the right an array of blue and white jars, wooden drawers in engraved and enamelled cabinets, and the classic chemist's coloured-glass pots. This is the "Maire's pharmacy", formerly "Baratte's pharmacy", installed first in Besançon in 1738. It was brought to Nice in 1754. When it closed in 1909, it was bought by Paris Singer (of sewing machine fame and fortune) for his *château* in St.-Jean-Cap-Ferrat. Finally, in 1954, Frank Jay Gould bought it and offered it to Nice—for all to admire.

More modest in their ambitions, but perhaps even more influential in the creation of the image of the Riviera in American imaginations, was the couple whose name is closely associated with Cole Porter, Pablo Picasso, John Dos Passos, Scott and Zelda Fitzgerald, Ernest Hemingway—in fact all the cultural stars of the interwar years on the Riviera. They are Gerald and Sara Murphy. With the inevitable background of rich parents (Sara's from printing, Gerald's from luxury goods), they came to Europe with their three children, Honoria, Boath and Patrick, in 1921, settling first in Paris and then on the Côte d'Azur.

The Murphys are credited by many with inventing the summer season. This is doubtful. For one thing complaints had been heard for years, decades even, that there was no need for the "season"—at a time when life for the rich was dictated by seasons—to end abruptly at the end of April. In 1889 the *Eclaireur de Nice* ran a campaign to encourage visitors to arrive earlier and stay longer. In Juan-les-Pins the new Grand Hôtel opened in 1894 and began to stay open all year round. An editorial in the 28 March 1908 edition of the *Anglo-American Gazette (& Continental Advertiser)* declared: "We confidently look forward to the day when the season at Nice will no longer be an affair of three or four months, but of at least six, and it is not beyond the bounds of possibility that we may see a summer season here in addition to a winter one."

This was wishful thinking at the time, hoping, no doubt, to turn into a self-fulfilling prophecy. But the pressure was on. Cole Porter gave the idea a nudge when he rented the Château de la Garoupe on the Cap d'Antibes for the two whole summers of 1921 and 1922 (but he was too busy to linger long, and never returned to the Riviera). The villa's owner was the American singer, Mary Garden, who later endeared herself to the citizens of Peille (see p.210). Little by little the prohibition against taking the sun was beginning to break down. When Antoine Sella, manager of the Hôtel du Cap, succumbed to the Murphys' pressure to keep the establishment open for the whole summer of 1923, the floodgates, or rather the sun barriers, burst. Coco Chanel set the seal on the fashion for tanned skin, looking, it was said as she stepped off a yacht onto Cannes harbour, "like a cabin boy".

The summer season was sexy. It was an exciting part of the post-war dash for pleasure and fun, to come out of the shadows and into the sun. In 1925 the Murphys moved into their new Villa America and the party really got under way. As the writer Donald Ogden Stewart, another of their famous guests, wrote in his memoirs, *By a Stroke of Luck!* (1975):

> They were both rich; he was handsome, she was beautiful; they had three golden children. They loved each other, they enjoyed their own company, and they had the gift of making life enchantingly pleasurable for those who were fortunate enough to be their friends.

The most sober account of life inside the circle came from someone who consciously kept himself on the fringes, John Dos Passos (1896-1970). He was the one who told tales of the Fitzgeralds' crazy antics, such as crawling around the garden during a dinner party given by the Murphys and lobbing tomatoes at the unamused guests. His, in *The Best Times* (1966) was the famous description of the sunbathing group on the beach, Gerald Murphy sweeping the seaweed off the sand, serving cold sherry, before everyone set to work on Sara's

> poached eggs with Golden Bantam corn cut off the cob and sprinkled with paprika; home-grown tomatoes cooked in olive oil and garlic on the side. Sometimes to this day when I'm eating corn on the cob I recapture the flavour, and the blue flare of the Mediterranean noon, and the taste of vin de Cassis in the briney Mediterranean breeze.

Yet Dos Passos admired Gerald Murphy, observing he "had the knack of a Beau Nash for making discoveries that later proved fashionable".

LITERARY REFRACTIONS

Scott Fitzgerald's *Tender is the Night* is a kind of template of American Riviera fiction. But he wrote it soured by experience, unnerved and upset by his wife's instability and his own intake of alcohol. At the start, in 1924, writing with tongue in cheek rather in the manner of a Guy de Maupassant short story—but still anticipating the kind of excitement and success that Sylvia Plath would enjoy a couple of decades later—he set out his reasons for heading off to the South of France in his essay, *How to Live on Practically Nothing a Year.*

Speedboats etching the sea with their wakes

Now when a family goes abroad to economise, they don't go to the Wembley exhibition or the Olympic games; in fact they don't go to London and Paris at all, but hasten to the Riviera, which is the southern coast of France and which is reputed to be the cheapest as well as the most beautiful locality in the world. Moreover we were going to the Riviera out of season, which is something like going to Palm Beach for July.

When the Riviera season finishes in late spring, all the wealthy British and Americans move up to Deauville and Trouville, and all the gambling houses and fashionable milliners and jewellers and second-storey men close up their establishments and follow their quarry north. Immediately prices fall. The native Rivierans, who have been living on rice and fish all winter, come out of their caves and buy a bottle of red wine and splash about for a bit in their own blue sea.

Soon the "native Riverans" would be catering all year round for the needs and demands of the thousands of foreigners taking advantage of favourable exchange rates and the prospect of a never-ending future of peace and prosperity. Not all expatriates—or "transatlantics", as long-term American visitors were called—lived a life of generous bonhomie, however. A Fitzgerald character in a short story called *One Trip Abroad*, a self-confessed sponger by the name of Oscar Dane, warns the heroine, Nicole: "Do you call that crowd of drunks you run with amusing people? Why, they're not even very swell. They're so hard that they've shifted down through Europe like nails in a sack of wheat, till they stick out of it a little into the Mediterranean Sea."

The later Nicole, heroine of *Tender is the Night,* and her husband Dick Diver are unquestionably conceived in the mould of the Murphys in the early scenes of the novel. This is the Riviera at its most seductive, swept clean, like the Garoupe beach, by American energy, made to glitter with physical beauty, money and a sexuality perfectly matching the uncomplicated sunshine. Of course it does not end happily. European cynicism and the innate vulnerability of the American dream overwhelm everything that seemed so perfect. At the end of the story a drunk, self-destructive and Fitzgerald-like Dick Diver is forced to retreat to rural America to practise medicine, possibly to redeem the once fine healthy, family-minded soul and the once fine healthy athletic body contaminated by old-world morals.

Ernest Hemingway, another self-consciously physical American, was a much less frequent visitor to the Riviera than his friend and rival Scott Fitzgerald. Indeed, he really only stayed there at all because his wife Hadley, whom he was about to divorce, summoned him to help look after their child, who had contracted whooping cough. Dos Passos referred to Hemingway as "ill at ease" among the Murphy's friends

> though he loved Sara Murphy. Fishermen never seem to take much pleasure in swimming. He would have felt silly sunburning on the beach. To enjoy the Villa America you had to fall in with Gerald's carefully staged ritual. Hem was already too much the showman to take part in anybody's else (sic) charade.

The only fictional trace of the Riviera in Hemingway's work is the setting of his last, posthumous novel, *The Garden of Eden*, but that was a legacy from a single later visit, in 1954, to the coast near la Napoule. He turns the resort into a fictional paradise, just after the First World War, when the English writer hero David and his two competing women are swimming and drinking and—in his case—writing his heart out, in the "dead summer season". The descriptions are conventionally Edenic: the blue sky and sea, the red rocks, the pine-scented dunes, except for one moment when David's new wife Catherine is spooked by the "strange" light as she looks down at a battle cruiser entering Villefranche bay. "All the colors were too bright," she says. "Even the grays were bright. The olive trees were glittery… it wasn't very nice." Actually Catherine does not like the *villages perchés* either, complaining to her husband that "it's so closed in and picturesque. I hate those hanging villages." But given the amount of alcohol consumed in the novel, it is a mark of the three main characters' potency that the pleasures of the Riviera sun and sea can still be experienced by them all with appropriate rapture.

James Thurber (1894-1961) and his wife stayed with the Murphys and indeed lived a while in Nice in the mid-1920s. His short story *Memoirs of a Drudge* tells the tale of his life as a "leg man" for the Riviera edition of the *Chicago Tribune*, a job made much less of a drudge by the practice of using large print and lifting most of the copy from the *Eclaireur de Nice* or from guest lists provided by the Ruhl or the Negresco hotels (or simply made up). There were the nights of battling with obstinate printers, won only by consuming large quantities of *grog américain*. And then…

We had the long days of warm blue weather for our own, to climb the Corniche roads or wind up the mountain in a char a bancs to the magical streams and the million springtime flowers of St-Martin-Vésubie. Sometimes we sat the day out on the terrace of a restaurant overlooking the Bay of Angels and gave the tireless Albert suggestions as to where he might find Henry James. Albert was a young Englishman who did interviews for us with distinguished visitors to the Riviera, and he had got the curious idea that the celebrated novelist was hiding away in a pension somewhere between St Tropez and Mentone, rewriting "The Golden Bowl". We decided that Albert had got his tip about the whereabouts of the great dead man from some ageing aunt who lived in the parlours and the gardens of the past. It was one way to spend an afternoon, sitting over our glasses of vermouth-cassis, bringing back to life the poor, sensitive creator of Peter Quint and Mme de Vionnet, figuring him lost and wandering, ever so wonderfully, somewhere among the bougainvillaea and the passionflowers. Thus in fancy and in dream passed the long days of warm blue weather.

Like the Divers' (and Hemingways') marriage, like Riviera newspapers trumpeting the arrivals and departures of the rich and famous, the glory days were not to last. They contained the seeds of their own destruction. Even the Murphys' Riviera sojourn ended badly, though for a very different and tragic reason: both their boys died of illnesses aged sixteen. Gerald never painted again, and soon the family returned to the United States.

The memoirs of the American dancer, Isadora Duncan (1877-1927), contain many echoes of that tragic decline which is so central to Fitzgerald's fiction and to the lives of many of that circle. At fifty, frequently drunk and running to fat, Duncan, mourning the death of her two children who had drowned in a freak car accident in Paris, was desperately seeking comfort in much younger men.

One day in late summer 1927 she met a handsome Bugatti salesman, Benoît Falchetto, twenty years her junior, at a party given at Chez Tétou in Golfe Juan in honour of the surrealist poet, Francis Picabia. Next day she managed to persuade Falchetto to take her for a test drive in a Type 52 Electric Grand Prix—way beyond her means, but an exciting prospect and, anyway, maybe, just maybe, her ex-husband Rene Singer would pay. A rendezvous was made for 14 September, *chez moi*. Her companion in her modest flat, Mary Destie, suggested Isadora wear a cape, since the Bugatti had an open top. Isadora chose instead a long red crêpe de chine scarf. It was an unfortunate choice. The wind blew Isadora's trailing scarf into the rear wheel of the car as it sped down the Promenade des Anglais. The dancer's neck was immediately snapped.

By the 1930s the American presence on the Riviera was far less striking than in the previous decade. Henry Miller and Anaïs Nin met up, and corresponded, there—Nin frequented St.-Tropez and lived a while in St.-Raphael; Miller enthused about Grasse and Nice. Gertrude Stein stayed briefly with Picasso but preferred the Haute-Savoie.

Post-war, James Baldwin, the black American author of *Go Tell It on the Mountain* and *Giovanni's Room*, found a seventeen-year-long sanctuary in St.-Paul-de-Vence, dying there in 1987. His haunt was the bar of the Colombe d'Or, where the ghosts of Scott Fitzgerald and Isadora Duncan mingled with the boisterous actuality of Yves Montand and Simone Signoret. Baldwin rented rooms in a nearby house, but only because the French actors persuaded the racist landlady that he was harmless—though she still barricaded the connecting door with a large cupboard. (Perhaps that was also due to his overt homosexuality.) But he did win her over in the end; indeed, she sold him her whole house when she moved out.

Some black Americans were unhappy with Baldwin's escape from the civil rights struggles in his native America. His reply was, "I am *not* in exile and I am *not* in paradise. It rains down here too." Only in a late play, *The Welcome Table*, does the Riviera feature explicitly in Baldwin's writing. But his years spent in Grasse—and in Europe as a whole—did give him something that he regarded as essential for a writer, the "sanction to become oneself".

Generally speaking, from the second half of the twentieth century onwards, when American writers came to the Riviera at all, they did not stay long. It was the more commercially minded American architects and artists, such as Dierks and Nall (see Chapter Eight) who were most attracted to settle there, and who made the biggest splash.

Is there an obvious explanation why Americans never returned to the French Riviera with the same enthusiasm that Fitzgerald and Plath brought to it? Perhaps the real California came to appeal more than "La Californie"? Perhaps Florida pushed all the right buttons? Perhaps there were just too many pushy (and equally rich) Europeans around, squeezed into the same tiny space? Whatever the truth, the power of the dollar and the romance of "gay, exciting things" beside the "screaming blue sea" are still waiting for their second coming.

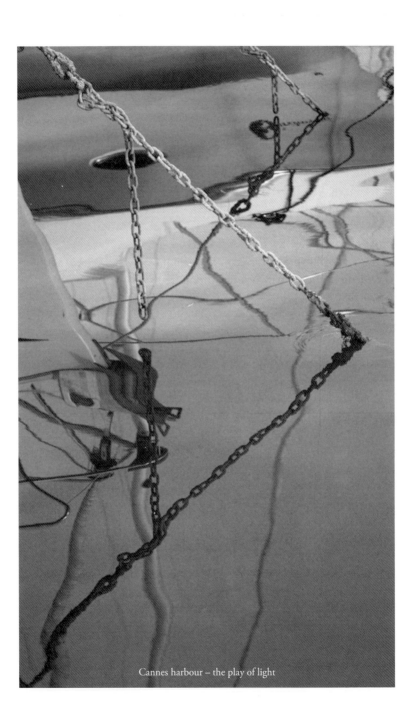

Cannes harbour – the play of light

Chapter Seven

NATIVES AND NEIGHBOURS

THE FRENCH

Nice and the Riviera eastwards, as far as Menton and the modern Italian border, feel French. They are French. But Italian influence has never gone away. Italian is spoken in many shops and restaurants. Many buildings on the *circuit touristique* date from the centuries of control by Savoy and Sardinia. The 1860 vote confirmed that, even if the history of this stretch of the Mediterranean coast belongs to Ligurians, Greeks, Romans and to competing kings, princes and counts from miles around, and in recent times was taken over culturally and economically by intruders from across the English Channel and the Atlantic or from other northern countries, the logical political-cultural place for the modern Riviera to be is comfortably within the French hexagon.

On 2 February 1860 *The Times* of London received a report that showed the extent of opposition to the "annexation" apparently expressed by the people of Nice.

Our town has been extremely agitated for some days past by the intrigues of a few people who are terrified at the idea of annexation with France. Personal animosity has played a principal part on this occasion; next, the private interests of the barristers, who fear to be eclipsed by the French lawyers; and, finally, the Italian feelings of a few, who believe they are serving the interests of the country and of the Government by agitating the population. The fact is, that for the last three days a letter of Garibaldi has been hawked about the streets and read in all the shops, in which the General declares that the King has assured him that he will never give up Nice. It is added, that the King would not be sorry to see a manifestation made which would justify his refusal. This is not all; the most absurd reports are circulated among the operatives to render them hostile to the annexation with France. They are told that the price of sugar, coffee, salt fish, and wine will be raised so high that

St.-Tropez – favourite of the French

they will not be able to purchase those articles; that they will no longer
obtain any employment, and that any persons found in the streets or
in wineshops after 10 at night will be sent to prison. Under these cir-
cumstances the tranquillity of Nice is in danger of being disturbed, particularly as there are so few police to prevent a disturbance… One word
from the French Government would be sufficient to put an end to this
anomaly.

In the event there was no real opposition. *The Times*—and the Italians—were merely stirring things up. A high percentage of the voters
plumped for being incorporated into France, possibly too high to be absolutely true, but reflecting the majority's real wishes anyway.

One ardent supporter of the Emperor Napoleon III went so far as to
celebrate the region's new affiliation by writing a novel about it. *La Mer de
Nice* first appeared in 1861 in part form in the *Moniteur Universel*, known
disparagingly as the newspaper for "grocers and lawyers". It consisted of
letters lavish in praise of Nice and the Riviera. Its author, Théodore de
Banville (1823-91), had an ulterior motive, to attract his actress girlfriend
out of the clutches of the poet Charles Baudelaire—and he succeeded,
taking her on a whirlwind tour of the Riviera sights. Marie Daubrun made
further friends among the Nice public with readings from the stage of pa-
triotic poems. The couple timed their French nationalist enthusiasm just
right.

With the formal transfer of power imminent, they were joined by the
famous journalist Alphonse Karr and the novelist Alexandre Dumas. (Fortunately, Garibaldi was preoccupied with occupying Palermo with his 1,095
Redshirts, so this supporter of the Italian connection was unable to spoil the
party.) *La Mer de Nice* ensured that de Banville was at the centre of the pro-
French celebrations. His novel is even credited with "inventing" the *bleu
niçois*, so frequently and fervently did he evoke its seductive charms.

Here the soft climate, the warm blue sky in December, the winter
clothed in sunbeams, the constant mad, fairy-like flowering, the sea
above all with its loving lullaby, everything says, Go to sleep, nothing is
worth anything; let me die, let me live! Who can describe the irresistible
seduction of this Mediterranean sea scarcely ruffled by the wind into
tiny folds waving like the airy tunic of a sleeping nymph? Azure and

lapis drowning beneath the tender blue sky, darker and splendid in the distance, everywhere adorably blue and a thousand times more blue than the sky itself, it wishes to know nothing of the melancholy that tears you apart, everywhere is serene and implacable as joy…

He also penned a verse in praise of the marriage of Nice to France, rather ignoring the fact that foreigners other than Italians were poised to "invade" for the winter season.

Enfin Nice est heureuse;
Il n'est plus d'étrangers
Sur la terre amoureuse
Où fleurit l'oranger…

Fortunately the quality of French writing about the Riviera improved, although not until *after* Stephen Liégeard (1830-1925) had his turn to gush. He is the very minor poet who aspired to the Academy and never reached his goal or immortality, but who invented something that caught on even more widely than "Nice blue" when, in 1887, he published his book called, with all the panache of a born salesman, *La Côte d'Azur*.

There is a delicate distinction between such "purple" evocations of the blue Mediterranean and the subtle coloration of the prose of Colette (1873-1954), who made St.-Tropez her almost mythical home. Occasionally she flirted with hyperbole; when she wrote in 1949 a short and now rarely read series of minutely observed prose poems on the theme of flowers—*Pour un herbier* (published in English as *for a flower album*)—Colette was all but carried away.

There are connoisseurs of blue just as there are amateurs of *crus*, or wine vintages. For me fifteen consecutive summers at Saint-Tropez were not only a course of treatment in blue, but also of instruction by no means restricted to the contemplation of the Provençal sky to the exclusion of the Mediterranean. I did not go off to canvass the blues in the pellucid beds of clear sand where the wave is at rest, knowing full well that from earliest dawn the blue of the sea would be cruelly encroached upon by the insidious green that puts out the last star in the sky, and that each cardinal point, quit of unstable blue, is free to choose its particular heavenly shade: East purplish, North an icy pink, West an ever deepening red and grey the South.

At the height of a Provençal day, its zenith is cinder-crowned. With lean shadows huddling under the trees and hunched at the foot of the walls, no bird singing, the cat plucking one by one the drops of the fountain drip, by the midday hour every particle of our vital ration of blue and of serenity is in dispute.

We used to await the little wing of dust fluttering at the street corners, the curl of white foam at the lip of the Golfe de Saint-Tropez, sure signs of the resurrection of all the blues. One, the colour of hard lapis lazuli, now returned to the sea, would come bounding shoreward to scintillate under our tunnelled arbour, where suddenly every wine glass was seen to cradle a cube of sapphire ice.

Above the still gilded Alps, a storm-laden cotton-wool wad, blue as a wood pigeon, lay along the summit of the peaks. Within a few hours the full moon would be journeying among the snow of stars, and the white sand lilies, closed throughout the day, would be blue until first light.

"Provençal" may not be used quite accurately, but this is a wonderfully well-observed description of Riviera colours. St.-Tropez was to become the most "French" of all the towns along the Côte d'Azur, in the sense of being visited and enjoyed mostly by French people. It still is. In 2007 the town's long-serving mayor and member of parliament, Dr. Jean-Michel Couve, extolled the intimacy of its "village life", especially in the winter. There does indeed remain a trace of that old fishing village, but it would be an exaggeration to say that it can compete with the lifestyle of those who lunch at Club 55 or party the night away in the VIP Room or Les Caves du Roy during the summer season.

Littérateurs by the Sea

The French Riviera has no *Chanson de Roland* to celebrate its romantic past, no local troubadour, no bard, no epic poet of its own. Instead, writers from the north, mostly Paris of course, began from the middle of the nineteenth century to come down to this neglected south-east corner of France partly to relax and partly to re-charge their creative batteries. Names that come to mind immediately are Guy de Maupassant, Alexandre Dumas,

Jules Verne, Jean Cocteau, André Gide, Jacques Prévert, Roger Martin du Gard, Guillaume Apollinaire, Sartre and de Beauvoir, Colette, Françoise Sagan... but of none can it be said that they are "Riviera writers". They all spent some time on the Côte d'Azur, they all made at least some use of their experiences here in their writing—locations, characters, moods—but in no case did the Riviera feature as a major part of their lives, fictional or real, with the exception of the last two mentioned, for whom St.-Tropez became a kind of literary talisman.

One of the first fascinating figures of French nineteenth-century intellectual life to have a profound connection with the Riviera was Prosper Mérimée. Mérimée (1803-70) was a man of wide interests. Not only was he Inspector-General of Historic Monuments, but he was also the author of *Carmen* (published in 1845 and made into an opera by George Bizet exactly thirty years later). Opinions about him were divided. "As soon as you saw him, you sensed in him a chilliness," wrote Hippolyte Taine. "Especially on ceremonial occasions his features were quite impassive. Even in private, when he was telling some ridiculous story, his voice remained monotonous, utterly calm, without brilliance or vivacity..." But the Russian writer Ivan Turgenev saw that "behind the external show of indifference and coldness, he concealed the most affectionate of hearts."

Mérimée rather resented the common assumption that Cannes was "invented" by Lord Brougham whereas, he claimed, *he* had seen it first. Later he was to complain that the English had settled in Cannes "as if in conquered territory... they deserve to be impaled upon the architecture they have brought into the area." These aesthetic objections were, however, overridden by his innate anglophilia; indeed, he evidently did not feel much resentment, for one of his many official functions was that of president of the English Archery Club. Patrick Howarth wrote that his arrows "were regularly picked up to the two English sisters [Emma Lagden and Fanny Ewer] who accompanied him whenever he went out, and whom the ex-Lord Chancellor Brougham described as 'scarcely appropriate Psyches for such a large Cupid'."

Mérimée was an ardent supporter of the construction of Anglican places of worship. For the last fourteen years of his life he spent his winters in Cannes. At his funeral the Protestant minister made such a virulent attack on the Catholic Church (Mérimée declared himself to belong to the "Augsburg confession", though he was profoundly anti-clerical) that his doctor made a protest and the proceedings were brought to a halt. He is buried in the "English square", the Protestant cemetery within the Cimetière du Grand Jas, not far from the Nobel Prize-winning writer Jacques Monod, the goldsmith Carl Fabergé and Lord Brougham himself.

Aided by his photographic memory, (Henri René Albert) Guy de Maupassant (1850-93) wrote some of the most elegant descriptions of *belle époque* Cannes. His congenital depression would lift as he gazed at the Riviera from his yacht, *Bel Ami* (named after a successful novel). Among many entries in his *Chroniques* are pages of intricate and intimate observation of life along the coast from St.-Tropez to Menton. In August 1884, for example, he found himself in the middle of a pine wood marked out by "avenues—not a single house, just traces of streets through the trees. Here are the boulevards, here are the squares." What is more,

> their names are even written on metal plates… boulevard Rysdael, boulevard Rubens, boulevard van Dyck, boulevard Claude Lorrain. One wonders, why all these painters? Ah! Why? It's because the development company has declared, like God himself, before switching on the sun: "This will be a resort for artists!" Bang!

He knew it would all happen and be a success because there were signs up already saying, "Lot bought by M. Carolus Duran; lot for Mlle Croizette, etc. etc." He was equally outraged by the pretentious mayor of the "village" of Ste.-Maxime, who had posted up in this "hamlet at the end of the world" signs that it was forbidden to "trot" in the streets. With heavy irony he appealed to the mayor that since it is not forbidden to trot in Paris, where there are many more carriages, nor even in Marseille, "why the devil shouldn't we trot in Sainte-Maxime… we won't suddenly crush your sixty inhabitants." Though he was consoled by the "magnificent" scenery all around, one does wonder how he would react to the modern town.

Maupassant's first of many visits to the Riviera happened three years earlier, as he returned from Algeria. There were family connections. His *grande hystérique* of a mother, Laure, spent some miserable years in Nice, and her separated husband Gustave actually lived for a time in Ste.-Maxime, while Guy's troublesome and rather backward brother Hervé was briefly a horticulturalist in Antibes before becoming dangerously insane.

The 1880s was the decade—Maupassant's own thirties—of his most productive writing. In 1884 he rented the Villa Monplaisir in Cannes, and he continued to come and go, from north to south and back, always in a different residence, restlessly seeking through his writing and his travels an outlet for his energy and a solace for his melancholy. The epitaph he wrote for himself, "I have coveted everything and taken pleasure in nothing," is given the lie, however, by his obvious delight in the sensual impact of the South of France. Only as his mind became increasingly clouded by paranoia induced by the syphilis he contracted as a young man were these pleasures submerged beneath suicidal bouts of depression.

The opening of one of his three hundred short stories, *Madame Parisse* (1886), provides a graphic account of the blissful impression that the Riviera made on him—and on everyone who experiences it—as he contemplates Antibes from the sea.

> Between the white foam at the foot of the walls and the white snow on the sky-line the little city, dazzling against the bluish background of the nearest mountain ranges, presented to the rays of the setting sun a pyramid of red-roofed houses, whose facades were also white, but so different one from another that they seemed to be of all tints.
>
> And the sky above the Alps was itself of a blue that was almost white, as if the snow had tinted it; some silvery clouds were floating just over the pale summits, and on the other side of the gulf of Nice, lying close to the water, stretched like a white thread between the sea and the mountain. Two great sails, driven by a strong breeze, seemed to skim over the waves. I looked upon all this, astounded.
>
> This view was one of those sweet, rare, delightful things that seem to permeate you and are unforgettable, like the memory of a great happiness. One sees, thinks, suffers, is moved and loves with the eyes. He who can feel with the eye experiences the same keen, exquisite and deep pleasure in looking at men and things as the man with the delicate and sensitive ear, whose soul music overwhelms.

Perhaps, in the story, it was the beauty of Antibes itself, not just love for Mme. Parisse, that made its *commandant* place the town literally "under siege" so that no-one, especially not her husband, should be allowed back in to disturb his much-postponed single night of illicit passion.

For all that, Maupassant was never far from seeing the dark side of the sunlit coast. In his 1888 collection of offshore observations, a kind of literary scrapbook called *Sur l'eau: Saint-Tropez à Monte-Carlo*, he described Menton (slightly outside the strict remit of his title) as an "antechamber of Death, perfumed and sweet, where so many families, humble and royal, princely and bourgeois, have almost all left behind a child." He was fascinated by the old cemetery above the town.

> What a place it would be to live, this garden where the dead are sleeping! Roses, roses, everywhere roses. They are bloody, or pale, or white, or with scarlet veins… Their violent scent dazes you, makes your head and your legs tremble… It is a cemetery of children, like those white balls to which married people aren't admitted. From the cemetery the view stretches out, on the left towards Italy, as far as the point where Bordighera's white houses line the shore; on the right, as far as Cap Martin, dipping its leafy hillsides into the water. But everywhere along this adorable coast we are in the presence of Death. Yet it is discreet, veiled, full of the knowledge of life and good manners, in fact well brought up. You never see it face to face, even though it is always rubbing up against you.

Menton's cemetery is, in fact, almost a presage of Maupassant's own imminent death. After an unsuccessful attempt at suicide in a chalet in Cannes (having seen his own ghost in the road, according to his inseparable *valet de chambre*, François Tassart), he succumbed on 6 July 1893.

The Riviera could be not just a source of inspiration—or indeed despair. It could also be a refuge. The Riviera as writers' retreat is epitomized by a property near Cabris, a pretty *village perché* in the hills behind Grasse. La Messuguière was built there in 1937 by the widow of a rich Luxembourgeois industrialist. Aline Mayrisch (and later her daughter Andrée Viénot) was accustomed to entertaining men and women of letters; both during and after the Second World War her large house—dubbed the "house of tired intellectuals"—became a Mecca for those in need of a quiet place to write, read proofs or just chat to each other. André Gide came eight times. Albert Camus and Henri de Montherlant were there, as were Paul Valéry, Antoine de Saint-Exupéry, Marcel Pagnol, André Malraux, Henri Bosco and many others. The publisher Gaston Gallimard used to advise his authors to stay at La Messuguière so that they could get on with their work. This tradition lasted until the late 1970s, when Andrée Viénot died. The architect, Léon Loschetter, recalled a typical scene, with the guests reading under the great lime tree, strolling through the woods or swimming in the small pool. The setting was idyllic and tasteful.

> The light oak bookshelves in the library take up most of the walls. A big dancing figure of Krishna, in bronze, dominates the hall. Sketches and engravings by the big contemporary names decorate the walls. In the dining room is a painting by Theo van Rysselberghe. Outside, under the olive trees, is a large bronze of a woman without arms, by Despiau, and several bronze vases brought back from China.

Writers wanting to re-charge their batteries were in fact spoiled for choice in Cabris. Nearby was the house called Les Audides, belonging to the elegant, monocled Pierre Herbart and his wife Elizabeth, whose daughter Catherine was the result of a fleeting relationship with the homosexual André Gide. Les Audides was another hive of literary activity. Roger Martin du Gard wrote to Gide towards the end of 1950: "My dear good friend, you know how it is, in such a community… Get up, work; meal, chat, work; meal, chat, bed: the hours go by, the days go by, you get used to it, living an exquisite life, but there's no room for anything else except what's essential."

As if that were not enough, Cabris was also where the mother of Antoine de Saint-Exupéry lived, in the Villa Fioretti, while the nearby Moulin des Pradons provided a shelter for Marcel Pagnol during the Second World War.

An important figure in French literature and the early years of film associated with the Riviera though not born or raised there is Blaise Cendrars. He was in fact born in Switzerland (as Frédéric Louis Sauser of a Swiss father and Scottish mother) in 1887. He took French citizenship at the age of twenty-nine. Cendrars lost his right arm when fighting in the French Foreign Legion during the First World War and was sent down to Cannes to recuperate with his wife and two young children. He was by then already a poet of growing importance in the modernist movement. A friend of Apollinaire and Cocteau, he became a prolific novel writer as well as being involved with the cinema, working with Abel Gance at the Victorine Studios in Nice.

One project in 1920 was *Ecce Homo*. Gance asked Cendrars to find him urgently a very precise location—a large and beautiful property, enclosed in walls, if possible a villa built of pink marble with a gilt roof or dome. He needed it within five days to serve as a "Temple of Beauty". Not only that, Gance also required there to be *another* house just twenty yards away and immediately below the other, if possible in the Byzantine style and built of red brick. Cendrars set to work right away.

> In three days I visited Cap Ferrat, Cap Martin, Beaulieu, Menton, and having gone round a dozen villas none of which was quite right—if the house was of pink marble, the roof wasn't gold, or if the roof was gold, there was no Byzantine building nearby—and then I found exactly what was needed… Roman statues all over the park, ancient yews forming an avenue and a hundred and eighty steps leading down towards the sea. I just couldn't get over it.

Almost immediately—this being the movies—Gance changed his mind. The film was never made. Later on Blaise Cendrars settled in Villefranche with his long-time mistress, drinking a favourite concoction of white wine, lemon and sugar. He kept writing prolifically—novels, autobiography and criticism—and entertained a stream of visitors.

COLETTE AND ST.-TROPEZ

The writer who, almost more than any other, represents the Riviera is Colette. She had enjoyed wild times in Monte Carlo and Nice in the first decade of the twentieth century when she was performing on stage and mixing with a very racy crowd. But staying at the Hôtel Eden Cap d'Ail in the spring of 1925, she became wary of the "pretty, false Midi". This was making no allowance for love. The more she felt attracted to her new lover, Maurice Goudeket, the more she fell in love with her "native element", the sun and the sea. The couple—he was thirty-five, she fifty-two—first rented a pink villa near Ste.-Maxime, sleeping on the terrace, waking to the "sombre, dark orange dawn". It was the start of a long love affair on both counts, with man and Midi. After just a fortnight, Colette decided to look for a farmhouse of her own and eventually found one near St.-Tropez that she named La Treille Muscate – but very much under the influence of her new lover, according to the writer Markie Benét.

It was Maurice who convinced Colette to transfer her allegiance from Brittany to his beloved Mediterranean, and in the years before the little fishing port became crowded with the beautiful people and their Ferraris, Colette, Maurice and their painter friends lived the idyllic life of beach, garden, local wine, and Provençal cooking that searchers for the "good life" have been trying to emulate ever since.

In fact, by the start of the 1930s St.-Tropez was already becoming fashionable, with titled ladies posing for *Vogue* beside the yachts moored in the harbour and restaurants charging Deauville prices. Fortunately La Treille Muscate was just isolated enough and "out of the fray". One of Colette's biographers Judith Thurman described the house and garden tour she gave to her guests while the "melons, vegetables and grilled fish" were being laid out on the terrace table.

She started with her workroom, one of the additions which had caused her so many headaches. It was a simple concrete cube whose thick walls retained the cool even at midday. The furnishings were spare: there was a handsome Breton cupboard filled with books, a huge divan swagged with mosquito netting, a big writing table, and a collection of pottery whose "vegetal green" stood out against the milky whitewash of the plaster. [Her guest] noted two stacks of blue paper on the desk, one pristine, one "covered with the famous writing, firm and upright." He also noted the balled and crumpled wads strewn over the floor. "What a penance," exclaimed Colette, "to shut oneself in here for fifteen hours a day when it's so beautiful outside."

In the first year of the Second World War, however, Colette sold La Treille Muscate and ended her happy, intense relationship with St.-Tropez—but not entirely with the Riviera. From the spring of 1950 she and her husband Maurice Goudeket made the first of a series of annual trips to Monaco as guests of Prince Rainier. These dips into celebrity and luxury were soothing and flattering, despite her complaints about the "fake cosmopolitan society", and good for her increasingly crippling arthritis. One evening in early spring 1952 Jean Cocteau came to dine with the Goudekets and recalled the evening in a memoir.

Maurice wheels her chair into the bar. Then into the amazing velvet and gold dining room filled with draperies, caryatids, huge frescoes of naked women, peacocks and tigers… Colette does not disturb the world, and is surrounded by respect… Sometimes I envy her isolation, her wheelchair. I have all the afflictions of youth and none of its advantages.

Back to see Colette this morning… She is transformed, and quite renewed. She hears us. She comes into the bar, wheeled by the barman. I recognise her fine eyes swimming in the liquor of the best Marennes oysters, her olive-tree hair, he mouth like an arrowhead wound.

The mantle of champion and mythologizer of St.-Tropez was about to be taken over by another writer highly sensitive to its heated charms. Françoise Sagan published *Bonjour Tristesse* in 1954 at the age of nineteen. The title came from a Paul Eluard poem. This story of a manipulative girl breaking up her father's love affair under a hot Mediterranean sun was made into a film in 1957, directed by Otto Preminger and starring Deborah Kerr, David Niven, and Jean Seberg. It was shot in monochrome for Paris and colour for the Riviera and was a very big success in France. Later Sagan became disillusioned with the commercialized, loveless social round of St.-Tropez, where people "no longer go from pleasure to pleasure, secret rendez-vous to secret rendez-vous, from one corner of a beach to another, from one room to another."

The catalyst for this change was not so much the success of *Bonjour Tristesse*, which bought into the sensual, personal tradition of Colette, but the arrival in the mid-1950s of the film crowd with the big money, notably Roger Vadim and Brigitte Bardot. When Bardot danced on the kitchen table in *Et Dieu Créa La Femme*, released in 1956, the days of the old innocence were numbered. Bardot herself, however, has long given up the famous bikinis and *choucroute* hairstyles in favour of campaigning for animal rights and controversial far-right causes—though she returned to live in St.-Tropez and remains one of its most potent symbols.

Bardot and Sagan used to circle each other warily at the Hôtel-Bar La Ponche, Sagan blaming the film star for "ruining" the atmosphere. Like Colette, Sagan expressed rapture at experiencing the simple pleasures. She loved to look out of her window, "open the shutters, and the sea and the sky would throw into my face the same blue, the same pink, the same happiness." Though she called St.-Tropez "indestructible" in her memoirs, where she could hold the sun "in the palm of my hand", she lamented the noisier, flashier place it became, perhaps conscious that she herself had been partly responsible for that change.

The Dark Side: Simenon and Sartre

If any writer in French is immediately associated not with Riviera heat but with the cold foggy north, it is the Belgian-born Georges Simenon (1903-89). His detective hero, Inspector Jules Maigret, is in most people's memory swathed in mists while he puffs his pipe and peers at clues in dank basements. But in fact even Maigret gets to enjoy the Riviera sun in many of his adventures, and his creator spent many years in nine different Riviera locations, from Hyères to Nice. In his *La Côte d'Azur de Georges Simenon* (2005) Paul Daelewyn plays the detective and tracks every movement of both Simenon and Maigret, from simple descriptions (for example, in the early *Maigret et l'Indicateur*) to a time when the Riviera begins to "flesh out the reality of the man breaking away from his context, from himself, finding himself face to face with his destiny and with his existential malaise: a Simenon leitmotiv."

Simenon saw himself as a man like any other: his autobiography bears the title *Un homme comme un autre*. Like at least most people, he enjoyed the discipline imposed by the austere north, but then "a mere gust of warm air, the scent of eucalyptus or rosemary, make me feel the need to rush towards the south." He revelled in what he called the "illusion of the tropics". Not that when he got there, he did not manage to find the sinister beneath the seductive exterior. In *Le Cercle des Mahé*, for example, the fort on the island of Porquerolles, reached by walking along a dry path "with red berries crackling under foot", is described as windowless and doorless: "its walls seemed to be made of a white dust that the sun, over the centuries, had petrified. Here too the doctor felt uneasy."

An aura of menace did not stop Simenon spending several months a year, from 1936 to 1938, in a little house on the port of Porquerolles, with an odd square tower and an "even odder minaret". Here he would get up at four in the morning in the relative cool and write, sometimes "at the end of a chapter, finding myself naked in front of my typewriter." He found inspiration for his narrative by taking long walks, enjoying the scent of the strawberry trees.

The only Riviera town that shares with Simenon's birthplace, Liège, a street named after the writer is Hyères. Its huddled streets, he felt, have some of the same qualities of anonymity and intimacy that are comforting to a northerner. The modernist villa where Marie-Laure de Noailles entertained her avant-garde friends features in Simenon's 1963 novel *Les Anneaux de Bicêtre*. The house was the brain child of Robert Mallet-Stevens and is the backdrop of Man Ray's surrealist film, *Les Mystères du Château de Dé*. Antibes was another fruitful source for Simenon's fiction. He spent almost a year there in 1937, writing and working with Jean Renoir on film scripts, while Maigret also turns up in Antibes, in *Liberty Bar*, observing how, in the brilliant sunlight, people appear like shadows: "shadows wearing straw hats and white trousers and carrying tennis racquets. The air was humming." In that year Georges Simenon published *Cours d'Assises*, set in Nice, whose buildings in the old town he described as having "the colour of sweets", where the air "smells as sweet as a confectioner's shop". It is a place for his characters to disappear into, to merge into the crowd of marginal people who make up its "floating population".

During the war Simenon lived in the Vendée, on the Atlantic coast, and then spent the ten years after the Second World War in the United States. His main Riviera homes, when he returned in 1955, were to be further east along the coast in Cannes, Mougins and Haut-de-Cagnes, until he left for Switzerland in 1957. This became his base, and he made only occasional sorties to the south of France, mostly to his tiny but secret refuge, his Simple Abri, in Haut-de-Cagnes. But in Cannes a new Georges Simenon appeared in public view, much richer, attracted as much to the smart shops along the Croisette and the luxury of the Golden Gate villa in the Californie quarter as to the simpler pleasures of the gardens and seascapes. In May 1960 he was president of the thirteenth Cannes Film Festival, which gave the main prize to *La Dolce Vita*, a choice that was curiously unpopular at the time. From now on, very little local colour seeps into his fiction, with the exception of the squid ink spilling into the risottos in his novel *Dimanche*.

Jean-Paul Sartre shared with Simenon a dark side to his personality, particularly with regard to manipulating women, but there was little else they had in common. Sartre and his constant companion Simone de Beauvoir (1908-86) used the Riviera as a locale for only occasional recreation—and it always ended in tears. Beauvoir's first visits, however, were made alone. She was teaching in a Marseille *lycée* in the early 1930s and was sent to examine *baccalauréat* candidates in Nice. In the second part of her autobiography, *La Force de l'Age* (*The Prime of Life*), she wrote that "the countryside lacked that intimacy which characterized the area round Marseille, but it was even more striking." A few years later she was prescribed a three-week rest (in the mountains, not by the sea) and headed for Bormes-les-Mimosas.

> The station was a deserted shack, and I was the only person who got off there. Not a porter or ticket collector anywhere in sight. It was midday; I was sluiced with Provencal sunlight and all the scents of the Midi. It was a glorious resurrection from the foggy atmosphere of my convalescence. There was a man setting off up the steep path to the village just as I appeared, and he relieved me of my bag. From the village square I could see the sea quite close below me, and the Iles d'Hyeres too; but I decided that the distance separating us was just about adequate. I put up at the best hotel (full pension for thirty francs) and stuffed myself full of good food, and as I ate I watched the old girls playing *belote* down under the veranda. I walked over the hills, through pinewoods that were intersected by beautiful sandy paths known to the inhabitants, somewhat pretentiously, as "the boulevards". Here I rediscovered those heavy, hairy, brightly coloured yet scentless flowers, and the pungent-smelling herbs I had once so loved to rub between my fingers. I read some of Faulkner's short stories, and basked in the sun for hours on end. But after three days of this I found I couldn't stand seeing the same faces at every meal; so I slung my rucksack over my back and moved on.

Sartre and Beauvoir's first visit together was in the summer of 1939. They stayed with a rich Argentine friend, Mme. Lemaire, who had a villa at Juan-les-Pins known as Puerta del Sol. Here Sartre tried to teach Beauvoir to swim, but, according to their recent biographer, Hazel Rowley, "he would suddenly become terrified of the slimy creatures he imagined lurking in the depths, and would swim back in a panic." The more real threat—of war—he dismissed as "bluff". Margaret Crosland attributed the fear of undersea monsters to Beauvoir herself. "This calm, this sunshine were deceptive," she is quoted as saying: "suddenly everything would be torn asunder." Bored by the "vie de château", she was uncomfortable and tetchy, preoccupied by all their various overlapping affairs which, not for the first time, were turning sour. In Beauvoir's words, "as usual we took a passionate interest in their problems, we discussed them with Madame Lemaire, constructing hypotheses and distributing censure with equal partiality."

When relations became really rough, and Sartre started losing his temper and strong men began to weep under his verbal lashings, they all headed off to Cannes "to make a round of the transvestite *boîtes*," as a way of achieving reconciliation.

The pattern kept repeating itself. In 1953 the pair spent their Easter holiday in St.-Tropez with a lover each, Michelle Vian for him, Claude Lanzmann for her. The only two restaurants open were next to each other on the harbour's edge. According to Lanzmann:

> Simone de Beauvoir has always had a loud voice, and while she dined with Sartre in restaurant X, I was the only customer in restaurant Y. And I heard Beauvoir tell Sartre everything because they told each other everything, that was the rule. I heard Beauvoir tell Sartre everything she had done with me during the day, where we had been walking, what I had said, which book I had been reading, which book she had been reading… When I met her again, after dinner, she told me everything that Sartre had said, which I had just heard. And when it was my turn, when I dined with Beauvoir, and Sartre was all alone in his corner, in his restaurant, reading a book or the paper, it was the same thing.

A few years later Lanzmann and de Beauvoir ended their affair, to their mutual relief, in the calmer atmosphere of Menton. St.-Raphael was then the scene of another complicated series of liaisons in December 1965 when Sartre this time brought along his Russian mistress/interpreter. His other women were not meant to know but, true to form, those least likely to react well found out. And as usual Sartre lied his way out of his predicament.

The last place to host the comings and goings of this increasingly famous pair was St. Paul-de-Vence, where they made several visits in different sets of foursomes. At the end of each visit they were usually happy to return to the relative comfort of the intellectual and political cauldron of Paris.

Poets and Drinkers

A whole slew of left-wing poets descended on the Riviera—to play, not to work. Rather on the model of Sartre and Beauvoir, they came to do a little revision perhaps, or to touch up a manifesto, but mostly to exchange views and each other's wives or lovers. By no stretch of the imagination were they "Riviera poets".

Among the better-known poets, regular visitors included the symbolists Stéphane Mallarmé (to Cannes in 1866) and Paul Valéry, who spent holidays in Grasse, founded the Cannes College in 1931, and was chief executive of the institution that later became the University of Nice. Surrealists as well as symbolists came down south in great numbers, among them Paul Eluard, André Breton, Louis Aragon and René Char, but it is hard to pin down any influence that these visits had on their body of work. Raymond Roussel penned many alexandrines describing minutely the Nice Carnival in his self-published poem *La Doublure*. Jules Romains (the self-styled "unanimist", came to Nice, but probably did not have that city particularly in mind when he declared famously that "the world is an enormous injustice." He taught philosophy there at the end of the First World War and dabbled in psychic experiments. Romains frequently came back, visiting Hyères as well, and died in Nice.

Some very strange poets had brief brushes with the Côte d'Azur. There was, for example, the British-born lesbian and drug addict Pauline Tarn (1877-1909) who went under the name of Renée Vivien. Too addled to appreciate Nice, despite renting a beautiful villa and garden there in 1904, she described the sun as "insolent" and the buildings "ignobles"; she detected, in a letter to her American lover Nathalie Barney, "no striking difference between Paris and Nice—a few more oranges here—comic-opera palm trees—an illusion of heat—that's all." The right-wing anti-semitic poet, journalist, traveller and diplomat Paul Morand (1888-1976) was more in tune with the Riviera and spent fifteen years in Villefranche-sur-Mer. He attributed semi-mystical qualities to the Mediterranean Sea but shuddered at the thought that crowds of people from all races and classes were permitted to interrupt his undiluted exaltation. André de Richaud (1909-61) was dubbed by his biographer the "cursed archetype of the romantic Orpheus". When he came to Vallauris in 1958 as a barely-alive alcoholic, he felt compelled to write a piece entitled *Je ne suis pas mort*; another work, *La fin du monde*, never saw the light of day.

The nearest to a proper Riviera poet—also a journalist, playwright and novelist—is Jacques Audiberti. Born in 1899, the son of a stonemason, he was brought up in Antibes (a *lycée* there is called after him). His earliest memories were the stuff of his poems (with titles such as *La Colline de la Garoupe* and *Nuit d'Antibes*). *Rempart* was published in 1953 and evokes the old Antibes of his childhood.

> Son père faisait des maisons.
> L'enfant, le soir, cherchait des astres,
> comme on prétend que font les pastres,
> blancs petits soleils de ciment
> dans les cheveux, noir firmament
> du maître au parfum de chaux grasse
> que celui de l'aïl seul surpasse.

> His father used to make houses.
> The child, in the evening, would look for stars,
> as they say shepherds do,
> little white cement suns
> in his hair, black firmament
> of the master smelling of lime,
> with only garlic a stronger scent.

Dangerous Liaisons

Most Anglophone readers find it hard to relate to those many hundreds of intellectuals, writers, journalists and artists whose work has resonance only in the French motherland, but whose names may nevertheless be half familiar. Their books and articles are rarely translated and certainly not available except through extracts or second-hand sources on the Internet or in specialist libraries. The passage of time tends to erase even the faint traces they left during their lifetimes. Those traces themselves, in the context of the Riviera, were as often as not stories of sensational or tragic liaisons. The fascist Pierre Drieu La Rochelle (1893-1945), who haunted the western Riviera in the inter-war years, is more known for his unsavoury politics and as the "man covered with women" than as the author of Gilles (1939). The wild life of Roger Vailland (1907-65), who wrote of his conquests in Cannes, was beset with suicides and ended with his own. The paedophilia of the poet Henri de Montherlant (1896-1972) in the southern zone during the years of the Second World War overshadowed his literary reputation.

Jean Lorrain (1855-1906) is remembered best for his flagrant homosexuality and debauchery at a time of harsh social repression, the era of Oscar Wilde. Lorrain penned a sarcastic but amusing description of a "salon littéraire sur la Riviera":

> Out of fifty guests at this intellectual joust there will be an average of ten listeners and forty participants. And for the listeners, condemned as it were to the scaffold, there is no escape. The artists watch the door, more keen to stop any victims escaping than to take their turn; yet what feverish urge they have to be heard, to be admired and to produce—what concerns they have, this one with his diction, that one with her gestures and her profile, and what cordial jealousy they feel towards each other, what battles over the programme! You will recognise it: the pianist glued to his piano, the poet sheathed in the fireplace like a caryatid, the cellist clamped to his cello and the harpist, her arms tangled in the strings of her instrument, like an eel in seaweed, refusing to give up her turn: *the harp is dying but refuses to surrender.* Yes, this is the horrible spectacle facing you.

The prolific novelist Gaston Leroux (1868-1927) was another larger than life figure with Riviera connections that were more than casual, though his chief claim to fame is as the author of *Le Fantôme de l'Opéra* (the first film version of which came out in Nice in 1926). He created the character of Jacques Rouletabille and made himself into a kind of French Conan Doyle. From 1908 to his death Leroux lived first in Menton, then mainly in Nice. What his neighbours made of the wild celebrations that always, according to his own account, accompanied his completion of a book, one can only imagine.

> When I had put the final full stop at the end of a novel, I would leap out onto the balcony and fire off my revolver into the air. That was the signal: my wife, my daughter, my son would all rush and get the crockery. Glasses and plates would fly across the garden. Once there was

nothing left to smash, we would get the saucepans and bang on them: it was a wild Sabbath.

Leroux's involvement with the region extended to editing, along with Vicente Blasco Ibañez and others, a luxury magazine, *Sur la Riviera*.

A remarkable, if minor, figure who established a name for himself on the Riviera in two quite separate fields is Alphonse Karr. He was born in Paris in 1808 and died in St.-Raphael in 1890, where he is commemorated by a plaque, with his bearded face hiding beneath palm trees on a busy crossroads near the sea front. His semi-autobiographical novels were extremely popular, and his journalistic career was crowned when he became editor of *Le Figaro*. He started up a satirical magazine, *Les Guêpes* (The Wasps), in which many of his famous epigrams appeared (the most endearing as well as enduring is certainly "Plus ça change, plus c'est la même chose"). But to people in the flower business, Alphonse Karr is the name of a dahlia.

Another extraordinary character on the Riviera, with curiously similar overlapping interests as writer and garden enthusiast is a man whose father was the illegitimate son of Jérôme Bonaparte, King of Westphalia. Ferdinand Bac was born in Stuttgart as Ferdinand-Sigismond Bach in 1859. He moved to Paris with his mother in 1870, became a famous caricaturist as well as journalist and painter, mixed with absolutely everyone who was anyone and who survived until he was ninety-three after fifty years spent fearfully anticipating an early death.

He was a presence on the Riviera social scene from the very start of the twentieth century. His family connection to the Empress Eugénie on Cap Martin in addition to his reputation as an eminent man of letters made him a much sought-after house guest. But his greatest triumph on the Riviera was as a garden designer (see Chapter Ten).

FOOTNOTE 1: THE LANGUAGES OF THE RIVIERA

Nissard or *Nissart* is a language still spoken and taught in schools. It is one of many offshoots of Low Latin that resisted the spread of a version of French derived from the northern *langue d'oïl*. You can hear it spoken on the streets of Nice and see it on street signs. A cultural-historical review, the *Lou Sourgentin,* has been going for the last thirty years and claims a revival not just in academic interest in *Nissard* but in its day-to-day use.

Certainly it thrives better than the neighbouring Provençal languages, despite the efforts to revive these by Frédéric Mistral in the nineteenth century.

Similar claims are made for *Monégasque* (*Munegascu/Munegu*), *Mentounasque, Turbiasque* and a multitude of other boutique languages (or perhaps more accurately dialects) along the French Riviera and in the more isolated *villages perchés*. Menton boasts a thriving local society that publishes a monthly illustrated journal as well as a local choral society that sings in dialect. In the areas formerly controlled by the Kingdoms of Savoy and Sardinia, the Italian/Ligurian influence (or contamination) is more obvious. Though often described as a "blend of Provençal and Italian", *Nissard* and its local variations in fact have equally valid, and independent, derivations from a common Low Latin source.

Every year a *Monégasque* language competition is organized in the *Principatu de Munegu* (Monaco). Throughout schools across the principality, close to 400 juniors are subjected to questions relating to the language while the more senior students have to answer more substantial tests (language, comprehension tests, vocabulary, grammar, translations and questions concerning the history of Monaco). *Monégasque* was introduced in schools in the principality in 1976 but is compulsory only at primary level. The official language of the principality remains French.

At a recent wedding in Gassin, a village high above St.-Tropez, the guests (among them myself) were entertained by the local troupe of singers performing songs whose lyrics were in a distinctly local language. I asked them if this is what they spoke at home among themselves. They assured me that this was indeed the case. The sound—whether sung or spoken— would have been pretty much what John Ruskin heard in his travels in the spring of 1845. He called it

> a language of marvellous originality—a lingual Punch... Many of the words are quite untraceable, at least by me, "ara", for instance, for "à present" (now)—which is Greek by the by, but only accidentally so— and "gaio" for "peu" (little). I heard a woman call to another just now, Aspai ma picciota (as tu vu ma petite fille), in which the aspai is I fancy a corruption of apercevoir, and the picciota is the Italian Picciola. Many of the words are very grotesque & peculiar, a good many spanish, and the whole spoken with a spanish accent and sound.

The quirks of the local language of the self-styled "curious" village of Peille—*Pelhasc*—have even been made into a thick dictionary by the local historian, Pierre Gauberti. It is a rustic version of *Nissard* and known to the urban sophisticates as *le gaouot*—a pejorative expression that implies a language of the peasantry of the *arrière-pays*, and not therefore used by the locals. The chief characteristics of *Pelhasc*, apart from an inordinate number of special words to describe agricultural implements, is its suppression of the consonants "r" and "l"—so *carriera* becomes *carriea* and *balanca baanca*.

Above all these local ways of speaking confirm the unique and separate identity of the French Riviera. The differences between the "languages" are not as significant as some people like to make out for reasons of parochial pride. What *is* significant is that they have a great deal in common. They are in fact a record of unity in the region, a legacy of a shared popular heritage. They establish and maintain an historical consciousness that the Riviera is indeed, despite the vagaries of high-level political power and ownership struggles, a single cultural entity.

Riviera waterfront – lady with a little dog

Footnote 2: The Food of the Riviera

Auguste Escoffier was born in Villeneuve-Loubet (just west of Nice), and this high-class chef symbolizes the refined cuisine that has come to be associated not just with Parisian luxury but also with the Riviera, with its grand restaurants in grand international hotels. And indeed there is a long tradition on the Riviera of such refined and inventive cooking.

But there is also the regional *cuisine du terroir*, and it is the disgraced mayor of Nice, Jacques Médecin, who defined it best, declaring himself to "belong to the last generation which has had traditional recipes handed down to it." His is the "correct" way to prepare a Salade Niçoise (*Salada Nissarda*), avoiding above all any boiled vegetables, even the now popular boiled potato, or any vinaigrette dressing. He gives the "real" recipes for *Pan-Bagnat* (literally "soaked bread"), ratatouille, stuffed sardines, *Lou Pistou* soup (the name is derived, he says, from the dialect word for "pounded", not from the word for "basil", though the pesto itself is clearly Genoese in origin), stockfish stew (*estocaficada*), aïoli and many more.

Other still popular Nice specialities include the onion and anchovy tart called *pissaladière* (derived from a rare fish puree called *pissala* which is, or mostly was, smeared on the onions just before the tart is put in the oven) and the large chickpea flour pancake called *socca*, which is bland in itself but a fortifying snack if desperate. Better perhaps in the heat to sip *gratta queca* (mint-flavoured crushed ice) and nibble a *ganse* (a cake flavoured with orange flower water). Gratifyingly, such local treats have survived the flood of international and fast-food imports.

Chapter Eight
FINDING THE LIGHT
ART, MUSIC AND CINEMA ON THE RIVIERA

THE NICE PRIMITIVES

In 1960 the city of Nice wished to do something to celebrate one hundred years of attachment to France. The highlight of the celebrations, which attracted worldwide attention, was an exhibition of the art that flourished in and around Nice in the fifteenth and sixteenth centuries, a time best forgotten otherwise on account of the brutal oppression by the rich few of the desperately poor majority. What sustained them—and provided some distraction—was their religion, particularly the churches and chapels whose architecture, altarpieces, paintings and statues provided their only glimpses of another, perhaps more hopeful, life.

For the centenary exhibition, it was not an easy job for the director of Nice's museums to get his hands on most of the treasures—a reminder of the difficulties faced by the artists themselves. The names of most have been lost to history, and a name alone is all that is known about others. The artists worked exclusively at decorating chapels all over the countryside from the Var to Genoa. An altarpiece done in Nice would be carted up the mountains by donkey, panel by panel, so it is easy to imagine why village authorities in the mid-twentieth century were reluctant to see their pride and joy disappearing down again to the coast, even on loan.

The names that have survived are mostly members of the Ligurian Brea family, a dynasty of artists descended from a barrel-maker (in Nice's rue de la Barillerie), consisting of the three brothers Pierre, Louis and Antoine, plus Antoine's nephew, François. There is one other early master of note, Jean Miralhet, who was born in Montpellier at the end of the fourteenth century and died in Nice in the middle of the fifteenth.

JEAN MIRAHLET AND THE PENITENTS

Of Miralhet's work only one masterpiece survives, the *Virgin of Misericordia* in the Chapel of the Black Penitents, known variously as the Chapelle

In Renoir's garden – a bronzed nude

Saint-Gaetan, the Chapelle de la Miséricorde and even the Chapelle de la Saleya, in Nice. This is a stunning piece of work, an altarpiece painted around 1430 depicting a tall elegant virgin holding out at her sides an enormous black cloak, under which shelter the citizens of Nice, or perhaps the world, protecting them from plague in particular and their troubles in general. The problem is getting to see it, as the chapel has been closed for years and, despite placards making ambitious claims, appears in 2008 far from ready for public inspection.

The confraternities of penitents (black, white, blue, grey, red, violet, green, even multicoloured, depending on their habits) flourished particularly in France from the early thirteenth century. Their robes, cords and hoods were signs of anonymity and humility and also served as funeral shrouds. Their charitable role was to care for the sick, bury the dead, even to give dowries to poor girls; the Black Penitents' speciality was accompanying condemned criminals to the gallows and giving them a Christian burial. The Riviera and its back country, the highlands of the Alpes Maritimes and Liguria, seem to have attracted a disproportionate number of their chapels, which in turn have hosted the finest art of the region up until modern times. In the little town of Sospel alone, nestling in a hollow in the hills between Menton and the high Alps, there were five groups of penitents: blue, red, black, grey and white.

Such has been the influence of the penitents on the Côte d'Azur that there is now quite a revival in their numbers and practices, especially in Nice. If you are there in Holy Week, you will observe the penitents playing a prominent part in the processions and services. The Chapelle Sainte-Croix is the headquarters of the White Penitents in Nice. As late as the 1750s this group continued the practice of self-flagellation, emphasizing one of the penitents' most important *raisons d'être*, to take upon themselves the sins of others, despite the official Church's proclamation that the practice should cease. For the feast of the Holy Sacrament, or *Fête-Dieu*, in the hilltop village of Gorbio, penitents of different brotherhoods process around the medieval streets, while lights burn from the oil in thousands of snail shells.

In the chapel of the White Penitents in Eze is a cross which, the official website charmingly tells us, is "allocated to the paint shop of Ludovico Brea".

THE BREA CIRCLE

Louis (Ludovico) Brea (c.1450-c.1523), generally agreed to be the pick of the Brea bunch, painted prolifically in churches and chapels from Genoa to his native Nice. His small Pietà in the Church of St.-Martin-St.-Augustin, one of the city's oldest parish churches, where Martin Luther gave a sermon in 1514, is hard to see, being high up on the left wall of a side chapel in a rather dimly lit, heavily ornate baroque interior. But it is well worth contemplating for its high emotional impact, derived especially from the tender pose of a limp, prostrate Christ held by his mother almost as if he were a dead child rather than an adult victim of a crucifixion.

The Franciscan monastery beside the Roman ruins in Cimiez contains two major works by Louis Brea, both altarpieces, an early one depicting the *Vierge de Piété* and the other a Crucifixion. The monastery and its attached museum contain some fine early examples of paintings, frescoes and sculptures from the thirteenth to the eighteenth century, while the garden is worth a visit in itself; it has very much the feeling of its original purpose as a restful place, with flowerbeds and lemon groves and ponds, where life can be contemplated on a hilltop looking down over the town and out to sea. A copse of cypress and holm oak marks the spot where the old Ligurian town used to be.

In the square outside (now a car park) stands a strange cross of false marble with a winged seraph in place of the crucified Christ. It represents a vision of St. Francis of Assisi (whose image features on the right hand side, while a pelican regurgitating its food sits in a nest at the top). It is a replica of the original fifteenth-century cross. Also in the square is a First World War memorial portraying a gallic cock killing a Prussian eagle; this was hidden under the sea during the Second World War, then stolen, then recognized by the mayor on a stroll round the flea market in the Cours Saleya, where it was being offered for sale. The one you can see now is also a copy, however.

One of the finest Brea pictures is housed in the (relatively modern) cathedral in Monaco. Louis Brea's altarpiece of St. Nicholas is in eighteen sections, although the eight at the sides are quite small. There are some beautifully defined faces, particularly that of John the Baptist. Sadly, it is put away behind glass in a gloomy space within a side chapel and is hard both to find and to see. Ironically, a much inferior Brea picture—a *Mise au Tombeau* by Antoine Brea, modelled on his brother's Pietà in the St.-

Martin-St.-Augustin church but with much more wooden, inert figures—is well lit and displayed prominently on a wall of the nave.

In Antibes the Church of the Immaculate Conception, once Romanesque, then seventeenth-century classical, contains another splendid 1515 altarpiece by Louis Brea; thirteen small panels surround the larger central panel, but these have had some heavy restoration.

THE ACCEPTANCE OF ART
On 10 November 1764 Tobias Smollett wrote to his (perhaps fictional) "Doctor" friend back in London:

> You desire to know the state of the arts and sciences at Nice; which, indeed, is almost a total blank. I know not what men of talents this place may have formerly produced; but at present it seems to be consecrated to the reign of dulness (*sic*) and superstition. It is very surprising, to see a people established between two enlightened nations, so devoid of taste and literature. Here are no tolerable pictures, busts, statues, nor edifices: the very ornaments of the churches are wretchedly conceived, and worse executed. They have no public or private libraries that afford any thing worth perusing. There is not even a bookseller in Nice. Though they value themselves as being natives of Italy, they are unacquainted with music.

What Smollett chose to ignore was the fact that "men of talents" did indeed exist in Nice. But they were artists who flourished three hundred years before his time, before the Renaissance and before the baroque – the "Nice primitives".

A rare artist of international renown actually born and brought up in the Riviera region was Jean-Honoré Fragonard (1732-1806), younger than Smollett by only a few years. Fragonard's father was a glove maker in Grasse. In fact, the young artist was soon despatched to study in Paris, returning to Grasse only briefly, when the Revolution deprived him of rich patrons. On view in his home town today is an early, academic painting, *Christ Washing the Feet of his Apostles*, hanging high up and not well lit in a dingy side chapel of the cathedral. It is a far cry from his frivolous, sensual pictures such as *The Swing* (or *Les hasards heureux de l'escarpolette*) in the Wallace Collection in London.

The great achievements on the wider Riviera arts front are associated with post-Fragonard times. Even so, the climate for the arts was slow to improve. A French archaeologist noted in 1816 that Nice's bookstores sold only prayer books and schoolbooks and that not a painting or statue was worth mentioning.

Fifteen years later, in 1831, on a mission to Paris to kill his girlfriend who had jilted him and married another, the composer Hector Berlioz had occasion to experience at first hand the local philistinism. He arrived in Nice to find a letter forgiving him his precipitous departure from the Rome Academy (on account of his girlfriend trouble) and anticipated a moment of rare calm.

> "And supposing now I were to lead a quiet, happy life, and give myself up entirely to music, would not that be too curious? Let us try."
>
> And so I drink deep draughts of the sunny, balmy air of Nice, and life and joy return to me, and I dream of music and the future. I spend a whole month in Nice wandering in groves of orange trees, bathing in the sea, sleeping on the heather on the Villefranche hills, and looking down from those glorious heights on the silent coming and going of the distant ships. I live entirely alone. I write the overture to *King Lear*. I sing. I believe in a God. Convalescence!
>
> These were the three happiest days in my life. Oh, Nizza!

But he was forgetting about the darker side of this Italian outpost. The King of Sardinia's police were a vigilant bunch—and unaccustomed to itinerant artists. Berlioz was spotted playing billiards with two officers of the Piedmontese garrison. Conspiracy! He was obviously a spy. First he was summoned and interrogated.

> "What are you doing here?"
>
> "Recovering from a painful illness. I compose and dream, and thank God for the sunshine, the beautiful sea, and the green hills."
>
> "You are not a painter?"
>
> "No."
>
> "Yet you are always drawing something in an album. Is it plans?"

"Yes, plans for an overture for *King Lear*. The designs and the instrumentation are ready, and I think the beginning will be somewhat formidable."

"What do you mean by the beginning? Whom do you mean by *King Lear*?"

"He is a poor old English king."

"English!"

"Yes. Shakespeare says he lived about eighteen hundred years ago, and he foolishly divided his kingdom between his two wicked elder daughters, who turned him out of doors when he had nothing more to give them. You see there are few kings…"

"Never mind the king… What do you mean by instrumentation…?"

"It is a musical term."

"Always the same excuse! Now, sir, we are well aware that it is impossible to write music walking silently about the sea-shore, with nothing but an album and a pencil, and no piano. So be good enough to tell us where you want to go, and you shall have your passport. You cannot stay here any longer."

With which Hector Berlioz was promptly ejected—a scene worthy of Tobias Smollett himself.

Berlioz was a visitor. Fragonard is an exception as a native-born artist. Yet in the eyes of the wider world, the Riviera is inexorably associated with all those painters who, from the end of the nineteenth century onwards, came down to escape from darker, colder climates or from the hurly-burly of the Parisian art scene.

Riviera Collections

Who first discovered the Riviera as the place to come to in order to create art? Should one credit Paul Signac, who settled in St.-Tropez in 1892, declaring that "all I ask is the sky, the sea, the setting sun"? Or Renoir and Monet, in 1883, when they went to paint together on the Mediterranean coast? Or should one go back a little earlier, to the travel boom in the 1860s, when thousands of people, many rich and with good contacts in Paris, Europe and even America, began to dabble in watercolours and oils and, above all, to spread the word?

No matter. What drew them all was the light—a light that Matisse described as "soft and tender, despite its brilliance". For some, worn down by the dour climate of the north, health was a closely allied factor. Renoir, claimed his son Jean, had a feeling, when he was in the "hothouse" of Menton, of "roasting his rheumatism in the sun".

Today, strung all along the French Riviera from St.-Tropez to Menton like a multicoloured necklace, are museums and galleries devoted to the greatest of the artists who succumbed to its allure. The individual artists are discussed later in this chapter, but first here is a survey, in west-east order, of the most important places where their work can be seen.

Some, like the Musée de l'Annonciade in St.-Tropez, house collections of several artists. The Pointillists, such as Signac himself and Seurat, are prominent, as also are the Fauvists; the collection includes works by Derain and Dufy as well as paintings by the many artists who came to the locality, from Matisse to Vuillard and de Vlaminck. Above all, this is a *local* collection, homage to the colours and charm of the little fishing port that is now a byword for the rich and famous.

The most eccentric of the Riviera museums is surely the Château de la Napoule. Any castle with the motto "Once Upon A Time" carved into the arched lintel over its front door hints at pretentiousness. The château-museum created by Henry and Marie Clews, rich Americans from Newport, Rhode Island and Paris, was a refuge from the harsh world immediately after the First World War and an ultra-romantic setting for Henry's humorous, erotic, often grotesque sculptural outpourings. Henry Clews hated anything modern, "scientific hooligans, literary morons, mechanized submen, gold brick swamis, willy-nilly silly Fabians and Shavians" included. A lover of fancy dress married to a strapping beauty who shared and indulged his tastes, he lived out his fantasies beside the sandy beach of la Napoule. Thousands of visitors are now attracted each year to his converted fourteenth-century, pseudo-Saracen castle.

The majority of the Riviera art museums are dedicated primarily to a single artist. Antibes and nearby Vallauris are virtually shop windows for the Picasso industry. The twelfth-century Château Grimaldi, with its spectacular views across the Bay of Antibes, first captivated Pablo Picasso in the early 1920s, when he followed a group of children crawling into its ruins. In 1946, when the château had already become an archaeological museum, its curator offered the now-famous Spanish artist the unoccupied third floor. It currently houses the Musée Picasso. This museum also contains works by other local or locally inspired artists—and many works in ceramic by Picasso himself. It had an extensive two-year makeover, re-opening in the summer of 2008.

Vallauris had been a ceramics centre for a thousand years but had fallen on hard times. The little town now hosts a complex of art museums, exhibiting pottery from the most humble to the most exotic. It is not to everyone's taste. The acerbic critic Ian Nairn called it "a right load of old ceramic rope". Nor was Picasso welcomed by all the traditional potters—"crack-pot" is probably too apt a term for their opinion of this elusive, obsessive man. He became so enamoured of working in clay that he made about 4,000 pieces—plates, jugs, birds, animals, even bottles in the form of the female figure, Tanagras. For lovers of ceramics, the mix cannot be too rich, and Vallauris is the essence of that variety; here the art of pottery goes about as far as it can go.

A few miles inland is another ceramics centre, the village of Biot. Fernand Léger, a Norman by birth, preferred the cooler north but was a frequent visitor to the Riviera in later life. He joined his former student, Roland Brice, in the early 1950s, at a time when many artists—Matisse and Chagall, for instance, as well as Picasso—were enthusing about ceramics. Five years after his death in 1955, a museum dedicated to his work was created on the site of his last studio in Biot.

Up behind Cannes, just north of Mougins, the sixteenth-century Château de Mouans, in the village of Mouans-Sartoux, houses an extraordinary collection of "concrete art". A rotating exhibition of concrete, minimal and conceptual art invites the visitor (with help from questioning and advising guides) to consider what (on earth) it is all about.

Cagnes-sur-Mer brings one back to tradition, as the home of Auguste Renoir, who settled here in 1903. Earlier trips to the Riviera—he had rented houses in Menton, Grasse, Maganosc and Le Cannet—had made him see the attraction of living in the south to his now ailing body as well as to his aesthetic senses. In Cagnes, just to the west of Nice, he built a big house (his wife's idea, as he preferred the small Provençal farmhouse on the plot they bought) surrounded by olives, oranges and roses. Les Collettes now houses the Renoir Museum. It is a place to visit not so much to view his paintings, though some of course are exhibited here, but to savour the atmosphere of untended nature and to experience at first hand the lush but simple, warm and radiant place which allowed a very sick man to live, continue to work and remain inspired. This is the most intimate of all the Riviera's art museums.

The view from its west-facing windows is of the Château Museum of Haut-de-Cagnes. Grimaldis lived here from about 1300 until the French Revolution, when a certain Citizen Gerbaud bought it. Almost a century later it was sold on to Dr. Gerecke and his wife, who restored and re-furnished it. Now it is a temple devoted to the worship of the olive, but it also houses a rotating collection of modern art and, every summer, hosts an art competition, the International Painting Exhibition. Until 2007 a *faux poivrier*, a kind of wild pear tree, used to grow up inside the château until it grew old and expired; *normalement* the tree will be replaced, claimed a none too optimistic guide.

The most fascinating collection this museum houses is contained in a single room—portraits by forty artists of one woman. Born in Brittany in 1900, Suzanne Marion became Suzy Rocher when her single mother married, and then became famous as a model, singer of risqué songs, film actress and androgynous lover of both men and, preferably, women, under the name of Suzy Solidor. As a kind of publicity stunt, she set out to become the "most painted woman in the world". Many excellent and famous artists were happy to oblige, among them Marie Laurencin, Tsuguharu Foujita, Kees van Dongen, Raoul Dufy, Francis Picabia, Jean Cocteau and Tamara de Lempicka. The war and occupation did not stop Solidor; indeed, her Paris nightclub was especially popular with German officers. Afterwards she kept her head down in the United States for a couple of years. Then in 1960 she moved to Haut-de-Cagnes, opened an antique shop and sang songs in a cabaret decorated with no fewer than 224 portraits of herself. The best of these (though not the products of her sitting for Picasso and Braque) she left to the town, and it is they which make up the "Suzy Solidor donation".

Since its foundation in 1964, the Riviera museum best known around the world is surely the Fondation Maeght, just outside the ramparts of St.-Paul-de-Vence. This is the creation of a remarkable couple, Aimé and Marguerite Maeght, who started as lithographers and part-time art dealers in Cannes before hitting the big time in Paris after the Second World War. They were an intelligent and generous couple trusted by the (often very suspicious) artists they represented and helped. Pierre Bonnard spotted Aimé's talents as a lithographer and encouraged him from early on. The foundation collection, housed in and around an extraordinarily beautiful building designed by the Catalan Josep Lluis Sert, has become virtually a place of pilgrimage for all lovers of modern art. Many artists such as Braque, Miro and Léger created pieces specially for display here.

The collections in Nice itself are a mixed bag. The Musée des Beaux-Arts (Jules-Chéret) promises much but delivers only a few real delights. The building, a pale apricot *belle époque* palace of a Russian princess, later expanded by a rich American, shows signs of wear and tear and suffers from the encroachment of surrounding apartment blocks. It is (timidly, because in brackets) named after the early exponent of poster art, Jules Chéret, whose pretty pastels of flouncing blondes decorate the mezzanine walls. Works by the *Niçois* Mossa family, father and son, who were the first curators, are strange, Klimt-like, symbolist works of considerable charm and interest. The quality of the portraits is surprisingly high—especially one self-portrait by the wild but intelligent young Russian, Marie Bashkirtseff. But the best of the collection is without doubt the roomful of works by one of the Riviera's most colourful adopted sons, Raoul Dufy. Nice's landmark steel pier, the Grande Jetée, has never been more vividly brought back to life.

The huge museum of modern art at the other, eastern end of town, the Musée d'Art Moderne et d'Art Contemporain, is, by contrast, purpose-built (it opened in 1990) and impressively stocked. The "New Realists" known as the "School of Nice" occupy a significant space—the individual items are displayed on a rotating basis. A local boy made good, Yves Klein, has a room to himself. Most famous for his use of nude models as human paint-brushes writhing on the floor covered in bucketfuls of paint, he also painted series of canvases and objects in a bright, vibrant blue—another variant of the obsession with the "Azur". An adjoining room is filled with the huge, exotic, multi-coloured creations of Niki de Saint-Phalle. Other rooms contain fine examples of American Pop Art.

At the foot of the hill rising behind Nice's old town and leading to the hilly suburb of Cimiez is a remarkable museum devoted to the work of Marc Chagall, a low building made of stone from La Turbie and opened in 1973 on the artist's 86th birthday. It is a kind of companion piece to the Musée Matisse, higher up the hill and set among the remains of the Roman arena.

The Matisse museum consists largely of modern extension to the col-

Shadows of Miro at the Fondation Maeght

lection, which is housed in a seventeenth-century Genoese-style villa. It still only manages a rather cursory cross-section of the master's work—although this is not surprising, given how most of his paintings and sculptures were scattered round the world, from Baltimore to Moscow, during his turbulent lifetime.

As for Monaco's collections, they are more devoted to dolls, old cars, stamps and coins, rococo ceilings, Napoleonic souvenirs, oceanographic phenomena and Grimaldi memorabilia than fine art. Menton, on the other hand, has some unexpected artistic treasures. The original Palais Carnolès, on the west side, was built in 1640 as a summer palace of the princes of Monaco. It was in fact Princess Grace who inaugurated its much expanded structure as an art museum in 1977. Although its main claim to fame is that its garden contains the world's biggest collection of *agrumes*, or citrus trees (137 varieties and counting), inside the palace one or two things stand out among the worthy local exhibits. These include some fine ceilings, a Dufy portrait and an eclectic collection (mostly Italian and Flemish, as well as contemporary French works) donated by Charles Wakefield Mori, an Englishman, in the early twentieth century, as well as another collection donated by Graham Sutherland. The garden and palace both feature a number of impressive statues by Léopold Bernstamm (including one splendid bust of Louis Blériot with droopy moustache and hooded eyes). But the most significant artistic presence—and legacy—in Menton is that of Jean Cocteau (see the section on individual artists below).

One slightly odder contribution to the artistic scene on the modern Riviera is the roadside art commissioned by the companies that build and manage the *autoroutes*. There are examples by the St.-Raphael toll station—white concrete Roman galleys and sections of aqueduct—and a fifteen-foot-wide juniper wood "Sunset" off the A8 near Puget-sur-Argens and Le Muy.

Artists on the Riviera: Renoir, Matisse and Chagall

"Artists on the Riviera" is a better subheading than "Riviera Artists". It is not that some of the most famous names in French art history just "happened" to come down south and install themselves at various locations along the Côte d'Azur. They all had good reasons to be there. But the Riviera—above all its light—was rarely part of their formative experience.

Nice: the Musée Matisse

On the other hand, the Riviera was not only influential on their work, but it defined much of it in the popular imagination. The images, the shapes, the colours are one very important part of the way we conceive of the South of France in our minds. Yet all these artists had their own stories to tell, their own reactions to the place which they made their home and the subject of their work.

Auguste Renoir (1841-1919) was the grand old man among Riviera-based artists, one of the most celebrated and popular of all the impressionists and post-impressionists. He was "the Master", famous for his expression of feelings of joy, of delight in feminine beauty, gorgeous colours, fêtes and multicoloured nature. In that sense he was a true heir of Fragonard. His arrival on the Riviera in 1903 can be seen as a logical culmination of his tastes for everything sunny. In fact, Renoir already knew the South of France well, having made frequent visits to Provence as well as to the Riviera.

He spent the last sixteen years of his life at Cagnes-sur-Mer on doctor's advice. His rheumatoid arthritis was becoming increasingly debilitating. But these were amazingly productive years, given his acute disabilities, and his pictures from this period are as full of optimism and energy as before. His son Jean wrote that he exulted in "the profusion, variety and sumptuousness of the Mediterranean landscape (which) he seemed to discover anew with each painting." His many visitors marvelled at the way that, from his special folding chair, his paintbrush in his crippled and bandaged hand (some say it had to be tied with string, others hotly deny this), he still managed to produce paintings of dazzling radiance. One observant visitor described him painting "like a pecking hen".

Robust and pink-cheeked local girls were employed as models. Renoir was famous for the range of reds in his palette to bring out the best in their luscious flesh. (He revealingly remarked that "when I have painted a buttock that I feel like spanking, I know that I have finished.") It was in Cagnes, too, that Renoir began to sculpt. Mostly he was compelled to seek the help of an assistant (Richard Guino, himself trained by the local sculptor, Aristide Maillol), but the old man was able to direct the process with a long stick, used as an extension to his hands.

Renoir's legacy—both his painting and his house—is a reminder of just how pastorally beautiful the Riviera was, and still (in places) is.

Claude Monet did not specially enjoy his sortie to the south with

Renoir. He said that "as much as it was agreeable to travel with Renoir as a tourist, it would be awkward working as a pair. I've always preferred working alone, following my own impressions." He did indeed come back by himself, several times, and was captivated particularly by the varying light around Cap Martin, where he painted his very first picture of the Mediterranean, doing a sequence of views at different times of the day. He declared in February 1884 that he was "daring to use earth-coloured and pink and blue tones… it is magical, delicious". Four years later he was on the Cap d'Antibes and in Roquebrune. All Monet's Riviera paintings are now in the United States.

The prolific and long-lived landscape artist, Henri Harpignies (1819-1916), who worked in oils and watercolour, discovered the Riviera light in Menton in 1885, when he was already nearly seventy. Anatole France called him "the Michaelangelo of trees", and Harpignies was indeed a fine and sensitive draughtsman, much influenced by Corot. One of his last paintings, in 1913, was of the village of Castellar, up behind Menton.

Henri Matisse (1869-1954) was an archetypal northerner. His first experiences of the Mediterranean in Collioure, near the Spanish border, had alerted him to the other world of blazing light and colours. But temperamentally he was not one to be seduced by the superficial ease of the south.

Even on his first visit to join Paul Signac in St.-Tropez in 1904, his reworking of the older painter's *Time of Harmony* introduced distinctly discordant notes and colours in an apparently pretty setting, anticipating the spirit of the Fauves—the wild beasts. The same sense of irony as in Baudelaire's "luxe, calme et volupté" infuses Matisse's painting. He brought down with him all his obsessions, his passionate work ethic and his penetrating eye. He was on one level indifferent to the most significant thing that attracted most visitors, the weather. When, according to Hilary Spurling's *Matisse the Master*, he arrived in Nice, on Christmas Day 1917:

> the town was bleak windy and deserted ("It's freezing in this pig of a place," he told his wife). His hands would scarcely hold a brush, and he had to wear sheepskin foot-warmers to paint views of the castle above the old town. When it snowed on his birthday, 31 December, he bought himself a new canvas and stayed indoors, painting his room at the Beau Rivage in sunshine reflected off snow and sea: "From my open window

you can see the top of a palm tree—white lace curtains—coat-rack on the left—armchair with white lace cover on the back—on the right a red table with my suitcase on it—sky and sea blue—blue—blue."

It is hard to imagine Matisse now out of the context of his homes in the old town of Nice or in the huge double apartment in the old Hôtel Regina Excelsior or the unpretentious little villa in Vence (so dull from outside that Picasso knocked on the door of a smarter place up the road on his first visit). His paintings (and, later, cut-outs) lined every wall. Sculptures and hundreds of souvenirs and props, birdcages, plants and all the apparatus of a painter who never stopped working filled every available space. So many times at death's door, Matisse found inspiration and consolation in his immediate surroundings, isolated from the seductions of the Riviera almost as much as from the hostile world beyond.

Nice itself was both a refuge (from war, from Paris, from his dour northern roots) but it was also ambiguous and disturbing, a stark symbol of the rootless, disintegrating world after the First World War. "Even the wealthy in Nice," Spurling reminds us, "were elderly, convalescent, tubercular, dispossessed in one way or another, marking time in retirement or exile." Catherine Bock wrote in an article on Matisse published by the Art Institute of Chicago in 1986: "In these Nice portraits of a handful of models, he recorded the restless anxiety of women gazing at the sea, pining at open windows, neither dressed nor nude, going nowhere, twisting in their chairs, inert on their couches with unread books and unplayed instruments in their hands, never facing themselves in the omnipresent mirrored vanity table, indifferent to bouquets, absorbed in their mute presence."

Perhaps it was because Matisse lived and worked on the Riviera that most people in his lifetime, and indeed for many years after, marked him down as a painter of languid prettiness, a decorator. Yet his ferocious approach to his work, his agony over each brushstroke and his almost solipsistic immersion in the act of painting or drawing should have given a clue as to the far more complex depths behind the superficial splashes of Riviera colour.

When Marc Chagall (1887-1985) moved to Paris in his early twenties, he brought with him intact his childhood self, a poor Jewish boy from Vitebsk, his head full of Hasidic rituals, folklore and images. As soon as he encountered the Fauvists and Cubists and the whole wild excitement of the

Montparnasse art scene, his imagination overflowed, fusing newly developed techniques and styles with his vivid imagination. His return to Russia in 1914 to marry found him caught up in a world war, revolution, civil war and cultural mayhem, first in Vitebsk and later in Moscow. After an uneasy year in Berlin, Chagall was back in Paris at the end of the summer of 1923.

In the increasingly violent, antisemitic 1930s Chagall visited both Palestine and Poland. Granted (eventually) French citizenship, he only just escaped the German net and spent the war years in the United States. Here his devoted wife, Bella, died. But he soon met, and had a son with, Virginia McNeil, the much younger daughter of a British diplomat, and returned to France. It might seem surprising to someone with such a "Mediterranean" palette that it was only in 1950 that Marc Chagall moved to the South of France—first to St.-Jean-Cap-Ferrat and then to Vence. He was now well into his sixties. At once he found himself in the territory of the "giants" of twentieth-century art—despite his lifelong desire to be independent of all movements and groups. With Matisse, in the words of Monica Bohm-Duchen: "Chagall had a relatively unproblematic relationship: there was mutual respect, a certain amount of jealousy on Chagall's part (he apparently found it irksome that *Les Collines* (his house) happened to be located in the avenue Matisse), no overt hostility or animosity, but equally no real warmth."

Relations with Picasso, however, had always been difficult—a classic clash of egos, made worse when Chagall started to use the same Vallauris studio to make his ceramics. The showdown came one lunchtime when Picasso, after teasing Chagall about not going back to Russia, started making sarcastic remarks about there being "no money to be made there." That was it. They never spoke again, despite a deep respect for each other as artists.

In 1952 Chagall remarried—not Virginia, but Valentina (Vava) Brodsky, with whom he remained for the rest of his very long life. Vence and St.-Paul-de-Vence were never sources of inspiration on the scale of Vitebsk or even Paris, but the Riviera provided a congenial, unthreatening base for many years of creativity. There is no finer proof than the extraordinary Museum of the Biblical Message in Nice—a beautiful building designed by André Hermant (with Chagall's help) and a perfect setting for the mix of *joie de vivre* with his dramatic, radiant interpretation of the stories and spirit of the Old Testament.

PICASSO, LÉGER AND BONNARD

An artist of such celebrity and complexity as Pablo Picasso (1881-1973) is deeply resistant to quick judgements. He cultivated ambiguity as much as fame. Although he spent many years on the Côte d'Azur, it is impossible to define the influence he had on the French Riviera any more than the influence it had on him.

Perhaps his most exuberant reaction to finding a home in the Château Grimaldi (which now houses the Picasso Museum) in Antibes is the dancing "flower woman" (his lover, Françoise Gilot) surrounded by frolicking goats and flautist-fauns set against a bright blue sea and sky in his painting *Antipolis ou la joie de vivre*. It is an extraordinary outburst of postwar joy and celebration of Mediterranean mythology. The pictures of this period were very much of the place, and Picasso would always say, "If you want to see the Picasso of Antibes, come to Antibes."

Picasso was nothing if not daring and original. He was a hard act to follow. As the critic David Sylvester observes, "Picasso is the fastest gun in the West, the one every budding gunfighter has to beat to the draw in order to prove himself." Nowhere did this rivalry play itself out so much as on the French Riviera, where the art scene revolved around Picasso, as inspiration and aspiration, as the object of jealousy and the object of admiration, not always unmixed. The constant comings and goings and communications with other Riviera artists, notably Matisse—his "cherished rival", as Sylvester describes him—fed into the intensity with which Picasso approached his art. These relationships were often teasing, sometimes hurtful, but fascinating—always to the others, sometimes to Picasso too.

A perceptive pen portrait was made by another artist (though mostly writer) who knew Picasso through their mutual friends, the Murphys, during the heady days of the 1920s in Antibes. John Dos Passos described Picasso as:

a small dark closed man. He had none of the off-hand geniality that makes Spaniards in general easy to get along with. He was sardonic, earthily cynical in a special Spanish peasant way—the cynicism of Sancho Panza. He seemed to me impenetrable even in moments of relaxation and laughter. He was very much the master bricklayer, the master stonemason, the artisan. He was skill incarnate. It was humanity that was lacking. The Greeks would have called him *deinos* as they did Odysseus. You couldn't approach him or his work—the man and the work were inseparable—without profound admiration for the sly elbow, the cunning fingers, the accurate eye; if he had had the gift of compassion he would have been as great as Michelangelo.

Picasso's home for the last twelve years of his life was on a site overlooking the bay of Cannes at Mougins, in a priory near the Chapelle Notre-Dame de Vie. It was built in the twelfth century as a place where stillborn babies could be brought to be baptized and so avoid being sent to limbo. Picasso's art is certainly unlikely to languish in any limbo.

Fernand Léger (1881-1955) was exceptional in our context in that he really did not like the south, its heat, bright colours and seductive landscapes. Formed artistically in the heyday of pre-First World War Paris, he was shocked by the mechanical brutality of the war into a preoccupation with machine-like shapes and the forces that drove industrial society. Son of a Normandy butcher and a self-styled "Purist", Léger remained true both in politics and art to his left-wing, modernizing ideals.

Léger's trademark "industrial" style led him to prefer monumental works. Even before coming south he had experimented with stained glass, tapestry, mosaic, three-dimensional sculpture, huge polychrome murals and billboards. For someone suspicious of heat and bright sunlight, the extraordinary vibrant effect of his works en masse is a brilliant complement—and compliment—to the spirit of the Côte d'Azur.

Pierre Bonnard (1867-1947) started his artistic life a so-called "Nabi", or prophet, hostile to the idea of naturalism and natural colour. His early life in Paris was spent in the company of anarchists and representatives of contemporary radical chic such as Alfred Jarry and Félix Fénéon and the writers and illustrators of the *Revue Blanche*, before he moved into rather grander Parisian society. After rejecting symbolism, he became what was once described as a "degenerate" impressionist.

Bonnard retained, however, the impressionist ideal of freedom—in terms of expression and technique. His first visit to the Riviera was in 1906. Immediately his colours became far more intense. He painted with Signac in St.-Tropez. His themes became increasingly connected to the Mediterranean. He had a liaison with a golden-haired model, Renée Monchaty, whom he almost married, but instead returned to his neurotic, dif-

ficult, anti-social long-time girlfriend, Marthe—a rejection that caused
Renée to commit suicide. In 1925, already a frequent visitor to the Riviera,
he retreated into marriage with Marthe (once described as a "touchy elf")
and bought a villa, Le Bosquet, high above the village of Le Cannet, near
Cannes. His paintings were most often of domestic scenes, with his wife
as the almost obsessive subject, as often as not in or getting out of the bath.
This bathroom has been compared with Proust's cork-lined bedroom as a
closed-in place in which the mundane is transformed into art, with Marthe
his "muse and gaoler". Bonnard's Midi landscapes viewed through an open
window have been called his "coded messages from prison". As Timothy
Hyman noted:

> Yellow takes on a dominant and symbolic value in the later work. As
> Bonnard looked back at his Parisian and Normandy pictures, he re-
> coiled from their greyness; he had moved from shade into light. In the
> last year of his life, when a dealer commented doubtfully of a picture
> by Signac, "There is a lot of yellow in it," Bonnard replied, "You can't
> have too much." Yellow appears in all its variety, from the mimosa's
> lemon cadmium, through ochre, to a deep Indian yellow, often set
> against white. For Bonnard, as for Van Gogh, yellow is felt as the true
> Primary—the colour of the sun, of pollen, of life itself. But in the late
> work it can also carry a more complex invocation—of the golden light
> of anarchism; of a yearning for a lost state of well-being, as well as its
> rediscovery in the sudden illumination of visionary consciousness.
> Throughout these final years in the Midi, the latent process is his dis-
> solving the image into gold—the Golden Age being thereby restored,
> or imaginatively affirmed.

Bonnard's last act as a painter was to change a patch of green to yellow
in the bottom left corner of his talismanic painting, *The Almond Tree in
Flower*. He died in the intensely and unusually cold winter at the end of
January 1947. Very few of his paintings can be seen today on the Riviera.
His early painting, *Summer*, is at the Fondation Maeght. A pre-Riviera
painting, *Window Opening onto the Seine at Vernonnet*, is displayed in the
Musée des Beaux-Arts in Nice. But Le Cannet has yet to come up with a
Bonnard museum.

Jean Cocteau

Two Riviera towns are associated with the poet, novelist, filmmaker, painter and hyper-aesthete, Jean Cocteau (1889-1963): Villefranche-sur-Mer and Menton. In the first, Cocteau spent—and sometimes wasted—much of his time in and around the Hôtel Welcome by the sea wall in Villefranche. In the words of Bernard Minoret:

> With fishermen as their audience, Jean Cocteau's friends and disciples had sought to spend their days in an atmosphere of passion and intimacy, in keeping with the poet's teachings. Yet their endless round of opium, intrigues and love affairs did not stop Cocteau regarding Villefranche as a working retreat… Villefranche remained the symbol of his life.

Sailors—especially those from the American Sixth Fleet, anchored in the deep water harbour—were an added attraction. Fights were frequent. The model Kiki de Montparnasse had to be bailed out by Man Ray for hitting a policeman in a row with some prostitutes over who should have access to those same sailors. Picasso came and talked and went away under Cocteau's adoring gaze. Rebecca West, Paul Robeson, Isadora Duncan, Coco Chanel all dropped by. As Cocteau wrote later, the Hôtel Welcome was "a source of myths, a site which the young enthusiasts of lyricism should transform into an altar and cover with flowers. Poets of all kinds, speaking every language, lived there and by a simple contact of fluids transformed the extraordinary little town, whose steep chaos ends at the water's edge, into a veritable Lourdes, a centre of legends and inventions."

Cocteau did not invent the interwar image of the Côte d'Azur but he did much to define and publicize it. When Diaghilev staged his ballet *Le Train Bleu* with music by Milhaud, sets by Picasso and costumes by Chanel, it was Cocteau who provided the story.

Cocteau's chapel in Villefranche will be discussed in the next chapter. In Menton his contributions were more secular than religious; his Salle des Mariages is far from being either sacred or sanctimonious. The municipality is now proud, but was once shocked, that the theme of lovers should be so overtly displayed. Even the figure of Marianne, who is a compulsory presence at French weddings, is distinctly *louche*. Maybe an atmosphere more nightclub than town hall is a more hopeful (or at least accurate) introduction to married life. On the other hand, outsize depictions of a scowling mother-in-law, a jilted ex-girlfriend, centaurs and Saracens may not be wholly conducive to long-term wedded bliss and stability.

The seventeenth-century square bastion at the southernmost point of the old town is another transformed temple to Cocteau's lovers, with its series of brightly coloured pencil drawings of *Les Innamorati*. Other artefacts there include tapestries, mosaics and fantastic ceramic animals in the spirit of Picasso. In a couple of years the Wunderman collection of Cocteau's works will be opened in Menton—the largest single collection anywhere.

NALL

A rare contemporary artistic phenomenon on the Riviera is the Alabama-born, Paris-trained artist, originally Fred Nall Hollis but now known simply as Nall, who settled in Vence (buying Jean Dubuffet's workshop) and established a reputation as well as a foundation there. A disciple of Salvador Dali, he trained at the Beaux-Arts school in Paris and then wandered the world. Nall has an extraordinary range. He is a fine draughtsman and engraver, works with prints, mosaics, graphite portraits in elaborate frames, porcelain, glassware, jewellery, watercolours… and computer images. He has done the set designs for Puccini's Fanciulla del West as well as a portrait of Prince Albert of Monaco.

Nall created five studios on his large Vence estate to offer training and facilities to young artists under the auspices of his own N.A.L.L. (Nature Art and Life League) Art Association. He has described himself as "inspired by the material, haunted by the spiritual"—and his Vence museum is an eclectic mix of new and old, western and eastern: old sculpted doors from India, beams, ceiling and fireplace from the former Gould villa in Cannes, Syrian mosaics and Matisse tiles. Nall is a mix of Renaissance man and New Age man.

The Riviera, he says, settled him down after a youth that involved not just intensive artistic creation but a flirtation with self-destruction through alcohol and drugs. "I moved to nature and light, a Mediterranean influence—and introspection; I fell in love and cleaned myself up… I was spoiled aesthetically—and adored it." Nall cannot rank among the figures who preceded him on the Riviera. But perhaps that is a motto not just for himself but for all those great French masters too.

MUSIC

Up until 1947 no entire opera is set on the Riviera, although Kobbé lists three for Brittany. With the notable exception of the third act of Puccini's *La Rondine*, when Magda and Ruggero flee Paris to install themselves in a (sadly temporary) love-nest near Nice, the Côte d'Azur failed to inspire the great composers of opera. However, on 3 June 1947 Paris was treated to the opening of Francis Poulenc's outrageous *opéra-bouffe, Les Mamelles de Tirésias* (The Breasts of Tiresias). It is set in "Zanzibar, an imaginary town on the French Riviera, between Nice and Monte Carlo".

Short and utterly bizarre, its source is the play by Guillaume Apollinaire produced in 1917, in which he invented the term *surréaliste*. The heroine, who starts out as Thérèse, sheds her breasts, which float away like balloons, while the husband explains to an amorous policeman that France needs more children and he himself will provide them—40,000 of them. He plans for them to support him, and the first one he produces has already written a novel that has sold 600,000 copies. Others are more disappointing. A fortune teller appears, condemning the apparently sterile policeman, who tries to strangle her, but she reveals herself to be Thérèse—though her breasts are still missing. But no-one cares, and the opera ends with the moral: "Learn the lesson of the war, O Frenchmen, and make children, you who were making scarcely any."

A frothy enough plot, one might think, for the Riviera—and with music to match.

Poulenc's friend, Igor Stravinsky, lived happily and productively in Nice in the second half of the 1920s, where he worked on *Le Sacre du Printemps* and composed *Oedipus Rex*, which Cocteau said Stravinksy wanted to be "curly, like the beard of Zeus". In a letter written in July 1929 to his friend Charles-Ferdinand Ramuz, the Swiss novelist and essayist, Stravinsky made a rare comment about his daily routine.

> I am back in Nice again… Every day I go out in my automobile with my chauffeur. I have a chauffeur who, for the time being, is very nice, very expensive, and constantly introduces me to his chauffeur-colleagues: one became the proprietor of a bistro, the other a bicycle merchant, etc. He presents me by saying: "Here is my new boss…"
>
> Besides going for drives in the automobile, I compose regularly every morning, take a dip every morning in the sea (before composing), and

in the afternoon I write letters, prepare my next season, and practise the piano (in order not to lose the technique that I have acquired in the past year).

Clearly the atmosphere had improved in Nice since the days of Hector Berlioz!

Cinema: Nice's Studios and the Cannes Film Festival

The French Riviera has never quite matched Hollywood as a production centre for films, despite an early start and a climate that is eminently fit for purpose. Serge Sandberg was a Lithuanian-born film producer who worked all over Europe for Pathé-Frères and was a pioneer of French filmmaking. From January 1919 to August 1920 he developed a large movie production programme in Nice with producer Louis Nalpas. He commissioned the building of the Studio de la Victorine, where several movies were shot—eight from 1919 to 1922—but sold the premises to Edouard Corniglion-Molinier (in 1927) when they became precarious, after first renting them out to the Irish-American Rex Ingram (from 1925 to 1927).

Ingram's first production on the Riviera was *Mare Nostrum* for MGM, based on a novel by Blasco Ibañez, who had come to live in Menton. The directors were Powell and Pressburger. It was a First World War film mixed in with Greek legend, for which the French government, anxious to support the ailing studio, lent a couple of submarines.

The Victorine Studios' white arched gate, rather like the entrance to Paramount Pictures, has recently been smartened up (not for the first time; the studios have had as many re-launches as they have had hit movies). Indeed, technically, the name has changed to Studios Riviera. One (Damoclean) problem is that the city of Nice has the right to build all over the site after 2018. Another is the bad name the studios earned in the years of the corrupt mayor, Jacques Médecin, whose cronies were installed as studio bosses; they pocketed production money and failed to invest in the facilities. It is said that the grass was growing so high inside the compound during the filming of the Bond "classic" *Never Say Never Again* that it was hard just moving the equipment around; the director almost walked out over the nicotine-stained screens in the projection room. At the time of writing, television shows and commercials are managing to stave off the studio's threatened bankruptcy.

But there have been highlights too for Nice's studios. Marcel Carné's *Les Enfants du Paradis*, Jacques Tati's *Mon Oncle* and Roger Vadim's *Et Dieu Créa la Femme* all had the Victorine treatment. Truffaut shot *La Nuit Américaine* (Day for Night) here. *To Catch a Thief*, Hitchcock's matchless Riviera drama, was another Victorine triumph. David Lean was shooting *Nostromo* in Nice when he died. Even *Mr. Bean* was made here.

Truffaut was responsible for casting an unusual actor for the part of an insurance salesman in *La Nuit Américaine*—Graham Greene. Yvonne Cloetta told the story in her memoir. The first choice for the small walk-on part was rejected as "too intellectual". Hearing this, Greene immediately volunteered.

> We took that for a joke, but Graham insisted. After dinner, all four of us went to a villa at Cap d'Antibes rented by Jacqueline Bisset, the star of the film. A party had been organised by Truffaut and all the crew were there. Graham was introduced to Truffaut as Mr Brown. He was greeted favourably by the director, who asked his assistant to arrange a meeting at the Victorine studios. When he was summoned a few days later, Graham wore a grey-striped suit, cream shirt and bottle-green tie, and carried the indispensable umbrella, and caught the train to Nice, where a car was waiting to take him to the studios. Truffaut was very pleased with his performance, but when the time came for his assistant to disclose the hoax—in other words who Mr Brown really was—he almost fainted.

It is said that the ghost of Rex Ingram still haunts the Victorine Studios. They might need supernatural powers to survive for much longer.

Along the coast in Cannes the film industry has a glitzier image. After a false start in 1939, when the outbreak of the Second World War prevented the start of the first Cannes Film Festival, the annual event has put Cannes on the international map. Held every May (it used to be every September), producers and agents, directors and actors and every kind of hanger-on descend on the brutalist Palais des Festivals to tout their wares and argue about which films come away with the prizes. Jean Cocteau had a starry-eyed view of its role. "The Festival," he said, "is an apolitical no-man's-land, a microcosm of what the world would like to be if people could contact each other directly and speak the same language." Given the intensity of some of the disputes over the decades, it is hard to share that optimism.

Yet Cannes does have the merit that Hollywood and the European cinema industries compete here on level terms—the organizers constantly claim that the annual battle rages to the mutual benefit of both—and of the citizens of Cannes. The city has taken on the role of the Riviera's convention centre, and this is the highlight. The inaugural festival on 20 September 1946 was the first important international cultural event after the Second World War. It was financed not just by the city of Cannes but also by the French Foreign Ministry. Despite the national backing and a French concern to rival Venice as the world's most prestigious film forum, the early years were fraught. In 1948 and again in 1950 the "annual" event was cancelled due to lack of funds, but ever since there has been no lack of money. In 1968 it was revolutionary fervour that caused proceedings to be cut short and the jury to disband, when a group of filmmakers, including Louis Malle (who had resigned from the jury), François Truffaut and Jean-Luc Godard, took over the largest screening room on opening night and held the curtains closed, to show solidarity with the student protesters.

From the 1970s onwards, the festival became gradually, then speedily, more competitive. At the start most films were given some sort of prize, but from the late 1950s the festival's importance as a commercial showcase, and the rewards to be gained not just from international exposure but from the increased sales generated by the prestige of winning, created ever more intense competition.

In 1978 Gilles Jacob became president and introduced two new items, the Caméra d'Or prize for the best first film and a special section called "Un Certain Regard". He also reduced the length of the festival to thirteen days and cut the number of films that could be selected to be shown. Up to then the jury had been made up of film academics. Jacob introduced celebrities and professionals from the film industry. In 1983 the new and much bigger Palais des Festivals et des Congrès was built to host the festival. It was immediately nicknamed "the bunker". In the late 1990s Jacob created the last section of the Official Selection: the Cinéfondation, whose aim was to support filmmaking by selecting short and medium-length pictures from film schools around the world. Today there are prizes galore; just in the feature film section there are the Palme d'Or, the Grand Prix

Cannes – brutalism and luxury side by side

and the Jury Prize as well as special prizes, awards for the best director, actor, actress, screenplay and so on.

The burgeoning power and rivalry of and among the promoters as well as the publicity and marketing people has meant that those who award the prizes have come under increasing pressure. *Marty*'s award in 1955 (it also won the Oscar, which has not happened since) was controversial mostly for beating out Elia Kazan's *East of Eden*. In 1960 Fellini's stylish *La Dolce Vita* (which gave the world the word *paparazzi*) won the Palme d'Or when Georges Simenon was president of the jury, despite some opposition to its "free love" atmosphere. The 57th Cannes Film Festival in 2004 created a stir by giving the highest award to President Bush-bashing director Michael Moore for his documentary film *Fahrenheit 9/11* and then declaring a fourteen-year-old Japanese boy the best actor.

But mostly Cannes is famous for posing pouting starlets and sex scandals, both of which receive unusual and exaggerated hype simply because there are so many manufacturers of scandal gathered together in one place. In 2003 Vincent Gallo's film *The Brown Bunny* attracted vitriolic criticism for one explicit sex scene at the end of what was only an art movie. But that seems old hat now. In the popular imagination, if not among those who work in the movie industry and have a direct financial interest in sales, it is the celebrities—and their misdeeds—who count for more than the films. The Cannes Film Festival manages to satisfy all appetites and is a suitable heir to the extravagant founders and villa-builders of this glitziest among all the Riviera towns.

Menton's Eglise St.- Michel – the largest baroque church on the Riviera

Chapter Nine
BUILDING THE DREAM
RELIGIOUS AND SECULAR ARCHITECTURE

The French Riviera is not on the whole richly endowed with medieval religious architecture or art, although there are some remarkable exceptions. One very fine example is the cluster of buildings around the cathedral in Fréjus. The twelfth-century cloister that links the cathedral with the medieval streets is particularly fascinating for its ceiling, which dates from the fourteenth century. Visitors are issued with a powerful torch to shine up onto hundreds of small panels painted on the roof. This close inspection reveals strange combinations of human figures and animals, real or imaginary, a wildly inventive and sometimes pornographic array of Bosch-like creatures alongside more conventional images of everyday medieval life.

The nearby octagonal baptistery dates from the late fourth century. It is not hard to imagine the adult converts entering by the narrow door to have their feet washed in the terracotta basin before being immersed in the central pool, then proceeding inside the cathedral to celebrate their first mass.

Further east, on the island of St.-Honorat, the enormous "keep" of the eleventh-century fortified monastery is an immediately striking feature in any panorama of the Riviera, best seen from the sea or the air (being well sited on the usual flight path into Nice airport.) It was built to protect the monks from Saracen incursions. The gate was constructed some fifteen feet above ground and was originally accessible only by ladder, although now stone steps lead up to it. The cloisters enclose a square courtyard with a marble rainwater tank. At ground level the older buildings are dominated by an extensive monastery built in the nineteenth century.

This pattern of development is not untypical. Elsewhere on the Riviera many original medieval structures have been incorporated into, or overlaid by, more modern buildings. The eleventh-century convent of the Annonciade, just north of Menton, for example, went through countless transformations, and most of it now dates back to the seventeenth century. The panorama, with its modernized foreground, remains undoubtedly as fine as it ever was.

From Menton to Nice the "Italian" influence is obvious in the old towns and villages, the churches, the pre-modern public buildings. Menton's old town was—and is—far more like other towns along the Italian Riviera than comparable sized settlements deeper into France. Given the history, this is no surprise. There are, of course, castles and rich houses, even palaces, all along the Riviera, but few rate highly for originality or unusual beauty (though the settings can be spectacular, as for example the castle of Roquebrune). Between Nice and Hyères traditional Mediterranean-style seaside houses, narrow and high, prevail. Now of course they are dominated by massive apartments and villas, hotels and public buildings. Particularly around Grasse and Mougins many seventeenth- and eighteenth-century Italian-style *bastides*, sheltered by limes or mulberries or chestnuts, keep their distance in the back country. But the overwhelming of the coast by the constantly increasing demand and supply of living space for visitors and tourists is a much discussed, and often deplored, fact.

Unlike Provence, the Côte d'Azur saw little architectural development of real interest or originality between the Romans and the classical period (from the seventeenth century). The baroque style did, however, catch on, and many public and ecclesiastical buildings and Nice and elsewhere provide rich examples. But it is really only at the beginning of the nineteenth century—the time of the construction, for instance, of the grand Place Masséna in Nice, with its red ochre facades and arcades—that architecture peculiar to the Riviera can be said to flourish.

During the interwar years as well as in the decades after the Second World War, but especially in the 1960s onwards, rich incomers—particularly Americans—provided a market for smart modern villas; American architects, such as Pittsburgh-born Barry Diercks, worked alongside their French counterparts to supply this constant demand.

THE BAROQUE
The most elaborate example of local baroque architecture can be found in Nice's Ste.-Réparate Cathedral in the heart of the old town. The eponymous saint set a florid standard by arriving in Nice after her martyrdom

in Caesaria in the fourth century in a boat of flowers towed by a pair of angels (hence the Baie des Anges). Families and local corporations competed for spaces to decorate in the most elaborate manner of the times (from the early seventeenth century to well into the eighteenth). The baroque style was the showcase of the counter-reformation and of the power of the Catholic Church; in France it had an important secular connection, too, with highly ornate palaces and decorated sculptures and objects, but its religious expression was dominant in the far south of the country, which was of course in the Italian (Piedmontese and Ligurian) sphere of influence.

There are several fine examples, both in Nice (the hard-to-see Chapelle de la Miséricorde is one, the Chapelle de l'Annonciation, also known as the Chapelle Ste.-Rita, is another) and elsewhere. The Basilique St.-Michel-Archange in Menton is the largest baroque church in the region with an elaborate high altar and a vast organ casing; it also contains a splendid altarpiece by Puppo in a side chapel. In Roquebrune the pretty pink-and-orange Ste.-Marguerite contains works by the local seventeenth-century artist, Marc-Antoine Otto. In La Turbie the altar in Ste.-Dévote is made of seventeen different types of marble, while Sospel (where the Eglise St.-Michel contains also an altarpiece depicting the Virgin in a pretty landscape by François Brea) offers other fine examples of baroque architecture.

St. Rita, incidentally, has a fascinating history. A contemporary of Joan of Arc, Margarita Mancini was born in 1381 in Roccaporena in Umbria. In childhood she became well known because a swarm of bees flew into her mouth without doing her any harm. But more was to come, as the French journalist and author of a series of fascinating books about "secret" France, Jean-Pierre Cassely, explains:

> Married to please her parents, she lost her husband and two sons who died a violent death. She then devoted herself to what had always been her vocation: the love of Christ. Despite her widow's status preventing her from entering a convent, she was called by the Augustine sisterhood. Anything that was asked of her came to pass, her reputation grew steadily and she quickly became the advocate of lost causes and healer of smallpox. As she was praying in the church, a thorn from Christ's crown fell down and pierced her forehead. A pestilential smell later came

from the infected wound and she was isolated in a cell, where she died with her face restored to a supernatural beauty, while the perfume of roses spread around the convent. Her embalmed body remains perfectly preserved at Cascia, near her home village.

Requests for her help in the visitors' book in the Chapelle Ste.-Rita bear witness to a continuing belief in her efficacy in the most improbable causes.

The baroque Gésu Church (or St.-Jacques le Majeur) was built in 1612 by Jesuits who came to Nice to found a college on the site of the old salt storehouses. It houses some very fine Louis XIII panelling and frescoes painted by the nineteenth-century Nice-born artist Hercule Trachel. There are also 164 painted and 48 carved cherubs. The Chapelle de St.-Sépulcre on the south side of the Place Garibaldi belongs to the Blue Penitents and has a blue interior.

Up the Paillon valley behind Nice, the church of Ste.-Marguerite was "baroquized" between 1763 and 1779, but its origins can be traced back to the thirteenth century at the time of the construction of the château by the Counts of Anjou. Its treasury contains a wonderful gold and silver dragon, its head turned and looking up in apparent amazement as St. Marguerite herself rises calmly out of its back. The church's many altarpieces have suffered greatly over the centuries from a variety of sad fates, being cut down and squeezed into the baroque interior, split up, removed to the Musée de Nice, stolen (Ste.-Claude in 1992) or entirely repainted. Fortunately, enough panels are left to admire in the church, including part of an altarpiece depicting St. Peter and St. Paul and another of Ste. Marguerite herself, both attributed to Louis Brea.

One baroque gem in Monaco is the Chapel of the Visitation, rarely visited partly because it is now an integral part of the Lycee Albert I. It has kept its seventeenth-century decoration except for the paintings, which have been replaced by a series of old masters (including a Rubens) from a private collection.

THE NINETEENTH CENTURY

In 1821 an Anglican church was built in (Sardinian) Nice—on condition that it did not look like a church. It was the beginning of a prickly relationship between Protestant visitors and their Catholic hosts.

One of the most important Englishmen to follow Brougham to Cannes in the mid-nineteenth century was Thomas Robinson Woolfield. In 1847 he spotted the lack of a suitable place for English Protestants to hold their services, so he made a chapel in the grounds of his villa. The French minister invited to officiate was chased away by the local police. Woolfield persisted and won his case. Soon the market was expanding. In 1855 he petitioned—with the backing of the anglophile Inspector-General of Historic Monuments, Prosper Mérimée—to build a suitable church. This is how Christ Church, Cannes, was founded. A chapel for the Scottish Free Church followed not long after.

When the Italian border was rolled back in 1860 to the far side of Menton, and the railway began to make the same journey, the urge to build more Protestant places of worship for the many new visitors—with cemeteries to match—became stronger than ever. By 1890 Cannes had four English churches and one Scottish Presbyterian church. Menton saw its first Anglican church in 1863, on the east side of town; within ten years another, larger, one was built on the west side. Even St.-Raphael got one.

Patrick Howarth told a tale from the Anglican chapel in Monte Carlo, when a member of the British nobility "noticed that the number of the last hymn before the sermon was 32."

> He decided to miss the sermon, went to the roulette table, backed 32 and won £500. The story of his success spread, others began to adopt the same method, and instructions were issued that from then onward the number of the last hymn before the sermon was never to be below 37.

Queen Victoria's several visits to the Riviera prompted even more attendance at Anglican churches and chapels. Five years after the first royal visit to Menton, the queen went to Cannes in 1887 to see the Church of St. George, built in the memory of her dead son Leopold. When she travelled to Grasse four years later, the English church there, St. John's, had been finished just three weeks before: "very English looking", as Michael Nelson described it:

> half timbered with a steeple… The church, which contains three stained glass windows given by the Queen, is now called the Chapelle Anglaise or the Chapelle Victoria. In 1970 the owners gave it to the French Re-

formed Church, who had been using it since 1945, on condition that the Anglican Church would continue to hold services there.

The slow but steady decline in demand is not unusual along the Riviera. Queen Victoria herself attended her last church service in Hyères, in 1892, at All Saints in the suburb of Costebelle, between the old town and the sea, described by *The Times* correspondent as a "pretty little building of iron covered with lattice work, with a thatched roof"—though the church of that name today is a derelict, but distinctly neo-gothic, affair. From then on the queen preferred to worship in her various hotels. As for the architectural style of Anglican places of worship, it tended to reflect more a kind of cosy memory of the home country than the churches' French or Italianate surroundings.

The neo-Romanesque Monaco Cathedral was built in the last quarter of the nineteenth century, using white marble from nearly La Turbie. This showy building with a great deal of granite, marble, gold and mosaics throughout its interior, replaced a real Romanesque chapel. The tombs of the Princes of Monaco are lined up in the nave—as well as the tombs of Princess Grace and Prince Rainier, with a permanent supply of (plastic) flowers.

Grand Hotels and Casinos

As early as 1842, a mere eight years after Lord Brougham's arrival in Cannes, the Hôtel Beausite was opening for business. It was the precursor (though sadly no longer existing) of a spate of increasingly luxurious hotels, culminating in the belle époque's magnificent extravagances. The Beausite became famous for its seven hard tennis courts, which once featured a doubles match with Suzanne Lenglen, a certain Mrs. Beamish, the King of Sweden and the ex-King of Portugal. The hotels along the Croisette closest to the Film Festival venues now attract the most attention—the Carlton International still goes through the traditional motions of *grand luxe* (its twin domes were reputedly modelled on the contours of a famous *grande horizontale*, La Belle Otéro). The interwar hotels such as the Majestic and the (art deco) Martinez add to the glamour of the Croisette. An Englishman, Frederick Gordon, was responsible for the Metropole in Cannes, also with tennis courts and subtropical gardens, but in the 1930s it went into decline and was turned into a seminary. Gordon's Monte Carlo Metropole has lasted better but in rebuilt form.

The Grand Hôtel du Cap at Antibes (transformed from a convalescent home in 1863) and its Eden Roc extension down by the beach (Scott Fitzgerald's Hôtel des Etrangers) spread the reputation of the "paradise" hotel for the rich and famous. In fact, all along the Côte d'Azur the building boom was well under way in the second half of the 1900s. A thousand workers were employed to build the spectacular Hôtel Riviera in Beausoleil between 1898 and 1903. It sported a conservatory made with iron from the Eiffel factory, a wood-panelled library, a bridge room and chapel. Its guests included Diaghilev and Nijinsky, Ravel and Stravinsky, Colette and Sir Winston Churchill.

Nice's Hôtel des Anglais enhanced the Promenade des Anglais, but the most extravagant was yet to come. Opening just before the First World War, the Negresco, designed by the Dutch architect Edouard-Jean Niermans, was a culmination of the *belle époque* with its oval domed foyer, its interiors in styles from Louis XIV to Empire and its domed towers. The Excelsior Regina, whose 400 rooms dominated the Cimiez hills, opened in 1897, just in time to welcome Queen Victoria. The Château des Ollières is a modern conversion of a Beaux-Arts villa from the 1870s built by a Russian prince and set in an exotic park.

Meanwhile hotel building along the coast in Menton was reaching a peak at the end of the nineteenth century. The massive Riviera Palace (by Glena and Marsang) and Winter Palace (by Ceruti) are both now ghostly apartment blocks. Nearby, Cap Martin was filling up with royal villas, notably for the Empress Eugenie and the Austrian Empress (Sissi) in what Hugues de la Touche called "la valse des altesses". While waiting for their own mini-palaces to be finished, they would stay at the Grand Hôtel du Cap Martin, built on a massive scale by the fashionable Danish architect Hans-Georg Tersling and described by Stephen Liégeard as a "Leviathan de luxe et de confort" (now, once again, apartments). The anorexic Sissi would sneak out of the hotel at dawn to walk for a couple of hours around the Cap Martin. She would chat to local people she came across and was generous with hand-outs and tips; once she gave a gold coin to a man working on the road who turned out to be a security officer in disguise.

In Monaco hotel building was intimately linked with the establishment of Charles Garnier's lavishly decorated casino. The franchise holder, François Blanc, expanded fast into the hotel business, starting by completing the nearby Hôtel de Paris (designed by Gobineau de la Bretonnerie in 1862 and much remodelled later). Competition among hoteliers in the principality became furious at the turn of the century, with Charles Ritz trumping the opposition by installing the master chef, Auguste Escoffier, at the Grand Hôtel; a rapidly built royal suite was a further successful incentive to attract the Prince of Wales away from Cannes. The cliff-top Hôtel Hermitage was a confection of Jean Marquet (who invented marquetry). For a piece of modern spectacular, it is hard to beat the Hôtel Vista Palace, its three tiers cantilevered out into space high above the principality.

At the western end of the Riviera, in Hyères, the British were behind much of the hotel development towards the end of the nineteenth century, as with Mr. Waterblade's Hôtel du Parc, for instance, which now houses the town's *service culturel*. Another whopper, the Hôtel des Palmiers ("Fine Garden, Central heating throughout, Appartements with private Baths and Toilet"), has become a *lycée*. The "City of Palms" was the finest, indeed the only, grand winter resort in the Var *département*, that is to say west of Nice. But it suffered from the conservatism of its rich landowners who controlled its development. It was this powerful clique who refused to let the main Paris-Lyon-Mediterranean railway line run through their properties. So despite receiving a succession of grand and royal visitors, culminating in Queen Victoria, investment in grand hotels fit for royals migrated eastwards to Nice, Cannes and even Menton. By 1930 the art historian and dealer Daniel-Henry Kahnweiler was describing Hyères as a "sleepy town, with empty grand hotels, where seem to prowl the ghosts of English women dead from consumption." The Second World War destroyed much of what was still left after the economic setbacks. In fact, little remains now in Hyères of those palmy days of the *belle époque*.

The florid architecture of that era's hotels and casinos had absolutely no counterpart in public buildings along the Riviera. The big money was in private, not public, hands. It is tempting to stop right there, but recent decades have seen some fairly monstrous municipal projects, notably the theatre/art museum/Acropolis conference centre over the Paillon river in Nice and the bunker-like Palais des Festivals in Cannes. They have their practical uses but add little to the aesthetic of the Riviera.

The Modern Villa

Ever since Lord Brougham was halted at the Var in the dying (and cholera-infected) days of 1834 and elected to put up his Italian-style villa in Cannes, the Château Eleonor Louise, the habit began of rich foreigners making their architectural marks—some might say scars—along the Riviera coast. Prosper Mérimée, who chose to stay in Cannes at the same time as Brougham, decried the "cardboard castles... like paper flowers in the midst of a parterre". (But he had little time for the Mont St.-Michel in Normandy, either, so his tastes could be erratic.)

One building that is certainly not a blot on the landscape is the Villa Ephrussi de Rothschild, on a crest between Beaulieu and Cap Ferrat. Béatrice Ephrussi, whose father Alphonse de Rothschild was governor of the Bank of France and principal shareholder of the Paris-Lyons-Mediterranean railway, discovered Cap Ferrat in 1905, when she pinched a very desirable seventeen-acre plot from under the nose of the King of Belgium, who had the property next door and wanted to expand. What she did over the next seven years was to erect a kind of Renaissance fantasy palazzo and fill it with art treasures brought by the train-load to Beaulieu station. She designed not only the garden (see Chapter Ten) but also the multiple state rooms, galleries, bedrooms and boudoirs, and would appear dressed as Marie Antoinette (whose cherub-encrusted whist table she had also bought) so that her friends would be in no doubt about her sense of refinement.

The New Zealand poet Bill Manhire had an amusing take on the *Villa Ephrussi* in a poem of that name, where he imagined the scene in Cap Ferrat in 1911:

Beatrice Ephrussi waits at the station at Beaulieu,
while the ancient world arrives by train.

Stone and marble are laid out before her,
everything there on the platform.

Wife of a banker, daughter of a banker.

This, she says.
    And *this* and *this*.
Also those chairs.

Bare cheeks at the Villa Ephrussi

And that—what is it?—*pediment*,
perhaps it might go to the lapidary garden.

As for the rest, send them away.

Manhire goes on to comment sadly on the death of Béatrice's husband,
after which

She closed up the house forever.
It had been a love nest, you see.
Vast, but a love nest.

The poem ends with a description of couple after couple celebrating their
wedding at the villa, posing in front of its exotic sets—before the poet
himself returns to his "own few things in pots".

Curiously, the Riviera's other example of an extreme "theme villa" is
just nearby—in Beaulieu. This is the Villa Grecque Kérylos, a reproduction of a rich Athenian's house from the fifth century BC, with a huge
marble bathroom, and high windows inviting in the light. It was built in
the first decade of the last century by an archaeologist, Theodore Reinach,
as a sensual/intellectual playground for himself and his Hellenistic-minded
friends. It contains a mix of original and reproduction artefacts, furniture,
figurines, frescoes, and mosaics (including a tortuous labyrinth), while
carefully disguising anything modern.

One very different curiosity is the so-called Château de l'Anglais,
today a bizarrely crenellated pink concoction, which started in 1858 as
the brain child of an eccentric but energetic Englishman, Colonel Robert
Smith. He had cut his architectural teeth in India and Devonshire, then
spotted the promontory of Mont Boron, high above Nice's harbour, as a
perfect site for a Riviera palace of his own, even though it involved blast-
ing away tons of rock and importing more tons of topsoil. He rented a
whole floor of the Hôtel Royal below so he could see the building rise up
directly in his line of vision. Sadly, "Smith's Folly", with its smoking and
billiard rooms, boudoirs, dining rooms and theatre, attracted less praise
than criticism, notably from Stephen Liégeard. It also began to deteriorate
once it had become the property of the colonel's ne'er-do-well son. It was
abandoned, then bought by an Austro-Hungarian count, nearly but not

quite turned into a "Museum of Peace", added to, threatened with dem-
olition, remodelled, turned into a hotel, then into apartments. The result
is no longer a very pretty sight.

Another Englishman's folly can be found at the back of Eze. The
Château de l'Aiguetta was conceived at the end of the nineteenth century
by the nephew of the celebrated poet Alfred Lord Tennyson, who created
a kind of gothic fantasy but was forced to sell it after the First World War
when he lost a lot of money at the Monte Carlo Casino. It came into the
hands of a rich American and was then bought by Monaco's Société des
Bains de Mer. Plans to turn the grounds into a golf course were interrupted
by the Second World War. The German occupiers succeeded only in re-
ducing the property to an even more dilapidated ruin. There is a current
project to transform the fantastical castle (Disney apparently had the
château in mind when he created *Sleeping Beauty*) into yet another of Eze's
super-priced gastronomic heavens.

Cannes itself, once Brougham had set the pace, still contains an
array of luxurious villas, often pastiches of other styles from Indian
palaces to mock Tudor. All the same, Cannes had cachet. As the American journalist Mary Blume wrote: "Cannes was dignified and aristocratic; it was the Riviera equivalent of the Rue de Varenne in Paris,
Liégard said. Proust knew this when he gave Odette a cloudy past in
Nice or possibly Monte Carlo—Swann wasn't sure which—but not in
Cannes." Both Cannes and Nice introduced new suburbs named after
California, no effort being spared to identify their slice of the Riviera
with opulence and well-being.

In Hyères, a villa built in 1849 and bought by the novelist Edith
Wharton in 1927 now houses the Porquerolles park authority—this is the
Castel-Ste.-Claire. Its grounds still recall the time when its American owner
created her spectacular terraced garden. They contain the tomb of Olivier
Voutier, a naval ensign who found fame when he discovered the Venus de
Milo in Greece in 1820. Together with the grounds of the Villa Noailles,
on the other side of the hilltop, the property is now part of a beautifully
maintained public park, Le Jardin Provençal. Close by is the Chalet de la
Solitude, a faux-Swiss folly lived in by Robert Louis Stevenson, but it has
fallen off the maps supplied by the tourist office, and the memory of
Stevenson in modern Hyères has barely survived.

In 1922 the rich American couple, Gerald and Sara Murphy, rented the Château de la Garoupe on the Cap d'Antibes, then built their own Villa America by the Garoupe beach. Circling the Cap today it is hard to see, let alone penetrate into, the hundreds of grand houses and gardens that crown the cape, as they do on the Cap Ferrat, the Cap Martin and every other desirable promontory and bay along the Riviera. There is a strong aura of exclusion for those unlucky enough not to own, or be invited to, one of these luxurious properties.

American patrons and architects have had a significant influence on the Riviera, particularly since Barry Dierks teamed up with a rich English banker and attracted attention by redesigning Somerset Maugham's Villa Mauresque on Cap Ferrat in the mid-1920s. They have built or rebuilt over a hundred major properties, including the first house on the Riviera to have a swimming pool, the Château de l'Horizon in Golfe-Juan. The Bostonian architect Ogden Codman Jr. co-wrote *The Decoration of Houses* with the novelist Edith Wharton and went on to design the huge folly on the King of the Belgians' twenty-acre property in Villefranche, La Léopolda, which used to have a swimming pool over 250 feet long. This is the one which, revamped, was sold in 2008 by its owner, the widow of the Lebanese banker, Edmond Safra, to a Russian oligarch for a record sum.

Yet, architecturally, there are surprisingly few examples of exceptional quality, even in the modern world of the super-rich. The buildings may be enormous or exotic or weird, but to style purists they mostly lack real distinction or interest. Dominic Bradbury wrote recently in *Mediterranean Modern*:

> In some parts of the world, a "Mediterranean home" still stands as lazy estate-agency shorthand for mock pastiche—a neoclassical villa with loggias and balconies, coated in stucco and painted white. The breadth of contemporary architecture in the region suggests that there is so much more to Mediterranean style, and that the area continues to be a place of change, excitement, diversity, and innovation… it remains a region of countless possibilities and epic drama.

One of the realized "possibilities"—and also one of the finest examples of modernist architecture on the Côte d'Azur—is Eileen Gray's E-1027 villa on Cap Martin, between Menton and Monaco—a "crisp ocean liner moored on the hillside." Not only did the architect Le Corbusier stay here, but he built himself nearby a simple cabin and an even more basic work studio (also a very simple restaurant). What unites the grand and the simple is the setting among the rocks and pines, with a view over the calm blue sea.

Almost on the Italian border, just up from the Baie de Garavan, is a 1920s Spanish fantasy, the Villa Fontana Rosa, the haven conceived by the writer and politician, Vicente Blasco Ibañez (1867-1928). Now being recovered from dilapidation, it features a rotunda dedicated to Cervantes entered by a monumental staircase, statues of the writer's favourite artists: Dickens, Tolstoy, Goethe, Beethoven and many others. Ceramic tiles tell an eccentric version of the story of Don Quixote.

What make the news today are the properties of the new rich, the stars of our celebrity culture. The weekly French magazine *Le Point* featured in its edition of 31 July 2008 the "maisons des stars". They have in common their red tiled roofs (though Roman Abramovich's Château de la Croë is neoclassical and all white), green lawns and cypresses and brilliant blue swimming pools. Sometimes they build their own. More often they massively expand existing villas. The rock stars are equally divided between the sea (Sir Elton John, Bono—squeezed between the railway line at the rocky shore in Eze-Bord-de-Mer—and Tina Turner) and the hills (Rod Stewart and Bill Wyman). The fashion entrepreneurs and designers (Pierre Cardin, Domenico Dolce and Stefano Gabbana) favour the seaside. Microsoft's founder Paul Allen is among the many big money folk who enjoy the walled tranquillity of properties on St.-Jean-Cap-Ferrat. But sadly none of these large and opulent buildings have much architectural or aesthetic interest.

THE TWENTIETH CENTURY

In 1900 the Dowager Empress of Russia sacrificed her Villa Bermond in the heart of Nice's Russian quarter to make way for an Orthodox cathedral that would both serve the Russian community (which had grown too big for the church in the rue Longchamp) and commemorate the tsarevich, who had died of tuberculosis in the city thirty-five years earlier. No expense was spared. It was a massive and complex project, involving bringing bricks from England and Germany, granite and glazed tiles as well as gold crosses from Italy, marble from La Turbie, and mosaics and icons (many donated by exiles) from Russia. The architect, Preobrazhensky, modelled it on the church of Yaroslav, near Moscow. Lurking greyly in the far north-west corner of the park in which the cathedral is set is a Byzantine-style chapel dedicated to the unfortunate consumptive Tsarevich Nikolai, in sad contrast to the highly-coloured, onion-domed cathedral itself.

This still looks magnificent—it is in fact the largest Russian religious building outside the Slavic countries. Today, after some years of relative neglect, it has become a focus for the new breed of post-communist Russians.

At the other end of the size scale are a number of small chapels on the Riviera associated with twentieth-century artists. The most celebrated is the Chapelle du Rosaire in Vence designed by Matisse. At the end of 1947, a young and lowly Dominican monk with no connections with the art world and no knowledge of Henri Matisse became obsessed with the idea of a chapel whose stained glass would be designed by the master. It struck a chord with the painter, who yearned in old age to design something monumental. Their combined enthusiasm eventually won over sceptical church authorities, and Matisse charged ahead. "Of course we're spending money like millionaires," he wrote to the young Dominican monk, Brother Louis-Bertrand Rayssiguier, "even though we're rich only in dreams." Matisse's biographer, Hilary Spurling, described the effect this project was having:

> The news that Matisse was about to build a chapel, and could be seen going about town with a priest in tow, caused ribald disbelief in Paris at a time when it was increasingly accepted by the artistic and intellectual community that the best hope for the future, not just of France but of humanity itself, lay with the Communist Party. Picasso came round to inspect the model at the boulevard Montparnasse, and recommended building a fruit-and-vegetable market instead, in a scene reported with gusto by Matisse, who was proud of snapping back that his greens were greener and his oranges more orange than any actual fruit. Family legend preserved an altogether pithier version of this celebrated exchange: "Why not a brothel, Matisse?" "Because nobody asked me, Picasso."

Matisse used his cut-out paper technique to create the stained glass designs, driving himself to exhaustion. The chapel was to be little more than a rectangular box to display the coloured light through seventeen long windows, like—Matisse said—a "theatre décor… characterless in itself". The final design differed in significant respects from the first models made four years before the completion. The original windows were more kaleidoscopic, with many more colours as well as black and white squares. The end result was much simpler, with olive leaf shapes in mostly blue and yellow. On the right wall as you enter the chapel are white tiles with the outline figures of St. Dominic and a Virgin and Child. On the back wall—for me, much less successful—are the scrawled outlines of figures in the fourteen stations of the cross, naïve to the point of childishness. Matisse designed every detail in the chapel, from the altar (at a diagonal, facing due east) to the candlesticks in the form of anemones, the chandeliers and even the single priest's chair.

The project was a race against his own mortality. Matisse became what in some ways he essentially was, a monk, sacrificing himself for the higher calling of art. He kept making changes, driving builders, glaziers and roofers to distraction. His designs appalled conservative elements in the Church. The pretty young nun Sister Jacques-Marie who was in charge of the chapel along with Rayssiguier, came under enormous strain. No-one involved was given a moment of time off by an intransigent master. "It was slavery," complained one art student who had been roped into the project.

At the end of 1949 the first stone of the chapel was laid, though Matisse was too frail to attend. It took another year before the windows were finally installed. His reaction to it was a kind of sublime detachment. "Imagine a simple postman confronted with his son, who has become a general," he wrote to an old friend. The nuns were converted. Within a year the entire congregation, led by their Mother Superior, were defending its "consoling and contemplative calm".

At the far, western, end of the Riviera, in the remote and dusty hills above Fréjus full of cypresses, pines, oak and olive trees, Jean Cocteau designed his own, very distinctive chapel. It was conceived as part of the reconstruction of the region around Fréjus after the terrible destruction caused by the accidental collapse of the nearby Malpasset Dam in December 1959. At his death in 1963 Notre-Dame-de-Jérusalem was still not finished. Originally planned as part of an "Artists' Colony", an "ideal city", it is a low octagonal building surrounded by a green sandstone gallery. Cocteau decorated it with frescoes in his characteristic style. In the Last Supper over the central door he included portraits of himself as well as the actor Jean Marais (his friend and lover). The crusaders' "cross potent" is everywhere. Overhead in the dome is an oculus, a round hole which Cocteau designed to be permanently open, so that rainwater would sanctify the chapel, even if a transparent glass window was installed to protect the frescoes. The chapel seems to contain the very essence of Cocteau: mystical, whimsical, symbolic as well as naturalistic—and very beautiful. Every 15 September a service is held there.

A more modest creation of Cocteau's is the Chapelle St.-Pierre (the Fisherman's Chapel) in Villefranche-sur-Mer, just opposite the scene of some of his spectacularly debauched pleasures, the Hôtel Welcome. The chapel had fallen into disrepair and was being used to store fishermen's nets when Cocteau saw it and determined to make it his own. He had to overcome some fierce local opposition. In 1957 he was permitted (partly after promising to donate any receipts from entrance fees and postcards to the Fishermen's Benevolent Fund) to decorate its interior. He went to work at once, covering the walls with scenes of the life of St. Peter and local characters, like Matisse designing and decorating every part of it, including the altar, the candelabra and the door. It was again a labour of love. According to Claude Arnaud:

Vence – the Chapelle du Rosaire entirely designed by Matisse

Carried away by his work he even spent days on unstable scaffolding, watched by fishermen and a few curious bystanders. Dressed in a simple workman's overall with a tight scarf that made the blood beat in his temples, he huddled in the egg of the present moment... The child was taking control of a man undermined by death. Soaking up the walls that he was covering with paintings, he became one with his chapel, combining his own substance with the colour, his taut yet blissful face camouflaged with plaster, like that of a happy child in a Provençal crèche.

Visiting Picasso's Musée National in a deconsecrated chapel in Vallauris is a much more violent experience. *Scenes of War and Peace*, painted at a feverish pace on plywood in 1952, assaults the senses. Silhouetted figures hurl weapons, emaciated horses drag a cart over blood-red earth, swords drip with blood, while on the opposite wall serene blue and white figures picnic and work tranquilly under a tree and a huge sun. The dove of peace presides over the altar at the far end of what, inside, feels rather like a Nissan hut. The English critic Ian Nairn was profoundly unimpressed:

> Not Guernica, which was real, but platitudes recollected in the tranquillity that comes from well-heeled notoriety. The customers deserve it, the Riviera deserves it. Picasso might look back on his beginnings and think of the total honesty of Toulouse-Lautrec. He should worry? We all should.

There are also several minor curiosities of twentieth-century religious buildings along the Riviera. Near Antibes, for instance, the illustrator specializing in fey lovers, Raymond Peynet, created a kind of chapel next to the museum that houses his drawings and other works. Between La Turbie and Peille the very simple modern chapel of Saint-Martin-de-Peille, built by Guzzi, boasts stained-plastic windows, while the altar is made from the trunk of a huge olive tree.

SYNAGOGUES, MOSQUES AND PAGODAS

Those coming to the French Riviera with a particular interest in its Jewish culture and life are usually pointed to the villas and art works of those who happened to be Jewish: Beatrice Rothschild's Villa Ephrussi, Theodore Reinach's Villa Kérylos, the Chagall Museum or the Robert Rauschenbergs and Yves Kleins in Nice's Museum of Contemporary Art. Evidence of Jewish religious life is less spectacular. The synagogue in Nice is a modest reminder of a history soured by antisemitism, sometimes passive and occasionally active, in this corner of southern France (see Chapter Two).

Jews had little to be optimistic about in those dark days. Synagogues along the Riviera were either ransacked or closed or both, many never to re-open. There are now three in Nice, one orthodox, one Lubavitch and one "Conservative", plus a Lubavitch synagogue in Cannes.

As for mosques, there are very few in France—in fact there are only five in the whole country specifically built as mosques—although there is a programme to build more. The single one on the Riviera is among the strangest buildings to be seen there. The Missiri mosque is in a suburb of Fréjus, suitably on the rue des Combattants-d'Afrique-du-Nord, an initiative of Senegalese infantrymen stationed in Fréjus in 1930. It is a smaller copy of the Missiri mosque in Djenné, in Mali. Today the dark red building sits empty, open to the sky, inside an iron fence. It looks neglected. Bits of concrete hang off it like shreds of torn clothing. A couple of concrete ant-hills do little to enhance the "African effect".

The impetus for its construction was in part the erection of a Buddhist pagoda, in another part of Fréjus, by Vietnamese soldiers during the First World War. The Hông Hiên pagoda was transformed and enlarged in 1972. Indochinese soldiers and civilians who died in the service of France are now buried here, close to the biggest (concrete) statue of Buddha in Europe.

In Context

Religious art on the Riviera has had to live in the spectacularly colourful shadow of its secular counterparts, especially in the last century and a half. But this does not imply that the Catholic Church has not been favoured and supported in this part of southern France. The penitents are still active. There are even today stories of charismatic prayer groups, one of which in Cannes reported violently shaking walls and visions of Christ and the Virgin Mary in St. Paul's Catholic Church in Cannes; the Bishop of Nice's investigators are apparently taking this seriously. Some people also give some credence to stories of Christ and Mary Magdalene (and/or their son) having a family holiday on the Riviera, thereby presumably sanctifying the ultimate hedonism for all time. But there is a history of serious scholarship too, notably among the monks of the Iles de Lérins.

As for architecture, there is nothing on the Riviera to match the great cathedrals and churches in either the rest of France or in Italy. But there are fine baroque churches and a smattering of modern chapels that are both individual and beautiful—and above all suited to the colours, shapes and natural rhythms of the Côte d'Azur.

Chapter Ten
EDEN TAMED
THE ART OF CULTIVATION

One of the sights that most astonished St.-Tropez locals—and they have had many shocks over the years—was the green grass lawn grown by the English owners of a beachfront villa. A version of Bexhill on Tahiti Beach is not, however, an unnatural progression from the well-tended lawns of Cannes or Menton introduced by Brougham and his successors.

The art of cultivating gardens kept parallel with the development of houses and villas from the earliest years. The agent responsible for selling to the British many properties in and around Cannes during its rapid mid-nineteenth-century expansion was John Taylor, who had in fact originally been a gardener. Dr. Bennet, who introduced the British to Menton, created a flourishing garden of his own; Queen Victoria sat in its fern grotto. Some of the greatest *belle époque* villas and palaces had gardens to match—tons of imported topsoil and potted plants by the hundred thousand showing off the extravagant wealth of the owners.

The Château de la Garoupe on Cap d'Antibes employed twenty-five gardeners on its 100 acres. Alice de Rothschild's Villa Victoria near Grasse—"perhaps the most ostentatious garden ever seen," according to Vivian Russell in *Gardens of the Riviera*—covered 335 acres and demanded the services of no fewer than fifty full-time gardeners.

> It contained an enormous collection of ornamental plants: palms twenty metres high, Yucca filifera ten metres high, bamboos with thick trunks, a "debauchery" of agaves and flaming aloes… Alice advised her gardeners to plant yellow and white between clashing colours—a spectacle that would make even a municipal gardener blush, but with bedding and borders overflowing with 55,000 daisies, 25,000 stocks and 5,000 myosotis, perhaps no one would notice.

Everyone called the imperious owner *La Baronne*. She made all her

Water lilies at the Serre de la Madone

workers wear special uniforms: yellow berets for apprentices, red for workers, navy blue for shift supervisors, royal blue for foremen. When she appeared, they all had to make themselves invisible.

The grand scale of the *belle époque* is evoked by Louisa Jones:

> In pursuit of the ideal décor, many joined Beatrice de Rothschild in defying "the stupid laws of nature and common sense". When Lord Brougham wanted luxurious greenswards around his new villa near Cannes, he saw no difficulty in importing turf from England, by boat, every year… Russian nobleman Prince Cherkassky enjoyed variety in the flower beds of his park at La Californie, and every night his forty-eight gardeners were charged with replacing thousands of bedding plants. In this manner, he could be surprised by fresh color upon wakening each morning.

Many of these great Riviera gardens have been built over now, either entirely or in part. The problem for all the region's gardeners, past and present, is a lack of space. There are no empty fields in which to plant a new garden, only existing plots and terraces to re-imagine and remake. Yet these are still enough to ensure that garden design remains a flourishing business on the Côte d'Azur.

Untamed Beauty

The natural beauty of the Riviera is far from dependent upon its taming—by the English or others. "The Riviera! How the dweller in lands of mist and fog longs for it! How joyfully he greets it," gushed Messrs Devoluy and Borel in their account published by the Medici Society in 1924. The olive, lemon and orange groves, the vineyards, the figs and the palms seemed to them, as to most visitors from colder lands, part of an immemorial harmony.

But all these were the result of intervention by people who lived and settled on the land. Whether the raw landscape of the Riviera could be said to have an "inherent" beauty is more of a moot point. Early travellers had different opinions. Their reactions on their first sight of the cork-oak forests and pine-clad cliffs varied from the ecstatic to the sceptical. Catherine de Medicis was anxious to build a "royal house surrounded by gardens" near Hyères in the sixteenth century, so captivated was she by the natural scenery. But in September 1789 Arthur Young, the leading agricultural writer of his time and a noted farming innovator, had a different reaction. He was making his way with some difficulty up the coast from Marseille. When he reached Hyères, he recalled the positive impression it had made on Elizabeth, Lady Craven, but immediately he decided that she had sent him on a "wild-goose chase".

> One would think this country from her's and many other descriptions, was all a garden; but it has been praised much beyond its merit. The vale is every where richly cultivated and planted with olives and vines, with a mixture of some mulberries, figs, and other fruit trees. The hills are either rocks, or spread with a poor vegetation of evergreens, pines, lenticus, &c. The vale, though scattered with white *bastides*, which animate the scene, yet betrays that poverty in the robe of nature, which always offends the eye where olives and fruits form the principal cloathing. Every view is meagre, on comparison with the rich foliage of our northern forests. The only singular features are the orange and lemon trees; they here thrive in the open air, are of a great size, and render every garden interesting to eyes that travel to the south; but last winter's frost has shorn them of their glory.

Northerners in general were suspicious, even frightened, of the ruggedness of parts of the south. The hills of Esterel were notoriously viewed with terror from classical times. Aubin-Louis Millin, a northern French traveller in the early nineteenth century, saw the Esterel simply as a refuge for all the criminals who infested the area from Marseille to the Var.

> In general you can put no trust in the peasants of these parts. If you ask them the way, either they give no answer or they purposely misdirect you. Take good care that nothing is wrong with your carriage or harness, for they will not help you… They yell like tigers, they behave like madmen if anything puts them out.

The "porphyry wall" of the Esterel hills was widely dismissed as untameable country. It was the domesticated landscape that impressed travellers. Tobias Smollett had much the same reaction in Nice, a generation earlier, as his fellow countryman, Arthur Young, was to have.

> The plain presents nothing but gardens, full of green trees, loaded with oranges, lemons, citrons, and bergamots, which make a delightful appearance. If you examine them more nearly, you will find plantations of green pease ready to gather; all sorts of sallading, and pot-herbs, in perfection; and plats of roses, carnations, ranunculas, anemonies, and daffodils, blowing in full glory with such beauty, vigour, and perfume, as no flower in England ever exhibited.

Smollett described the thriving trade in carnations, which were sent in winter to Turin and Paris: "nay, sometimes as far as London, by the post". He went on:

> They are packed up in a wooden box, without any sort of preparation, one pressed upon another; the person who receives them, cuts off a little bit of the stalk, and steeps them for two hours in vinegar and water, when they recover their full bloom and beauty. Then he places them in water-bottles, in an apartment where they are screened from the severities of the weather; and they will continue fresh and unfaded the best part of a month.

This account reinforces a picture of steady progress in cultivating the less than hospitable terrain. The Riviera climate favours a mix of the subtropical and the temperate. Citrus groves flourish alongside cacti, vines with roses, oak with eucalyptus. John Ruskin was entranced by the journey from Fréjus to Nice, which he made in the spring of 1845.

> All the meadows about Fréjus were white with large arums, with golden centres, mixed with a lovely flower like a dog rose, but growing on a low shrub, with a scent of the orange—I think it must be a sort of gem cistus—and another & larger variety of it of a rich purple was growing all through the copses, making them look like gardens of rhododendron. Then the laurustinus, full of bloom, and the most exquisite smell, arbutus (but not now in flower), & hundreds more—and above all, *cork* trees in quantities… Down we came to Cagnes, and so all along the blue bay of Antibes—just before entering Nice we came on the first orchard

full of orange trees in full fruitage, to George's entire electrification. I jumped up as soon as I saw them—he was half asleep when I call to him, but woke up. I only wish you had seen the mouth he made, worth half a pantomime.

George was Ruskin's manservant, copyist and, later, daguerrotypist. His real name was John Hobbs, but he was called George so as not to confuse him with his master. Such, remarks Robert Hewison, Ruskin's biographer, is the power of money.

Charles Lenthéric, writing in the 1870s, cited an orange tree near Hyères "laden with 14,000 oranges, and of such a size that Charles IX and his brother the Duc d'Anjou, could scarcely surround it with their arms." He waxed lyrical about the Esterel "brilliant with its metallic lustre—a vegetation perhaps richer, certainly more varied, than any other in Europe." No terrors for him here. But he did also strike a cautionary note.

To tell the truth, Hyères is not blessed with eternal spring, neither is it the classic land of the orange, although the orange does grow there in the open fields. We are bound to own, indeed, that violent winds have on many occasions destroyed a great part of the plantations. Bachaumont and Chapelle must doubtless either have allowed their poetic fancy to run away with them, or have visited only some specially fortunate gardens, exceptionally sheltered in some of the little valleys of Coste-belle and Fenouillet, when they wrote in the *Voyage* at the end of the last century:—

On est contraint de chercher l'ombre
Des orangers, qu'en mille endroits
On y voit, sans rang et sans nombre,
Former des forêts et des bois.
Là, jamais les plus grands hivers
N'ont pu leur déclarer la guerre
Cet heureux coin de l'univers
Les a toujours beaux, toujours verts,
Toujours fleuris en pleine terre.

[You are obliged to find shade under the orange trees, which can be seen in a thousand places, without order or number, forming forests and woods. There the worst of winters could not declare war on them. In this happy corner of the universe they are always beautiful, always green, always blossoming in the open fields.]

Lenthéric was particularly taken by both the natural and the artificial beauty of the area around la Napoule.

The country looks like an immense hot-house filled with flowers in full bloom; on the little hills are olive woods and groups of umbrella pines, and in the plan long rows of cypress; by the side of the streamlets are oleanders crowded as close together as willows in an osiery; fields of orange and lemon trees are there, and at intervals one sees the trees characteristic of a tropical flora—the palm, the cactus, and the aloe shoot up their graceful stems into the blue sky, as they spread their think foliage in the hot sun. We cannot say that we are still in Provence; it is more lovely than Italy; one might fancy oneself in the East.

The particular microclimate of Menton has not only favoured the cultivation of lemons, but has also attracted gardeners, British gardeners in particular, ever since the town earned its reputation as the warmest, and healthiest, winter resort in Europe. Katherine Mansfield, whose lungs derived some temporary benefit from living in Menton, was a keen lover of gardens, especially the garden of the Villa Flora where she stayed.

It is raining here, but such lovely rain! The drops hang on the rose bushes and on every tip of the palm fronds. Little birds sing; the sea sounds solemn and full and silver gulls fly over. I can smell the earth and I can feel how the violets are growing and all the small things down there under my window. It is exquisite… And then the annuals that, sown in January and February, are flowering in Avrilo—there are at least 24 kinds and if you are clever you can grow them so that one kind marches up with banners after the other until the chrysanthemum is there. I think I shall become a very violent gardener. I shall have shelves of tomes and walk about the house whispering the names of flowers.

On the Riviera there are many kinds of garden and many microclimates. The transition as you go inland was well summed up by the author of *Riviera Nature Notes* at the start of the twentieth century:

> The Olive is gradually replaced by the Chestnut: pass up higher still through the pleasant Chestnut groves of Bollena, Valdebore, and St Martin Vesubia, and you reach the Alpine region where the Chestnut gives way to the pine, the larch, and the birch.

The writer, who hid behind the initials "C. C.", enthused about the "aromatic fragrance" that makes one so aware of being on the Riviera.

> Firstly, there is that little Crucifer, the honey-scented *Alyssum mariti-mum* which sprinkles the stony ground, distilling sweetness from its myriad small white flower. Then Thyme and Mint and other Labiates about, shedding, as we walk over them, a stronger and more penetrating perfume. Here and there the neighbouring Orange grove sends a waft of rich scented air to mingle with the breath of humbler plants. And when we come upon a bit of broken ground, we are wrapped in the resinous exhalations of the Aleppo pine.

George Edward Comerford Casey, as we now know "C. C." to be, noted that Napoleon was particularly fond of the white-flowered shrub, *Cistus monspeliensis*. What with the olives, myrtles, rosemaries, jasmines, lavenders and even scented ferns, the Riviera air is indeed still charged with enough perfume to overcome the most revolting pollutants.

The *Riviera Nature Notes* were dedicated to, and originally published by, Sir Thomas Hanbury. No account of Riviera gardens could omit his extraordinary achievement on the slopes of the cliffside village of Mortola Inferiore—even if the Hanbury Gardens are just on the Italian side of the border.

The Hanbury Gardens

In 1511, when Niccolò Machiavelli stayed at the Palazzo Orengo, he would have had much the same view out to sea as today, looking straight out at Corsica from the rocky promontory of Capo Mortola, but he would scarcely have imagined the botanical riches to be introduced into this rugged place three and a half centuries later. In 1867 Sir Thomas Hanbury, who had made a fortune trading silk and tea from Shanghai, joined with his brother, Daniel, a chemist specializing in plant-based drugs, in buying the dilapidated *palazzo* and its surrounding olive terraces.

The results were spectacular. Already by 1893 the director of Kew Gardens, Sir Joseph Hooker, referred to La Mortola as an "unrivalled collection". When Thomas died in 1907, his son Cecil and daughter-in-law Dorothy developed the garden. Inevitably there was a period of neglect during the years of conflict in the 1914-18 war, but work soon got under way again, opening up paths, creating vistas and fountains (inspired partly by the Villa Maryland on Cap Ferrat). It is now under the control of Genoa University.

The Hanbury Botanical Gardens cover almost 45 acres, some of which is wild. The cultivated areas that plunge down towards the sea are divided into zones and types of plants: tropical, sub-tropical, Mediterranean, South African, Australian—a richly varied collection that also serves the cause of botanical studies. Its visitors have included Queen Victoria, Winston Churchill (who was trundled up and down the slopes in a special chair made for his royal predecessor) and Edward Lear. In its time it was an important centre for research and acclimatization. Its principles and practices have been followed in gardens all along the Riviera and as far away as Hidcote Manor in Gloucestershire.

HISTORICAL GARDENS

Across the road from the ruins of the five thousand-seat Roman arena is the Cimiez Convent (Monastère de Cimiez—see also Chapter Eight). Matisse and Dufy are both buried in its cemetery. The garden extends southwards from the convent with views out over the Baie des Anges. This is the oldest garden on the Riviera, laid out in formal squares and rectangles in the middle of the sixteenth century. It has kept its original design.

From that time on the custom of building substantial gardens next to houses both big and small became firmly established, turning all the cultivable parts of the Riviera green. Orange trees became more and more popular. They were probably first introduced by Genoese emigrants to Biot in the 1500s, though they were known as "Portuguese" oranges in Hyères around the same time, so might also have come from the west. The climate for the most part favoured the cultivation of plants that needed heat to thrive, but the mistral was a perennial handicap, especially in the western end of the Riviera. This ferocious wind sweeps down the Rhône valley and turns eastwards. By the time it reaches Nice it has weakened and it never penetrates as far as Menton. A more unpredictable rogue intruder is frost. Over the centuries there have been brief but devastating frosts, even in the protected Menton area. Edith Wharton's garden in Hyères was ruined almost as soon as she had installed it by a flash frost, and she had to start virtually all over again.

The Villa Fragonard in Grasse was one of the finest examples of a seventeenth-century mansion with an extended walled garden, built just outside the town walls. The Villa d'Andon near Grasse has an eighteenth-century garden with traditional layout and an intact original irrigation system—though it has been recently modernized. In December 1782 the writer Antoine Leonard Thomas described the countryside around Nice in a letter to a friend: "Everywhere the blend of untouched and cultivated Nature, hills which are gardens and others that bristle with rocks, pine and cypress, and in the far distance, the snow-covered peaks of the Alps." By the start of the nineteenth century the whole Riviera was becoming almost obsessed with gardens as word spread that there was a piece of paradise just waiting to receive the finest examples of the flora that the world had to offer.

The tradition of royal and municipal patronage for public gardens on the French Riviera, especially those with an interest in botanical research, goes back over a couple of hundred years. In 1804 the Empress Joséphine donated to the city of Nice a collection of exotic plants that would not flourish out of doors in her château, Malmaison, near Paris. Prince Albert I of Monaco founded the Exotic Gardens in 1897—gardens now visited yearly by over half a million people. Another garden specializing in succulents and cacti, up on the summit of Eze, is a smaller version of that in Monaco. But most of the finest collectors' gardens along the Riviera have started as private initiatives.

The Hanbury Gardens are a magnificent example of what started as a site for an international collector, conceived as much in the interests of botanical science as aesthetic pleasure, but which evolved into a combination of research and harmonious design; in other words a combination of a classic "collector's garden" and a splendid "show garden". In the case of all the gardens featured in the final section of this chapter, there is inevitably

Hanbury Gardens and the Palazzo Orengo

an element of both. It is helpful to the visitor nevertheless to have an idea what the priorities are; which was, or is, the primary purpose of the garden.

COLLECTORS' GARDENS

The Exotic Botanical Garden in Menton, on the Garavan bay just beside the Parc de Pian with its thousand-year-old olives, is one of at least eight major extant gardens within the Menton boundaries. Val Rahmeh, as it is also called, is another beneficiary of the mild microclimate of this part of the coast. Again it was an Englishman who started it off. Lord (Sir Percy) Radcliffe, an army general and former Governor of Malta, bought and then developed the property in the 1920s. After the general's death in 1934, his second wife, Lady Florence Alice (née Coromandel Tagg), changed the name to that of her dead husband's first partner, the even more exotically named Rahmeh Theodora Swinburne.

The more serious botanical development, however, was the work of Miss (May) Campbell, who bought the property in 1957. The cat-loving daughter of the English colony's favourite doctor, she was known as the "Dame aux daturas"—Datura being a genus of (often poisonous or narcotic) plants with trumpet-like flowers. The garden has a wonderful collection of citrus fruits (from the Nagami kumquat to the Buddha's hand citron to the citrumelo and the Thornless Thai lime) as well as avocados, passion flowers and specimens from Africa, Asia, America and Oceania. One of the most interesting of the 1,400 plants at Val Rahmeh is the rare *Sophora toromiro*, a native of Easter Island and now thought to be extinct in the wild; in 1955 the explorer Thor Heyerdahl collected seeds from the last one standing and brought them to Europe. The garden was sold to the French state in 1966 and opened to the public by the National Museum of Natural History.

From 1912 to the present day the English gardening tradition in this part of the Riviera has continued under the guidance of members of the Waterfield family. The family's own garden, Le Clos du Peyronnet, is condensed into a single, steeply sloping, densely planted couple of acres. The basic plan was created in the 1950s: pergolas, urns, colonnades and patios, shrub groves, cascading pools and blossoms, rare and everyday species, an orchard of avocados, guavas, citrus and loquats, twisting wisterias, cypresses joined at the top to form "green smoke rings". This is one of the world's most romantic gardens.

Major Lawrence "Johnnie" Johnston, an American born in Paris but naturalized British, was the owner of Hidcote Manor in Gloucestershire. An intrepid plant hunter, despite being gassed in the First World War, he began to spend his winters on the Riviera, visiting his mother who lived in a rather superior nursing home in Menton on the route up to the hill village of Gorbio. From 1924, and for the next ten years, Johnston started buying properties next door. The finest of these was the Serre de la Madone, to which he added two wings, an orangery, statues, two large rectangular pools and an extensive garden to show off his shrubs, bulbs and flowers. He brought back a large collection of plants from expeditions to South Africa, East Africa and China. An article in the *Gazette illustrée des amateurs de jardins*, a prestigious French gardening magazine, described him in 1936: "He comes to greet you in corduroys straight from his terraces, with dirt on his hands like a gardener, or like a hunter with his dogs behind him. Yes, he is a hunter, a skilled plant hunter, but he gives life to plants instead of taking animals' lives."

As a retired major (from the First World War), Johnston was evacuated along with most French and foreign inhabitants of Menton in May 1940. The Serre de la Madone actually ran along the new frontier during the Italian annexation of Menton from 1940 to 1944, and it was greatly damaged during this time. A seventeen-year-old Belgian volunteer, Yves Monceau de Bergandal, arrived in an ambulance provided by the Anglo-American Ambulance Society based in Cannes, to transport the celebrated ex-officer to the Spanish border. De Bergandal recalled picking Johnston up on the roadside dressed in knickerbockers and accompanied by twelve dachshunds, three parrots and two cranes. The entire menagerie climbed in, loose. They made their journey successfully to Spain and freedom, leaving dogs and assorted birds with a pair of old ladies in Aix on the way.

The Menton property and garden have recently been restored to their former glory by an Anglo-French group of enthusiasts, working in a unique partnership with the Conservatoire du Littoral and the French state.

The Villa Roquebrune at Cap Martin, where the Empress Eugénie was a frequent guest, is the creation of Norah Warre (1880-1979), who cultivated her precipitous five acres for all of 75 years, devoted to her vast profusion of rare and familiar plants. The original plot was then subdivided and maintained with varying success by a variety of new owners, although it is back in one pair of hands now. Near Biot is another garden with British connections. La Chèvre d'Or was created by Pierre and Nicole Champin, but one of their advisers was the British botanist and horticulturalist Basil Leng, who was involved in a whole roll-call of great gardens along the Riviera—including the Serre de la Madone, the Villa les Cèdres on Cap Ferrat, and the Villa la Léonina in Beaulieu. Leng's own garden called La Ferme des Orangers, was on Cap d'Antibes. It was here, in May 1939, that the English apple specialist and gardening writer Edward Bunyard was invited to stay, with the enticement that "the roses are out and the orange blossom too". Bunyard remembered the occasion in an article he wrote just before he died.

> Who could resist such an invitation?—and I knew that the nightingales would also be singing!... At Antibes, the nightingales were already at work and, better still, my host had an excellent Italian cook, long resident in France, who combined the best of both cuisines. Next morning came marmalade made from oranges grown on the estate, my first experience of such a home-grown product. It was curiously Oxfordian in flavour, but that cannot have been due to the accent of my host.

Not all Riviera gardeners have been so English. Vicomte Charles de Noailles (1891-1981) was a serious collector, of plants as well as works of art. In 1947 he developed a spectacular garden near Vence. He had already created an avant-garde home and garden in Hyères and commissioned the first ever "cubist" garden there from Gabriel Guevrekian after the designer's success at the 1925 Paris Exhibition. In Vence de Noailles became more expansive and more traditional. As president of the French Society of Amateur Gardeners he was to exercise influence over a whole generation of post-war Riviera designers and collectors.

Another couple of world-class Riviera gardens which have done as much for botanical science as for aesthetic pleasure are Les Cèdres, the Marnier/Lapostolle research garden above Villefranche (funded by the royalties of Grand Marnier and re-landscaped by Harold Peto) and the botanical garden and arboretum of the Villa Thuret on Cap d'Antibes (named after a nineteenth-century specialist in seaweed, Gustave Thuret).

Jean-Baptiste Alphonse Karr was a gardener and horticulturalist with a difference. He started by writing popular novels with a gothic flavour (*Sous les Tilleuls* ends with the hero kissing his lover's decaying corpse) and in 1839 became editor of *Le Figaro* and proprietor of a satirical monthly journal (see Chapter Seven). When in 1855 he went to live in Nice he established, and then dominated, the market in cut flowers on the French Riviera.

Ever the optimist (one of Karr's quotes is, "You complain that roses have thorns—I'm just happy thorns have roses"), he put more and more of his energies into floriculture. There is a bamboo (*Bambusa multiplex* Alphonse Karr) and a pear named after him—as well as a street in Nice and a monument in St.-Raphael, where he died.

The Domaine du Rayol is probably the finest example on the French Riviera coast of a private garden—or estate—that has become a public asset. In 1910 a Parisian businessman, Alfred Courmes, and his young wife built themselves an Art Nouveau villa on fifty acres of land on the rocky coast between the St.-Tropez peninsula and Le Lavandou. Twenty-four years later, having moved to a smaller house at the other end of the property, he drowned himself in the sea—another victim of the alluring Monte Carlo Casino. In 1940 an aircraft manufacturer, Henri Potez, abandoned his factories on the Somme and moved south to Le Rayol. The *domaine* was later defended by local authorities and residents who managed to fend off the inevitable urge to subdivide and build.

In 1989 a government agency called the Conservatoire du Littoral took over (this is the body that also manages the Serre de la Madone in Menton, the Eileen Gray/Le Corbusier properties in Roquebrune/Cap Martin, Mont Alban (above Nice) and the Bois de la Garoupe on Cap d'Antibes). In Le Rayol it engaged the landscape designer, Gilles Clément, famous for his "Planetary Gardens", to create a space where plants from all over the world compatible with a Mediterranean climate could flourish and be studied. He later fell out with the French government over their stance on conservation.

Look out for Mexican cacti, Chinese bamboo and giant ferns from New Zealand. Le Rayol is also part of the "Mimosa trail". Lovers of this Australian native, brought over by Captain Cook, can sample here—and all along the Maures *corniche*—quite a few of the 1,200 varieties of this fragrant variety of acacia.

SHOW GARDENS

"Competitive" gardening followed inevitably on the development of more and more elaborate properties all along the Riviera from the middle of the nineteenth century. That is not to imply they were not designed for personal pleasure, and often to display collections of interesting plants from sources all around the world. The fashion of building stone steps down the steep terraces on which many of the gardens were built became fashionable, with one owner and designer vying with another to create the longest single stairway, and the finest vista. One Parisian politician said that all over the Riviera "staircase duels were taking place".

Visiting each other's gardens became a familiar pastime on the Côte d'Azur. Tours were planned. Towns organized beautiful garden competitions in order to promote their locality to potential visitors. Many of the great gardens, the most famous and prestigious, were opened to the public.

Ferdinand Bac, the all-round aesthete (see Chapter Seven), "repented caricaturist", critic and decorator was much in demand as a garden designer (even by Beatrice Rothschild, though she had no success). In 1912 he started work for Marie-Laure de Noailles on her Villa Croisset in Grasse. It featured huge "dark pyramids shading the patios" following the example of the cloister in Assisi. He then worked on the Villa Fiorentina on Cap d'Antibes. Both these gardens have now been lost to development and re-design.

After the First World War Bac came to stay with a couple of wealthy bankers by the name of Ladan-Bockairy, for whom he had already done a garden in Compiègne. He found them a square, squat, rustic house up behind the Baie de Garavan near Menton, belonging to the social philosopher Alfred Fouillé. The renovation took five years, from 1919 to 1924, after which Bac stayed on with the Ladan-Bockairys until 1939. His "total make-over" of both villa and garden that comprise the *domaine* of Les Colombières encompassed sculptures and frescoes in classical and Venetian style throughout the house. He also created a landscape garden whose colours have been compared to Cézanne's, which has echoes of Egypt (the lotus garden), Greece and Rome, as well as Andalucia and Tuscany. A bridge leads to a carob tree over a thousand years old. He said he wanted to "create a bouquet of travel memories… and bring them to life in order to relive the past."

Bac explained his ambitions:

> The idea was to start with small private spaces near the house, with a secret garden enclosed by walls and gates, and gradually, as one moved away from the house, amplify the movement with more daring geo-

graphical arrangements; these would in turn defer to a rebellious natural topography full of grandeur, full of hills and dales, ravines and rocks, stubbornly resisting any attempt to tame it… We set isolated, small garden monuments, placed with respect for the character of this natural setting which, if truth be told, required no help from human hands.

After an unhappy period of wartime neglect and then use as a hotel and tea room, the house and garden of Les Colombières have recently been restored to Bac's original conception, with the addition of sculptures by Ivan Theimer, new terraces, exotic plants and carpets of wild flowers.

The pine forests of Cap Martin had once been reserved for the Princes of Monaco's hunting pleasures. But in the latter third of the nineteenth century, writes Kathryn Bradley-Hole, "pigeon-shooting had become such a big draw for the Riviera's hivernants that in 1886 the wilds of Cap Martin were obtained for a shooting enterprise, whereby visitors who regretted leaving behind the Scottish moors each winter could at least take a potshot at the copious rabbits and pheasants."

Rising land values very quickly scotched that idea, and villas began to dot the promontory. Among them was the Villa Cypris, ten acres with a fabulous view across to Monaco. Its great feature was a triple flight of steps, the central one plunging down to the sea. All the steps were turfed, and plants made a strip down the centre. Walking today along the coastal path, if you look up at the right time you have an excellent view of the brick bridge and colonnaded cloister gallery above the rocks with its bell tower and Provençal tiles. Among the pathways and bowers in the steeply sloping gardens are a Venetian temple and a kind of Moorish pergola modelled on the Great Mosque at Córdoba. The original Dutch garden (a thin canal flanked by topiary and brick paving) is now a swimming pool. Much of the rest survives.

Villa Torre Clementina is the name of a *belle époque* extravaganza at Cap Martin commissioned by the eccentric spiritualist Ernesta Stern (1854-1926), with turrets and loggia, Japanese garden and Greek theatre—described by Ferdinand Bac as "China and Japan, Syracuse and Trebizond… an accumulation of effects which lack only the Christian sense of moderation." The property has undergone a complete (and suitably extravagant) make-over by American architects and designers.

Although it is hard to do more than snoop around most of the Cap
Martin villas today—the same is true of Cap Ferrat and all the other exclusive capes—a walk along nearby roads and paths, peeping through the
cracks and speculating on what is happening behind the walls and hedges,
does nevertheless have its appeal.

EZE AND CAP FERRAT: EXCLUSIVE PLAYGROUNDS

Only the fortunate few received an invitation to the grand villa, built in
1922 by the fashionable architect Achille Duchêne for Consuelo Vander-
bilt Balsan—and you would be fortunate indeed today to penetrate the
garden, let alone the house, as the owners' privacy is jealously protected.
On a crag across from the hilltop village of Eze, high above Cap Ferrat, this
property, called Lou Sueil (dialect for *seuil*—threshold), is a mix of "Cistercian" simplicity of style and no-expense-spared formal and terraced
garden, with its mimosas: "perfect specimens in varied sulphur, lemon and
orange hues, here and there underplanted with blue carpets of *Anemone
blanda*." Kathryn Bradley-Hole's description of its interwar years' heyday
is as colourful as the garden itself.

> One stairway led down to a magnificent walk proceeding between tall
> olive trees a-flutter with white fantail doves; beside the path, a long white
> colonnade was garlanded with the pink clusters of "American pillar" roses.
> The underplanting was a carpet of blue cinerarias and forget-me-nots,
> outlined by ribbons of nemophila. Further paths scurried through "bril-
> liant fields of antirrhinum", while sunlit banks were variously bathed in
> massed irises of mixed pastel hues, or sheets of pot marigolds, or, else-
> where, "a kaleidoscope of all colours of ranunculus". "Fortune's Yellow"
> roses engulfed a low wall beside an orchard to orange trees on the western
> side, framing the distant views of old Eze with gold in the springtime.

There are nine special mini-gardens within the 22-acre garden of Beatrice Ephrussi's fantasy world overlooking Villefranche and Beaulieu, the
Villa Ephrussi-Rothschild/Villa Ile de France. The Spanish includes a
grotto and pergola and a canal with aquatic plants; the Florentine has a
grotto and a cypress-lined path; bas-reliefs and gargoyles decorate the Stone
(*Lapidaire*), enlivened in spring by its azaleas, camellias, rhododendrons
and fuchsias; the Japanese, as one might imagine, features Koi carp, a tea

house, bamboo fences and azaleas; succulents including, of course, many cacti fill the Exotic garden; the flowers surround a hexagonal temple in the Rose garden; the Provençal with its olive trees and pines leads to the Temple of Love; the French garden is at the heart of it all, surrounding the waterfall and canal flowing from the Temple of Love down to the villa; finally the Sèvres garden's hibiscus, buddleia and orange trees set off the tea room at the west side of the villa.

A fountain playing patterns to your favourite Mozart tunes and Viennese waltzes adds a kitsch touch to the elegance of the gardens, now managed, as is the Villa Kérylos, by a company called Culturespaces.

The English architect and landscape gardener, Harold Peto (1854-1933) designed the Villa Maryland and its garden on a four-acre plot for a family of shipbuilders from Hull (he also designed the liner *Mauritania*'s interiors). His blend of Italian/Roman, Moorish/Spanish and North African styles became a kind of model for future designers of Riviera houses and gardens. Today the Villa Maryland is largely unchanged—but inaccessible to the public.

Another Peto creation on Cap Ferrat from the same time (very early twentieth century) is the Villa Sylvia, above the Baie de l'Espalmadour. This was commissioned by a rich American painter, Ralph Wormeley Curtis, cousin of John Singer Sargent, friend of Edith Wharton and Henry James—and father of Sylvia. His wife was from the Colt firearms dynasty. Its blue-green tile roof can be seen from across the bay from Villefranche, but, once more, it is itself very hard to visit.

La Fiorentina and the Clos Fiorentina are perched side by side on the rocky tip of Cap Ferrat. Designed in part by Ferdinand Bac and later by Rory Cameron, the larger property was owned by Hubert de Givenchy and was once rented to Elizabeth Taylor and Richard Burton. It is famous for its Aleppo pines and cypresses, patterned orange groves with white-washed trunks, and giant toads; the smaller Clos has a mandarin walk, again with white painted trunks. "It looks very effective when the lilies are out," Cameron wrote, "their white chalices catching the light filtered through the mandarins' pointed leaves."

Urban Oases

Among many fine parks and gardens in Nice is the Villa Arson, on the north side of the town; since 1970 it has housed the Ecole Nationale

Supérieure d'Art, where artists go to live and to study. The Palais de Marbre has many other names and has had a series of owners, including a Russian colonel who bought it in 1902 and turned it into a centre of Russian social life; its gardens are largely built over now and the building accommodates the city archives.

Antibes has long been a European centre for the commercial production of flowers. It also contains several fine estates, among them the Bastide du Roy, an old royal estate redesigned by the landscape architect/designer Jean-Claude-Nicolas Forestier (1861-1930) under the auspices of the singer, the Countess of Polignac, a friend of many musicians whom she and her husband entertained in the late 1920s in grand style. In one way it is a slightly less elaborate version of the Villa Ephrussi on Cap Ferrat, in that it contains within it many small gardens, seven in this case, one being the "yellow and white", another the "Spanish".

In 1882 much of the French Renaissance-style architecture of the Tuileries gardens in Paris was sold off and scattered. Caroline Miolan-Carvalho, the favourite singer of Charles Gounod, planted a garden in St.-Raphael which contained 43 fragments from the Tuileries in a magnificent tumble of pediments and capitals and cacti and exotic flowers.

PORT-CROS

The island of Port-Cros has been a National Park since 1963. It is largely covered with the usual Aleppo pines, holm oaks, strawberry trees, wild olives, myrtles and so on; but it also has some unusual plants such as Jove's beard (a kind of kidney vetch but several feets high), tree spurge, pink and white lavenders and its own variety of thyme. Among all these darts the rare leaf-toed gecko (more likely than not on some old juniper tree) and the equally rare Tyrrhenian painted frog—though they are apparently of a disappointing brownish colour and their most distinguishing mark is a round, rather than horizontally elongated, pupil.

Port-Cros is the only National Park in the Riviera region; the mountainous area of Mercantour (created in 1979) is the one nearest to the Riviera among the nine such parks in France and its overseas territories.

Chapter Eleven

HILLTOPS AND ISLANDS

TALL STORIES FROM THE BACK COUNTRY

The Riviera tourist authorities are keen on themed routes: the Roman road, the "Matisse route", the "Mimosa trail" (eighty miles from Bormes-les-Mimosas to Auribeau). A recent addition is the *route des villages perchés*. They expect you to take the road, of course, even if the best way to reach— and to see—these many hilltop villages, from the Esterel to Sospel, would be from a helicopter. It can be a little queasy driving round and round, curling up to each limpet-shaped village then down again.

There is, of course, a further back country, the high Alps. Since this is no part of the Riviera as such, I shall leave in peace the snow slopes, gorges and parks of Haute-Provence, Alpes Maritimes and Mercantour. The foothills, however, are studded with strange and wonderful places and worth the effort of reaching them, even by road.

These *villages perchés* were always meant to be inaccessible. Some, like Ste.-Agnès behind Menton, are visible from faraway, up *there*, on a little and round a corner—a glimpsed promise that you will be in the village centre in a couple of minutes. Instead, they seem to retreat as you get nearer, as indeed their ancient inhabitants must have hoped would happen to the Saracen invaders they were sheltering from. Today, the road up from Menton to Ste.-Agnès plays an elaborate cat's cradle with the A8 motorway, while a series of milestones and signposts seems to increase rather than decrease the number of kilometres still to travel. Officially the village is about two miles from the coast as the shell flies (see p.32) and six by road; in fact, that three-to-one ratio is surely an underestimate, as seems to be the case with all these winding roads.

And as in most hilltop villages, local painters and artisans have pre-ceded you up there. Huddled in semi-basements, down alleys slippery with cobbles, lurk the customary wares of garish canvasses, painted saints (*santons*) and battered ploughshares. Usually among the curios, however, are some objects with interesting histories. Even in the most crumbling

Old Roquebrune – saved by a gorse bush?

château or dilapidated fort or lovingly stocked eco-museum one can often find a medieval garden or torture chamber or herbal remedy—generally accompanied by colourful local legends.

Ste.-Agnès, Gorbio and Castellar

Ste.-Agnès' story concerns a certain Haroun, a Saracen who fell in love with a Christian girl, a *Marseillaise* called Anna. He abducted her, strangled his jealous wife, but then reached a religious deadlock until Anna prayed so hard that he abandoned his Muslim faith. After his death she retreated to her favourite rock, the highest hill village on all the Côte d'Azur. As for the eponymous Agnès herself, she had a less adventurous life, being reputedly a Roman princess who simply found shelter from a storm and vowed to build a chapel to her patron saint, namesake and protector.

Nearby Gorbio has less of a tale to tell, but it does have an olive tree planted in 1713 that doubles as the bus stop. Every June, on the holiday of Corpus Christi, the village holds a medieval ceremony, the Procession of the Snails (*Procession dai Limaça*), when the twisting streets are lit by thousands of flickering snail-shell lamps filled with olive oil.

Perched on a hill across the Carei valley is the village of Castellar, consisting mostly of two long parallel streets. The Counts of Ventimiglia—a troublesome family at the most peaceful of times—lived here from the thirteenth century, and their spirit still seems to haunt the place. There is a plaque on the wall of the *Mairie* that recounts the departure from the village in 1873 of no fewer than 74 "Castellarencs who, led by their mayor, Adraste Abbo, left their native village to found in Kabylie (in Algeria) the colony of the Holy Wood, which later became Abboville/Abbo." I imagined a kind of religious cult, but the reality turns out to be more mundane. The year 1873 marked a time of extreme poverty in Castellar, with a catastrophic decline in olive oil production. Nonetheless, it was a dramatic gesture by a high proportion of the population to follow their mayor across the Mediterranean.

Castillon and Sospel

In the old days you could take a tram up from Menton to Castillon, the halfway point, before carrying on to the route's final destination, Sospel. In a couple of places a remnant of the line swings out over the hillside high on stone columns like the elbows of a giant statue. But Castillon is no more. At least, it has been re-created as "the most beautiful new village in France", after being twice demolished—by an earthquake in 1887 and by bombs in 1944. It is now a nest of would-be chic artists and artisans.

Sospel has seen a decline too. The old bridge over the Bévéra river goes back to the tenth century. Its small central tower was the toll house on the salt road from Nice to Piedmont. It is hard to imagine now just how prosperous and important Sospel was. Its medieval population of 3,000 included rich merchants and traders and a bishop in residence as well as all the paraphernalia of government associated with being the *chef-lieu* of the region. Up until the Revolution it was thriving, but then Sospel began to lose its economic and political importance as the coast prospered and the little inland hill town became just a speck within the great body of France. The *Hôtel de Ville* and the cathedral (see Chapter Nine) are on a grand scale, and many features such as door frames, painted signs and decorated walls attest to the town's glory days, but the *trompe-l'oeil* façades of the riverside houses date from the nineteenth century—so not everything fell apart in the immediate aftermath of the political and economic upheavals around the time of the Revolution.

Even in Smollett's time, in 1765, Sospel provided a welcome rest on the arduous journey from the coast up to Piedmont. He found "Sospello" to be "agreeably situated in a small valley, surrounded by prodigious high and barren mountains. This little plain is pretty fertile, and being watered by a pleasant stream, forms a delightful contrast with the hideous rocks that surround it."

Not much more than a century later, speculators were eyeing the town up as a pleasure ground for those foreign visitors sated by the heat and glitz of the coast. A golf course was built—not the first one on the Riviera, since by the 1890s there were links near both Nice and Cannes. The great hotel architect Hans-Georg Tersling (1857-1920) was commissioned to design Sospel's 85-room Golf-Hôtel. In April 1914 a Parisian surgeon, Dr. Paul Hamonic, passing through Sospel, came across a mass of smart cars jamming the town. Assuming that people must be there for a "hydrominéral" cure, he was shocked to see that they had come from Nice and Menton and from even further afield to "jouer au golff (*sic*), mais personne ne sait pourquoi." But the developers did know why. The *belle époque* crowd had grown so numerous (2,950 foreign families wintering over in Menton alone in 1910/11) that people were prepared to toil all the way up to Sospel—many by tram—to smack little white balls into holes. But by the early 1930s the vogue had passed. The course reverted to pasture and the hotel to apartments.

Roquebrune

In 1468, at the height of the great plague, nine days of prayer were believed to have delivered the good people of Roquebrune from the epidemic's clutches. Ever since, even during the Revolution (and so at considerable risk), their descendants have celebrated this deliverance with a re-enacted *procession votive de la Passion*. The oldest families jealously guard the roles of the main characters. Grafted on is a celebration of another, earlier deliverance. In the seventh century an earthquake threatened to bring down the entire, almost vertical, cliff on which the old town of Roquebrune is built. It is told that a landslide was stopped in its tracks by a gorse bush.

In 1157 Guido Guerra, the Count of Ventimiglia, had to hand Roquebrune over to the more powerful Republic of Genoa. A garrison was stationed in a castle built at the very top of the village, which survives to this day, restored after centuries of wear and tear from fire, cannonballs shot by the Comtes de Provence and from siege and neglect. It is the oldest surviving *donjon* in France. The restoration was largely the work of an Englishman, Sir William Ingram, who bought the castle in 1911 and gave it to the town in 1921.

Peillon and Peille, Plus Eze

Almost twins, perched on hills less than three miles apart but at least three times as far by road, the two villages of Peillon and Peille each have their charms, with medieval streets and stairways, arches and cobbled squares. The first, however, is smaller, more accessible and boasts a chapel with frescoes by Giovanni Canavesio (1450-1500). The second, more isolated, has so many odd features that it describes itself on signs and in its publicity as "the most curious village in the Alpes Maritimes". It is hard at first to see what could justify such a claim. Admittedly it seems to cling on to the wooded mountainside rather than perch on top; indeed it almost seems to be sliding down. It does, moreover, boast a medieval picture of itself in the twelfth-century Church of Ste.-Marie… and a ruined castle. A volunteer in the tiny local museum with good sense of history claimed that the

actual reason for Peille's description as "curieux" has to do with its traditional olive jars. These three-foot-high wide-necked amphorae have been
made in the village since the earliest times. When they became holed or too
decrepit, the citizens of Peille, she said, would take them out into their
fields and bury them, flush with the ground. They would then be used as
lavatories.

This is not apparently the only example of Peille's curious behaviour;
another is the adoption of the *bousavouia*. Originally a hollow reed used
as a bellows, this was replaced, after fierce local resistance to the French
Revolution in 1792, by a metal tube made from the barrel of discarded
French guns, onto which two prongs of metal were welded at one end to
give the embers a good stir before blowing down the tube. As a further
curiosity, not only does Peille have its own dialect (see p.133), but there is
also a local legend. It is said that a shepherd-cum-sorcerer answered the
people's appeal that he should make it rain, on condition he married the
local lord's daughter. He seemed to have got away with it because the event
is still celebrated on the first Sunday of September, despite the disapproval
of the Catholic Church, with a *Festin des Baguettes*. There is indeed a
history of eccentric independence.

Mary Garden was a Scottish woman born in 1874, who went to sing
as a soprano at the Paris Opéra-Comique and then became famous as
Richard Strauss' Salomé. An "archetypal diva", she had a flamboyant and
sometimes scandalous career in Europe and the United States, once almost
causing a duel to be fought between the Belgian writer Maurice Maeter-
linck and the composer Claude Debussy. Her connection with Peille is
simply that she shelled out a very large sum from her own pocket to build
not only a memorial there to victims of the First World War but also a
road for people to get to it. Her motive was simply that she enjoyed the
beauty of the hilltop village.

The tourist industry flourishes more intrusively in Eze, a much gen-
trified hill village with the advantage of looking down from a precipice
onto Cap Ferrat and the Mediterranean. Even the Christ on the Catalan
crucifix held by a disembodied arm offers what seems to be a welcoming
smile in the Chapelle des Pénitents Blancs. There are a couple of hotels and
restaurants in Eze whose food—and prices—are as spectacular as the
panoramas from their terraces. But you can always slip away down the
Friedrich Nietzsche path to the sea shore below. The German philosopher,

however, preferred to walk up the path, not down, stimulating his imagination enough to inspire one section of his four-part *Thus Spake Zarathustra* (1883-85).

Behind Nice: From the Paillon to the Var Valleys

Further back up the Paillon valley, L'Escarène was an important staging-post on the salt road from Nice to Piedmont. An old bridge with a single arch and the Place de la Gabelle both recall those days. Lucéram, to the north, is much prettier, with some of the steep, crammed-together medieval town intact. It once had a Roman fort, but this was later destroyed, as its publicity leaflets say, by "Moors". Its rarest feature is the horseshoe-shaped tower, fifty feet high, with the opening towards the village. Still in excellent condition, it was put up at the very end of the fourteenth century to protect the village from marauders, mostly men from the Comté de Tende, as Lucéram was rich from the taxes it levied from its position along the salt route. Its church is well worth a visit (see Chapter Nine), and there are splendid walks in the surrounding hills. A long winding trip by road takes you to the village of Coaraze, whose name means "cut tail", since the Devil, it is told, trapped his tail here and had to shed it like a lizard to escape. Jean Cocteau left only some ceramic sundials behind.

Tourettes-sur-Loup, further west, is in violet country—there is a "fête des violettes" here every March. The outer houses of the medieval village form a rampart above a sheer drop.

Falicon is a typical village of the immediate Nice *arrière-pays*, perched on a rocky outcrop, host to Queen Victoria and the setting for a novel (by Jules Romains), with a pretty church and a short hike up to a panoramic terrace. Aspremont and Tourette-Levens offer similar fare. Pretty though they are, these villages and small towns between the coast and the high mountains, with their precipitous gorges, lakes and Alpine panoramas act on the visual palate more as an *entremets* than a main course.

Behind Cannes

St.-Paul-de-Vence, Vence itself, Valbonne, Grasse, Mougins and Auribeau make a more satisfying cultural meal. One has to disregard, however, the effect of their popularity and, if possible, see these towns at a time or season when the volume of tourists does not overwhelm the impulse to enjoy their beauty or their history. This is not a question of snobbishness, just a fact of life—for residents as much as visitors, as true for the hill towns of the Côte d'Azur as for Venice or Bath.

It is hard to imagine genteel, flowery St.-Paul as a frontier town, guns lined up on the ramparts, pointing towards the frontier along the Var, even if some of the cannon remain (unthreateningly). The *donjon* is now the town hall and a thick-walled tower houses the tourist office. The older generation of painters and film stars, those who paid for the meals at the Colombe d'Or with canvases and associated with the Scott Fitzgeralds, with James Baldwin or Simone Signoret and Yves Montand, have moved on, leaving the streets prey to the usual purveyors of local colour. It is best to take the road up to the Fondation Maeght.

When looking for a Riviera hideaway, the actor Dirk Bogarde, as he recalled in his *Snakes and Ladders* (1978), "stuck the point of a compass into the village of St Paul de Vence"—it was the centre of an area where he had filmed when it stood in for wartime Crete. Even in 1969 he was aware of it "slowly but inexorably turning itself into a kitschy ruin of faux art galleries, Provençal boutiques, Vietnamese restaurants, and tarty little shops selling postcards, hideous porcelain, olive-wood salad bowls and key rings." Yet this did not stop him from buying a run-down seventeenth-century farmhouse nearby in a remote, "by-passed" village, surrounded by "twelve acres of long-abandoned vines and jasmine fields", sheltered from the Mistral amid the "calm and peace which lay not so far beyond the cruelly ravaged coast" with its "new blocks which were spreading like white fungus along the coast from Juan-les-Pins to Antibes."

Vence is also filled with galleries and studios but still does a good impression of being a thriving market town. Its origins are Roman (see p.12). A Roman column stands in the Place Godeau, named after a seventeenth-century bishop famed for his wit and for being a founder member of the French Academy. Vence used to be an important Christian centre, boasting two saints and a pope among its bishops. Two daughters of the local lordly family, the Barons of Villeneuve, became Queen of England (Eleanor, wife of Henry II) and the Queen of the Two Sicilies, having married Charles of Anjou. D. H. Lawrence died in Vence and was buried, after a small and quiet ceremony, in its cemetery. Today the town is a popular film set, even more in demand than in Dirk Bogarde's day.

Winding through the International Science Park of Sophia-Antipolis (scene of J. G. Ballard's spooky novel, *Super-Cannes*) brings you to another "happy valley", Valbonne. Its grid system is due to Roman street planning. The main square was once the forum.

The name Grasse derives from the state of grace in which Jewish converts to Christianity found themselves in the Middle Ages. "If the Arrière-Pays is the Riviera's balcony," writes Ted Jones,

> Grasse is its royal box: it was Queen Victoria's retreat from the summer heat of the coast. Seemingly balanced precariously on a limestone ridge, from which it seems likely to slide off at any moment, Grasse was what the Brooklyn-born writer Henry Miller once called 'a superb decrepitude'.

Its reputation of sweet-scentedness, as the centre of the perfume industry, was due to a kind of cover-up, since from medieval times the chief occupation of the *grassois* was (leather) tanning, a notoriously smelly business. When (so the story goes) Catherine de Medicis demanded perfumed gloves, her demand was met to her satisfaction. Since then the balance has swung in favour of the manufacture of perfumes themselves. The only rival industry is the exploitation of its most famous native son, Jean-Honoré Fragonard.

Mougins, on an 850-foot high conical hill, is where Pablo Picasso ended his days. The photography museum has a great many images of him, but the many artists' shops and galleries offer less exciting fare than the Spanish master's. It has also been home since 1986 to the Haitian dictator, Jean-Claude "Baby Doc" Duvalier. He lived briefly the high life on the Riviera, driving around in a BMW and a Ferrari Testarossa, before he was fleeced of his millions by his notoriously rapacious wife, running up debts all over Mougins.

Behind St.-Tropez

The Esterel and Maures hills ensure that the next back-country villages of any size lie well to the west. Among the forests of chestnut and cork oak, La Garde-Freinet has the distinction of being actually occupied by the Saracens for over a century. They bequeathed their expertise in working with cork (as well as the tambourine and flat roof tiles). The bottle-stopper makers of La Garde-Freinet in the mid-nineteenth century won fame by standing up for their rights—and being shot down. The now sleepy town is also known for its natural dyes and a silk-worm cottage industry.

The name Grimaud derives from that of Grimaldi. The family castle, now in ruins, sits on the top of this hilltop village, full of arcades and fountains. The presence of the Knights Templar is retained in a house on the ruc des Templiers, formerly the rue des Juifs, while a reminder of ancient violence of another kind is the statue of St. Theodorit, seven knives sticking out of her chest in the Chapelle des Pénitents.

Cogolin is a seriously industrial, though small-scale town, famous for its briar pipes, wool rugs, bamboo furniture (from its own bamboo forest) and reeds for clarinets and saxophones. The Musée Raimu houses memorabilia of the (mildly antisemitic—see p.26) actor who starred in *Marius* and other Pagnol films.

The romantic and extremely handsome actor Gérard Philipe (star of *Fanfan la Tulipe*, 1952) is buried in Ramatuelle. This village stands high in the centre of the St.-Tropez peninsula, across the hill from the smaller but no less picturesque Gassin, which rather optimistically claims the narrowest street in the world, l'Androuno.

Collobrières, the biggest village in the western Maures, is the centre of chestnut purée and *marron glacé* production. Its name derives from the French for grass snake, *couleuvre*, not because they are specially prevalent here, but because the local stone contains snake-like patterns. Just outside the otherwise unremarkable small town of Gonfaron is the Village of Tortoises—a sanctuary for the rare local breed, the Hermann's tortoise. The presence of the nearby donkey sanctuary recalls the local legend whereby a seventeenth-century householder rebelled at the custom of cleaning one's porch in honour of St. Quinis during the annual procession in the saint's honour, declaring that he would only do so if the statue of St. Quinis flew over his rubbish heap. When it did just that, the householder found himself and his donkey on the top of a hill, from which they were both hurled into a ravine. It is truly amazing how tall stories abound in the *arrière-pays* villages of the Riviera. More rooted in reality is Gonfaron's cork museum, the Eco-musée du Liège.

THE *AVANT-PAYS*: ISLANDS OFF THE RIVIERA COAST

The Iles d'Hyères—Porquerolles, Port-Cros and the Ile du Levant—have also been known since Renaissance times as the Iles d'Or, seemingly due to the golden reflections from the mica shale of their rocks. (There is another Ile d'Or, incidentally, just off the shore in St.-Raphael. It is private and inaccessible; indeed, one owner, in his red stone tower in the island, declared himself "king". It is most famous as the inspiration for Hergé's *L'Ile Noire* in the Tintin series.)

The three Iles d'Hyères have a richer history. For a start, they are full of forts. The strategic importance of the islands in the centre of the Côte d'Azur and close to the port of Toulon has been obvious since Roman times. When the Germans occupied France the whole population of Hyères and its islands was evacuated to make way for the German forces. Besides the grim there is the sensual too. The powerful effect of these exotic islands on the senses is wonderfully evoked in Roger Martin du Gard's description of how, one midsummer dawn in 1922, his fellow novelist André Gide rose from his hotel bed on Porquerolles and

> went off at random, tearing across the island like a drunken savage, half naked, scratching himself on arbutus and tamarisk, chasing after butterflies, picking flowers and berries, plunging into every creek to find which was the warmest, jumping from rock to rock and fishing in the narrow clefts, for seaweed, shells and tiny sea-monsters, which he brought back in his handkerchief. It was past twelve when he reappeared in the hotel dining-room, with sand in his ears and bits of sea-wrack stuck all over his body, laughing, wild-eyed, drunk with light and heat and joy, reciting intoxicatedly Heredia's lines:
> Le soleil, sous la mer, mys-té-ri-euse aurora,
> Eclaire la forêt des coraux abyssins...!
> [The sun, beneath the sea, mys-te-ri-ous aurora,
> Lights up the forest of deep down coral…]

Not that the islands have always had that effect. Brenda Maddox, in her biography of D. H. Lawrence, describes how, in October 1928, he ended up with a group of sexual adventurers in the old Look-Out (La Vigie) on Port-Cros that offered

> the prospect of the kind of colony Lawrence once craved: private rooms round an inner courtyard, a communal great room with a big log fire, and the air full of the scent of pine trees, wild lavender and rosemary. At the pinnacle of the small craggy island, the walled Vigie offered dazzling

views of the blue Mediterranean—but at the price of a three-quarter-hour's walk uphill from the port... He staggered up to the fort, then was stuck, while the others descended daily to swim or to eat at the hotel, the only place of entertainment on the island. His coughing echoed round the compound.

During the interwar period La Vigie years became a kind of French writers' colony. Jean Paulhan and his wife Germaine held court. Writers published by the Paris publisher Gallimard and the crowd from the *Nouvelle Revue Française* would come to talk, swim, play ping-pong or *boules* and generally be "en accord avec la terre". Once Paulhan told a friend he had "caught an octopus and almost tamed it," while the poet Henri Michaux recommended adopting a cuttlefish. Paulhan wrote to another friend:

> The view you get from la Vigie is the most wonderful you can imagine: three islands, the Mediterranean coast from Toulon to Saint-Tropez (you can see the towns light up in the evening), the first Alps and the sea; sometimes, far off, the coast of Corsica. Indeed, the first impression is stunning. Only later, bit by bit, you tell yourself that it can't be quite serious; that the sun and the moon, to speak only of them, have odd ways of rising and setting; that you surprise them sometimes in ridiculous positions. But there's no doubt it's equally dangerous being seduced by the scenery as it is by wealth.

But, as so often, there is a darker side. The island can act as a kind of pressure cooker, where the emotional atmosphere becomes stifling, a place where personal revelations come too easily, and the blinding light of shared confidences is later regretted. The gay novelist Yves Navarre (born, as it happens, in Condom) described Port-Cros as "un étouffoir"—in other words, suffocating.

The French navy no longer uses the Ile du Levant for target practice, but it does continue to test engines and rockets here. This does not seem to put off the nudists who congregate in France's first nudist colony, Héliopolis—even the all-year-rounders.

The Iles de Lérins are much smaller. Just off the coast of Cannes, the Ile St.-Honorat and the Ile Ste.-Marguerite are named after two very early Christian saints who founded religious houses here. They have very different fauna and flora. There are pheasants only on Ste.-Marguerite, while St.-Honorat is full of snakes. In fact St. Honorat is said to have found his eponymous island so riddled with snakes that he was obliged to pray for deliverance from them. He prayed so hard they should all die that, when it happened, the stink of the corpses was overwhelming; he then had to climb a palm tree and pray they would be washed away. Some clearly survived to reproduce, however, and the island's symbol is a pair of palm trees intertwined with a snake. By the seventh century there were as many as 4,000 monks, with dependent monasteries all over the mainland. Among the twenty saints who trained on St.-Honorat is St. Patrick, who described the island as "an earthly paradise". As the nineteenth-century observer, Charles Lenthéric, put it: "For ten centuries the little island of Saint-Honorat, like a rock detached from the Grecian Archipelago, and stranded on the shores of Provence, was a real nursery of doctors, scholars, saints, and martyrs."

The monastery's modern website endorses this picture of restful industry and erudition: "Ici, ni agitation, ni pollution, ni spéculations". It was not always so peaceful, however. Disorder and lack of discipline had become so rife by the middle of the fifteenth century that a special meeting was convened in order to compel the monks to go to a minimum monthly confession and to take Holy Communion at least on the major festivals. The monks by this stage were barely monks. So many were fleeing scandals in Italy that the monastery became known as the "monks' galley".

Outside threats were just as grave. The Cannes shoreline is a key point on the sea route between Italy, Provence and Spain, but offers no easy mooring. Ste.-Marguerite became a base of both merchant and military ships. Work began on the Fort Royal there in the first half of the seventeenth century, after centuries of Saracen raids and incursions by Genoese pirates (which led to secret tunnels and heavy fortifications). Even so, it did not prevent two years of Spanish occupation during the Thirty Years War, from 1635-37, after which a garrison took up permanent residence on the island. The great Sébastien de Vauban, Louis XIV's General Superintendent of Fortifications, paid no fewer than three visits to bring the fort up to the highest standards. But the monastery was neglected. The monks were reduced to a contingent of four. Even worse was to come during the French Revolution. The island was bought by an actress, Blanche Sainval, who in a spirit of popular, not to say secular, frivolity, turned the place into a party venue. It was only in 1859 that the Bishop of Fréjus bought it all back, re-introducing monks of the Cistercian order to St.-Honorat. They are still there.

The Lérins monastery now has about twenty monks in residence, living a life of quiet prayer and hard work, and welcoming visitors to the Hôtellerie. One of their small number travelling back on the ferry after a rare visit to Cannes to visit his dentist declared that the glory days of scholarship are long past—but so are those of dissolution and disorder. Tourism sustains the Lérins monks now. You can sample their honey and wine and a yellowish liqueur called Lérina that tastes of aromatic genepy and contains the distilled essences of forty-four separate plants. Operating in a competitive commercial environment, the monks have added other varieties, including a wincingly named "Lerincello".

As for neighbouring Ste.-Marguerite, the legend of the sister of St.-Honorat (her austere brother would only come and visit her when a certain almond tree blossomed, so her prayers made it blossom every month) has been superseded by the scarcely less sophistical story attached to the Fort Royal, Louis XIV's favourite prison. For it is here that the Man in the Iron Mask (whoever he was, and anyway it was probably a leather or velvet mask) was locked up for eleven years in a cell with a tantalizing view

St. - Honorat – defending an "earthly paradise"

through a trellis of iron bars across the blue water to the hills above Cannes. The prisoner, possibly a mere valet rather than a brother of Louis XIV or some other royal, *aristo* or diplomat, was dragged from gaol to gaol for twenty years from 1669; it is probable that the iron mask story, popularized by Alexandre Dumas *père*, took wing as he was being transferred from Exilles in Piedmont to Ste.-Marguerite. But we know no more about his identity today than when Victor Hugo noted resignedly that "no-one knows his name, no-one has seen his face, he is a living mystery, shadow, enigma, problem."

Other prisoners in the fort on Ste.-Marguerite have included Abdel Kadir, an Algerian rebel leader, the Marquis Jouffroy d'Abbans, inventor of the steamboat, Marshal Bazaine, the only one to escape from the island, and six Huguenot pastors, who returned to France after Louis XIV's Edict of Nantes. Their persecution was particularly fierce and unrelenting; five of them went mad from being kept in solitary confinement.

One last story from the Iles de Lérins, however tall it might seem, is nevertheless (mostly) true. It concerns the remains of the violin virtuoso and composer Niccolò Paganini, who came to Nice for his asthma and for the distance it put between himself and his creditors in Genoa. He died in Nice in 1840. Although the Lérins were part of the Kingdom of Savoy, as was Genoa, the Piedmontese authorities declined to allow the corpse to return (claiming it was infected with cholera), while the Bishop of Nice refused a burial in consecrated ground because the wretched musician had failed to obtain absolution. Paganini's son hid the coffin in a number of cellars near the coast. During its stay below a former leper house in Antibes, passing fishermen are said to have complained of eerie music coming out of the cellar.

What happened then was described by Guy de Maupassant, from first-hand experience:

Approaching Saint-Honorat we pass by a rock, naked, red, like a porcupine so rough, so armed with teeth and spikes and claws that it's almost impossible to walk on it; you have to put your feet in the hollows, between its defences, and walk with care; it is called Saint-Ferréol…

It's on this weird reef, in the open sea, that was buried and hidden for five years the body of Paganini. The adventure is worthy of this brilliant and macabre artist, said to be possessed of the devil, so strange in looks, in body, in face, whose superhuman talent and prodigious thinness made him a figure of legend, a kind of character from Hoffmann.

Maupassant goes on to recount how the violinist's son was forced to turn back from Genoa, then was driven away from Marseille and from Cannes, before ending up out at sea,

cradling on the waves the corpse of the strange artist rejected by everyone. Not knowing what to do or where to take this dead body, sacred to him, he saw this naked rock of Saint-Ferréol in the middle of the sea. He took the coffin off and buried it in the middle of the islet. Only in 1845 did he come back with a couple of friends to find the remains of his father and take them to Genoa, in the villa Gajona. Wouldn't it have been better if the extraordinary violinist had remained on his spiky island where the waves sing among the strange fissures in the rock?

This is a fitting image with which to end the extraordinary tales told, and often re-told, of some of the Riviera's less accessible parts.

Further Reading

Adcock, Fleur, *Poems 1960-2000*. Newcastle upon Tyne: Bloodaxe, 2000.

Adleman, Robert H. and Walton, Colonel George, *The Champagne Campaign*. Boston: Little, Brown, 1969.

Arnaud, Claude, *A Life Assessed*, in *Cocteau*. Paris: Centre Pompidou, 2003.

Arthaud, Christian and Paul, Eric L., *La Côte d'Azur des écrivains*. Aix-en-Provence: Edisud, 1999.

Ballard, J. G., *Super-Cannes*. London: Flamingo, 2000.

de Banville, Theodore, *La Mer de Nice*. Paris: Poulet-Malassis et de Boise, 1861.

de Beauvoir, Simone, *The Prime of Life*. Trans. Peter Green. Harmondsworth: Penguin, 1965.

Benét, Mary Kathleen, *Writers in Love*. New York: Macmillan Publishing, 1977.

Bennet, James Henry, *Mentone, the Riviera, Corsica and Biarritz*. 1862.

Bennet, James Henry, *Winter and Spring on the Shores of the Mediterranean*. 1861.

Berlioz, Hector, *Memoirs*. New York: Dover, 1932.

Blume, Mary, *Côte d'Azur: Inventing the French Riviera*. London: Thames and Hudson, 1992.

Bogarde, Dirk, *Snakes and Ladders*. Harmondsworth: Penguin, 1988.

Bohm-Duchen, Monica, *Chagall*. London: Phaidon, 1998.

Cradock, Fanny and Johnny, *Bon Viveur: Holiday on the French Riviera*. London: Frederick Muller, 1960.

Bordeaux, Henry, *Le Calvaire de Cimiez*. Paris: Plon, 1937.

Bradbury, Dominic, *Mediterranean Modern*. London: Thames and Hudson, 2006.

Bradley-Hole, Kathryn, *Villa Gardens of the Mediterranean: From the Archives of Country Life*. London: Aurum Press, 2006.

Calder, Robert, *Willie: The Life of W. Somerset Maugham*. London: William Heinemann, 1989.

Cassely, Jean-Pierre, *Secret French Riviera*. Versailles: Jonglez, 2007.

Cassy, Rob (ed.), *Riviera Nature Notes*. Oxford: Signal Books, 2004.

Chekhov, Anton, *Letters*. Trans. Constance Garnett. New York: The Macmillan Company, 1920.

Cloetta, Yvonne, as told to Marie-Francoise Allan, *In Search of a Beginning: My Life with Graham Greene*. London: Bloomsbury, 2004.

Cocteau, Jean, *Le Passé Défini: Journal*, vol. 2. Paris: Gallimard, 1985.

Cocteau, Jean, *Professional Secrets*. New York: Farrar, Strauss and Giroux, 1970.

Colette, *For a Flower Album*. Trans. Roger Senhouse. New York: David McKay, 1959.

Collas, Philippe, *Edith Wharton's Riviera*. Paris: Flammarion, 2002.

Connolly, Cyril, *The Rock Pool*. Harmondsworth: Penguin Books, 1963.

Conrad, Joseph, *The Rover*. London: Dent, 1925.

Crosland, Margaret, *Simone de Beauvoir: The Woman and her Work*. London: Heinemann, 1992.

Curnow, Allen, *The Bells of Saint Babels*. Auckland: Auckland University Press, 2001.

Daelewyn, Paul, *La Côte d'Azur de Georges Simenon*. Nice: Serre, 2005.

Devoluy, Pierre and Borel, Pierre, *The French Riviera*. London: The Medici Society, 1924.

Dos Passos, John, *The Best Times*. London: Andre Deutsch, 1966.

Edwards, Anne, *The Grimaldis of Monaco*. New York: William Morrow and Co., 1992.

Facaros, Dana and Pauls, Michael, *South of France*. London: Cadogan, 2005, 7th edn.

Fitzgerald, F. Scott, *How to Live on Practically Nothing a Year*, vol. 3. London: The Bodley Head, 1962.

Fitzgerald, F. Scott, *Tender is the Night*. Harmondsworth: Penguin, 2000.

Freed, Barbara F., Halpern, Alan, *Artists and their Museums on the Riviera*. New York: Harry N. Abrams, Inc., 1998.

Greene, Graham, *J'Accuse: The Dark Side of Nice*. London: The Bodley Head, 1982.

Hare, Augustus, *A Winter at Mentone*, 1862.

Hare, Augustus, *The Rivieras*, 1897.

Hemingway, Ernest, *The Garden of Eden*. New York: Scribners, 1986.

Holroyd, Michael, *Lytton Strachey*. London: Chatto and Windus, 1994.

Howarth, Patrick, *When the Riviera Was Ours*. London: Century, 1988.

Hugo, Victor, *Voyage*, 1839.

Hyman, Tim, *Bonnard*. London: Thames and Hudson, 1998.

Johnston, Shirley, *Great Villas of the Riviera*. New York: Rizzoli, 1998.

Jones, Louisa, *Gardens of the French Riviera*. Paris: Flammarion, 2002.

Jones, Ted, *The French Riviera: A Literary Guide for Travellers*. London: I.B. Tauris, 2004.

Kanigel, Robert, *High Season: How One French Riviera Town has Seduced Travelers for Two Thousand Years*. New York: Viking, 2002.

Lenthéric, Charles, *The Riviera Ancient and Modern*. Trans. Charles Webb. London: T. Fisher Unwin, 1895.

Latymer, Hugo, *The Mediterranean Gardener*. London: Frances Lincoln, Royal Botanic Gardens, Kew, 2001.

Leslie, Peter, *The Liberation of the Riviera*. New York: Wyndham Books, 1980.

Liégeard, Stephen, *La Côte d'Azur*. Nice: Serre Editeur, 1988.

Manhire, Bill, "Villa Ephrussi", in *Lifted*. Manchester: Carcanet, 2005.

Mansfield, Katherine, *Letters*. New York: Alfred A. Knopf, 1920.

Martin du Gard, Roger, *Notes sur André Gide*. London: Andre Deutsch, 1953.

de Maupassant, Guy, *Sur l'eau de Saint-Tropez à Monte-Carlo*, 1888.

Médecin, Jacques, *La Cuisine du Comté de Nice*. Paris: Juliard, 1972.

Millin, A.L., *Voyage dans les départements du Midi de la France*, vol. II, Paris, 1807-1811.

Minoret, Bernard, *Cocteau*. Paris: Centre Pompidou, nd.

Nelson, Michael, *Americans and the Making of the Riviera*. Jefferson: McFarland & Co., 2008.

Nelson, Michael, *Queen Victoria and the Discovery of the Riviera*. London: I.B. Tauris, 2001.

Noailles, Vicomte de, *Mediterranean Plants and Gardens*. Calverton: Floraprint, 1977.

Plath, Sylvia, *Journals*. Ed. Karen V. Kukil. London: Faber, 2000.

Renoir, Jean, *Renoir, My Father*. San Francisco: Mercury House, 1988.

Ring, Jim, *Riviera: The Rise and Rise of the Côte d'Azur*. London: John Murray, 2005.

Rowley, Hazel, *Tête-à-Tête: the Lives and Loves of Simone de Beauvoir and Jean-Paul Sartre*. London: Chatto and Windus, 2006.

Ruskin, John, *Ruskin in Italy: Letters to his Parents, 1845*. Ed. Harold I. Shapiro. Oxford: Clarendon Press, 1972.

Russell, Vivian, *Gardens of the Riviera*. Boston: Little, Brown, 1993.

Smollett, Tobias, *Travels Through France and Italy*. Teddington: The Echo Library, 2006.

Spurling, Hilary, *A Life of Henri Matisse*, vols. I and II. London: Hamish Hamilton, 2000/2005.

Stewart, Donald Ogden, *By a Stroke of Luck!* New York: Paddington Press, 1975.

Thurber, James, *The Thurber Carnival*. Harmondsworth: Penguin Books, 1945/1972.

Thurman, Judith, *Secrets of the Flesh: A Life of Colette*. London: Bloomsbury, 1999.

Tolstoy, L. N., *Letters*. Trans. R.F. Christian. New York: Charles Scribner's Sons, 1978.

Treves, Sir Frederick, *The Riviera of the Corniche Road*. London: Cassell, 1921.

Trouillot, Paule et Jean, *Guide historique des 163 communes des Alpes-Maritimes et de Monaco*. Nice: Association des maires des Alpes-Maritimes, 2008.

Waterfield, Giles, *The Long Afternoon*. London: Review, 2000.

Wells, H. G., *Meanwhile: The Picture of a Lady*. London: Ernest Benn, 1933.

West, Rebecca, *The Thinking Reed*. London: Virago, 1984.

Wharton, Edith, *The House of Mirth*. New York: Charles Scribner's Sons, 1905.

Wharton, Edith, *The Touchstone*. London: Virago, 1970.

Woolf, Virginia, *Diary*, vol. IV. Ed. Anne Olivier Bell. London: The Hogarth Press, 1982.

Young, Arthur, *Travels in France*. Ed. M. Bethan-Edwards. London: George Bell & Sons, 1889.

Index of Literary & Historical Names

Index of Places & Landmarks